Between Two Worlds
A Canadian Story

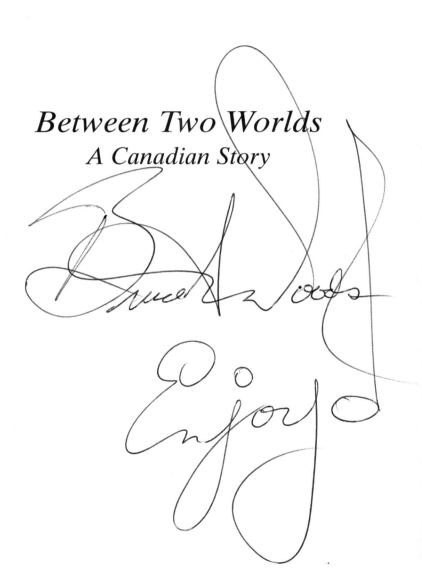

Enjoy

Between Two Worlds
A Canadian Story

Bruce Alexander Woods

Bramy Books, 167 Fallingbrook Dr.,
Ancaster, Ontario, L9G 1E7

Courtesy of Muriel Crawford, Peterborough
mcrawfor@pipcom.com

Bruce Alexander Woods, the Author

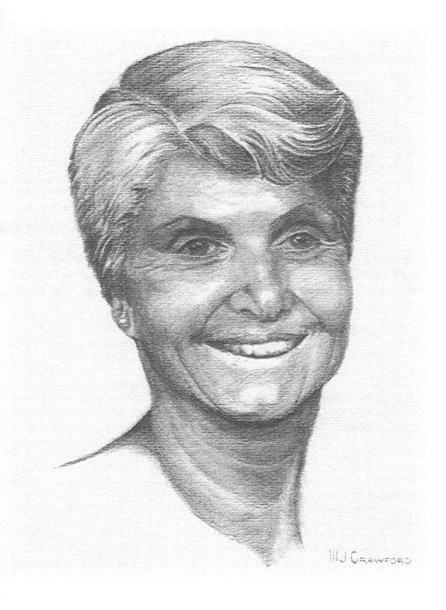

Joan Margaret (Amy) Woods, who urged me to write and suggested the title of my first book, the sequel named itself.

Between Two Worlds
A Stratford Story

National Library of Canada Cataloging in Publication

Woods, Bruce Alexander 1931-
        Between Two Worlds, A Canadian Story

ISBN: 978-0-9784236-1-2   First Edition

        1) Woods, Bruce A. 2) History 3) Memoirs

For more information contact
Bruce A. Woods
Web Page: www.betweentwowomen.net   Home Page

Bramy Books is an imprint of Maracle Press Limited, 1156 King Street East, Oshawa, Ontario. L1H 1H8 Toll Free 1-800-558-8604
Bramy Books ISBN: 978-0-9784236-1-2
Editors: Stacey Larin, Dorothy Alexander, Hugh Steven

These stories are true but some names have been changed to protect privacy.

Table of Contents

Tribute:
   To my readers who encouraged me to write a sequel to my first book.

In the first book, "Between Two Women, A Stratford Story", the author, Bruce Woods celebrates the "joy of living" in his rollicking Tom Sawyer existence that kept us chuckling right through to his happy conclusion.

In the sequel, our author turns serious and now he celebrates the "meaning of living". Although we occasionally see his ability to laugh at himself, now his maturity shines through – revealing a side of his personality hitherto undisclosed. His revelations on folk hero Terry Fox right through to his introduction of other Canadian unsung heros make for an insightful read. The reader is in for a disclosure that will endear the author to his growing number of admirers.

Introduction:

1948 was a watershed year. In my home town of Stratford, milk and bread were still delivered to the door by horse and wagon, but unbeknown to the workers involved, their days were numbered. The era of the stay-at-home mom who walked to the corner store for groceries was coming to an end. The automobile, previously a luxury, had become a necessity. We were in a world of transition that would revolutionize society as we knew it. We were passing from one kind of world to another. I was a part of a generation that was between two worlds. Earthly transitions sometimes can illustrate spiritual transitions. I was about to embark on a spiritual transition that would radically change my life.

September first, 1948. I became a citizen of two worlds. One cannot leave the world we already live in; that's just the way it is. To illustrate, stradling the horse and wagon world and the age of the automobile didn't happen overnight, but I was part of both. In 1948 I also became a part of two worlds. There is another world out there of which I was unaware. It is the Christian world. I knew the secular world; I was about to straddle two worlds, secular and Christian.

When I returned to Stratford to visit family and old friends B.C. (i.e. before conversion) I was, in their opinion, still the old Bruce. Needless to say, this made for some interesting conversations that began one way and finished another. My former friends noticed right away that I was no longer cussing and telling off-colour jokes. This cat is barking a new song. The impression given did not always elicit a favourable response.

Soon the word was out; "Bruce Woods has become religious!" My Aunt Margaret who always warned me I was irreligious, now told me I was too religious. I decided there and then, quite obviously, they think I am a religious fanatic. I am an on-fire Christian who loves Jesus too much. Others however accept the new me; when I dropped in to see Grandma, my aunt Elsie decides to be gracious. Wishing to accommodate Grandma, she invites me to say thanks (i.e. table grace) before the meal. Till now, this unheard-of thing is verboten. Elsie's

1

request is just too much for Uncle Gordon, who says, "What do you mean by thanks?" Looking straight at me, he protests, "If you want to say thanks, you can thank me. I'm the one who earned the money to buy the groceries." (Apparently my new tradition is going to take time to register with Uncle Gordon). An awkward moment at Elsie's expense is eased; I defer to the perusual. Changing the subject to the weather, we are picking up our forks to eat our meal.

When I visit my father and stepmother in Toronto, Phyllis remonstrates, "Religious quacks who make converts of impressionable teenagers ought to be hung up by the thumbs."

The only concession my father makes is that he is glad I have given up smoking, saying, "However, don't think by this admission that I approve of your decision to become religious."

I am a citizen of two worlds: the one temporal and the other spiritual. This dichotomy is destined to get me in trouble. Riding two horses at once is a skill that breaks down when the horses decide to part company. Anyone who decides to live the Christian life will understand.

Chapter 1
The Painting on the Wall

On February 1, 1905, my mother came into this world. As the song says, "You must have been a beautiful baby, cause baby, look at you now." My mother was beautiful. She was not only a beautiful woman, she was a beautiful spirit as well. You couldn't help loving my mother. She was talented but didn't brag. She was fascinated with the world and wanted to learn. She was an interesting person and unlike so many she was not provincial in her outlook like so many of her family. In short, Mom was one of those persons who was endowed with a full hand from birth. She should have been the person "most likely to succeed." She didn't. Her life was a tragedy. The man she gave her heart to abandoned her with a baby (me) for another woman. He paid a high price for such selfishness. Unfortunately for Mom, she paid as well.

No one knew Mother better than I did, yet I didn't know her. I was too close to understand her sorrows, too young to understand what had devastated her life. A child simply cannot appreciate the trials of a parent. That kind of comprehension only comes later when life's tangles are beyond any repair that a son can offer. I don't really think I understood how much she loved me until after she was dead. I did understand that she loved me and tried in life to put that in words, and in deeds, but never with the kind of insight that comes much later, when it's too late to have a conversation. Someday in heaven, and in a better place, the first thing I want to do is to set things right. With witnesses to share the data (mainly friends and family), I want to thank her for the incredible contribution to my life that she made. She gave me a story.

The adventures I related in my former book "*Between Two Women*" tell that story. It is a tale so mind-boggling that it made an author out of me retelling the story. Someday, I want to tell her that the dark depression that overwhelmed her was a classroom education second to none. I want to apprize her that everything I was able to accomplish in life, I owe to her investment that she lavished so unselfishly upon me. In short, I want her to know that all that I am, I owe to her, and that her life was not wasted. I could not have put my hand to the plough without her and I appreciate it. I never told her these things on earth.

I will tell her these things in heaven. Perhaps she knows this now, but that's beside the point. I want her to hear it with her own ears right from my lips. Mom, you were terrific. You were not the failure, you imagined yourself to be. You were a success story with a penultimate that required your own flesh and blood to finish the journey. It was my privilege to complete your narrative. In a previous volume, I told the unfinished drama as forcefully as I could. I now take up my pen to finish the story.

Mom, you were very much the artist, whether it was photography, piano playing or a landscape painting." I have a picture you painted hanging in the basement of our house. It is right in front of my treadmill. I look at that picture every morning when I do my twenty-two minute workout. You remember it. How could you have forgotten? Oh, I know it was just a copy of the work of another artist who had the satisfaction of seeing it printed in a calendar that hung on a thousand kitchen walls back in the thirties. You took that now forgotten artist and gave him (or her) a life beyond the grave. Your copy is an oil painting and nobody wants it. I didn't even want it. For years it was stored in a closet, but finally I had to do something with it, so I hung it in front of my treadmill to hide the unfinished basement wall that I face. Having run out of drywall, I used your painting to cover that ugly two by four that is still exposed. Placing my treadmill just below the painting, I suddenly made my austere basement wall look better. So there it hangs, making my dreary exercise corner look good. There you have it. Just like in life, when you made my life better; here you are at it again.

Mom, can you hear me? If you can't, I'll just pretend you can read my writing. Remember how I used to scribble. Your handwriting was always so much better than mine.

I have a window of sorts, right beside me. It is a casement set in a basement window well. You can't see out, but it lets the light in. To brighten the basement, I took some old mirrors that I had in storage and placed them in the window well. I tilted the mirrors so that they would catch the sunlight and reflect the sunshine right into my otherwise darkened basement. Now at the right time of day, it's as bright as our bedroom window where the large windows flood the room with light.

Mom, I'm telling you all this to say something really special that I'm sure you will appreciate.

In the morning when the sun shines brightly while I'm on the treadmill, the sunshine does an amazing thing with those positioned mirrors. Meantime, I have turned on my MP3 player complete with earphones. I am listening to the Bible. Food for the soul, while I am looking at your beautiful painting. At just the right moment, after the sun has climbed over the horizon and shines though the leafy trees, a stream of light illuminates your magnificent painting just where the pathway follows the rushing torrent of the stream.

Mom, there is nobody on the path. That's the way you painted it; but when that shaft of light comes coursing across the painting through the trees, I think of you.

And I think the path is the journey through life. The river flows alongside of the path and is rushing somewhere in the other direction because the pathway is ascending upwards. The shaft of light doesn't last long, but nonetheless there it is. So I choose to think of 'you' walking the journey of life, and I'm somewhere behind you doing the same thing. Someday, I'll come to the end of the journey and find myself right where you are; we'll talk awhile, and get caught up with all the adventures of my life that you haven't heard. Meanwhile, since I'm still on planet earth, I'll spin my yarn to my readers with happy anticipation that they too will enjoy my story.

Chapter 2
The Search

Here I am in church. Not a cathedral. Just an ordinary church. Lots of people of every age. Over 200 of them and it's July, 1948. I'm feeling very uncomfortable because my smoker's cough is disturbing the peace. Now you might ask, "What is a respectable pagan like Bruce Woods doing in a disreputable place like church?" Well, you can blame Margaret Dennett! It was all her doing, and to boot, right in the middle of the service, I have made a discovery. Put a smoker in a warm building and he will cough. All this requires some explaining, so let me start at the beginning.

"I've got five days off work, for the Canada Day holiday weekend," I say to mother. "I'm going to hitchhike to Goderich and see Graham Bogie."

I figure it will be good to get away from Mother's depressing establishment. How mother will cope with my absence doesn't occur to me. Loneliness seems to be her fate. That's her problem and I have no need to solve it. Her beauty shop is a far cry from the tidy business she had in Stratford. We sleep in a curtained-off area from the shop which is located on the second floor of a building on Dundas Street near Richmond. It is in downtown London where parking is limited. Not a good location to start a business, especially a beauty shop.

Mother is her own worst enemy. Her tragedy is the sadness of many who have had one too many disasters. Her downward spiral has cost her dearly. She has the impossible assignment of starting a hairdressing business from scratch where she is not known. She has a second rate location. She has consulted no one for business advice. She would not have trusted anyone for such matters. She taught her brother the business and he is doing well in Tillsonburg. Her location resembles Norman's. He also has a second floor location on the main street. I suspect she imagines she can duplicate Norman's success. It's a stab in the dark and the attempt is forlorn from the start. She is a prisoner of her shrinking world. I can get away, but she cannot. My absence compounds her boredom, and she doesn't even have a radio. I resolve this problem as best I can. I buy a radio from a local business. It's a dollar down and a dollar a week until the radio is paid for. At least Mother will have some company while I'm gone.

Early Friday morning, I'm off, and by noon, I'm walking up Bogie's road, six miles north of Goderich. There is no advance warning. Long distance phone calls are expensive, so I just show up and take my chances. Ethel Bogie gives me a warm welcome and tells me I don't even have to pay board.

"I can't tell you how pleased I am to have you pay Graham a visit. He gets very lonely here on the farm." Next we talk about mother and I explain that things are not going well. Mrs. Bogie expresses her regrets and returns the subject to her son.

"I'm glad for Graham to have a friend call;" she says, "he gets very lonesome here on the farm."

I explain that I'm living in London now and working on construction, building the Husband Transport warehouse. I have the blisters to show it, but there are advantages: the hard work is putting hitherto unknown bulk into my biceps. Fortunately for me, I am not asked to help in the haying, although at long last, I probably could accommodate. I'm a working man looking for a little relaxation, and I'm making eighty cents an hour. Something to brag about, to be sure. I came to see Graham and we have a great time of reunion. But then I get to meet someone who, like the stuff of angels, will alter my life's direction. Mrs. Bogie introduces me to a family from London that is staying with them for a week's holiday.

Casey Jones is a milkman. He supervises nineteen others each of whom has his own horse and wagon. He has married a widow who has three daughters, and instantly gained a family. Mr. and Mrs. Jones, Donna, and Margaret are vacationing at the Bogies.' Donna has red hair (I have a weakness for girls with red hair) but Margaret is the pretty one. Graham and I team up with them for afternoon swims at the beach. Margaret and I have taken a shine to each other. In fact, on Tuesday, I don't have to hitchhike back to London; I get a ride with the family and sit beside Margaret in the back seat of their brand new 1947 Ford. This is my lucky day. After that, I never miss an evening meal at 100 Briscoe Street. Mrs. Jones knows how to cook. On Mother's meager rations, I haven't been eating too well. In no time, Margaret and I are courting. Her parents seem to approve.

Every mother has the problem of having to slowly see her son spread his wings and leave home. For my mom, the break comes fast.

Mother is always patiently waiting to see her son.

"Now tell me everything you did today," she enquires.

Even when I get home late and would like to turn in, I have to share every detail and Mother seems glad to hear it. She knows intuitively that she must eventually share her son with another female. She wonders, as do I: is this the one? After I relate all the news, we turn in. Here I am, a sixteen year-old teenager and I am still sleeping with my mother on the double mattress that occupies the floor. Poverty and youthful innocence are oblivious to proper decorum.

George McBride is going steady with Donna. This twosome likes to sit on the couch after dark and neck till midnight. Milkmen get up early, so her parents are asleep early and leave propriety to oversee the rest. There are no competitors for the couch. It makes me jealous. Margaret limits me to one kiss per day. I share no similar discipline but I think, "What's a fella going to do when you're in love?" When we say good night, I just make that kiss last as long as possible.

We make a foursome wherever we go. I figure that surely George and Donna will get married. Nope. They eventually split up and they both marry another person. I never get to meet their eventual spouses. It's amazing how people that figure so largely in your life at a given time can drift into oblivion when fate separates your paths. I envy George. Since Margaret rations her kisses to one a day, I have to savour it as best I can and then cool down by riding my bike home to 80 Dundas Street. Maybe it was my smoker's breath; it was not until after I quit smoking that I discovered how obnoxious smoker's breath can be. Mother always wants to know how my evening went. Since Margaret and I always have to do something to pass the time, I have plenty to satisfy her curiosity. I would have preferred to have less to tell. Mother is more pleased than I am.

Meantime, Mother tells me she is giving up the beauty parlour. This is the end of her career as a hairdresser. Her hopeless situation was apparent to me from the start. Now the obvious has come home to Mother. She will sell off her equipment and live as cheaply as she can. It took Mother only seven months to use up half of her financial nest egg. Alas, she is a lost soul with no purpose in life. Factoring in her considerable gifts, it is a tragic waste of talent. At sixteen, I am in no position to understand or help. I accept things as they are. It is a bleak prospect for Mom; for me, it is the door to freedom and adventure. Mother is the one in crisis, but my only thought is "homeless again." No great challenge here. I'm getting used to stepping into the future with no plans in particular. Youth is extravagant in hope. Mother's hope is spent. She finds the cheapest room she can rent and rations her dwindling dollars for food. On the other hand, my hope for the future is in robust condition. Like most teens, I have the world by the tail. George offers me a place to stay at his house for a dollar a day till his parents return from holidays. I live with George for two weeks.

Margaret tells me about a week after our acquaintance that I can call on her after nine. She's going to church on a Monday night to see a movie about the Second Coming of Christ. I am a little miffed that she didn't invite me, but she says I can hang around the house till she returns from church. I am in for a surprise that night when she abruptly says, "We'll have to break off our friendship because I've decided to become a Christian, and I can't be having a worldly boyfriend."

Just like that she intends to dump me. Needless to say, I am surprised but not quite ready to give up.

"Now hold on here," I say. "Maybe I can do something to live up to your new standards. I can be a Christian, if that's what you want."

I see Christianity as some sort of communicable disease which, I assure Margaret, I am willing to catch, if she doesn't mind spreading the virus. When she hears that, she is encouraged, and tells me that if we are to date, we can't go to movies, dance or play cards. I figure that's okay, so long as my one rationed kiss isn't on the list. I go to church with Margaret the next Sunday. I am introduced to a world that is unfamiliar, a world to which I am a stranger. It's July; the building is warm and full of people. The ventilation is not good. The Reverend John Dunkin is preaching, and I discover smoker's cough in the middle of the sermon. Bad habits can get you into trouble. I am humiliated. I am disturbing the service. Just as I am about to beat a hasty retreat, a nice little lady behind us offers me a cough candy and saves the day. I make it through the church service. Margaret makes sure I shake hands with the preacher. He tells me that he hopes I will come back.

"This is a relief," I think, "especially when I just about broke up the service with my coughing."

Margaret is preaching to me that I have to be born again. I really don't know what she's driving at, but I humour her, because after work, I virtually live with the Jones family, and once again I savour the evening meal. I am now going to church Sunday evenings as well as Sunday mornings. Every Monday we go to Young People's where about thirty people from ages sixteen to thirty-five attend. Bart and Marg Pearse are the leaders. They are warmhearted and welcoming. By today's standards, singles and marrieds are an impossible mix, but in those days it seemed to work. Barry Moore, who is recently married, has a wonderful voice and leads the singing. Barry is a schoolteacher and is active in Youth for Christ. YFC, as it is called, holds rallies at London's Central High School attended every Saturday night by a thousand or more people of all ages. By the standards of 1948, it is a racy, slightly irreverent meeting, with rousing singing and a sermon from a visiting pastor or evangelist. One Saturday night in 1948, we hear a relatively unknown evangelist from Chicago whose name is Billy Graham.

Audrey and Barry Moore 1948

Barry is active in our church as a song leader and organizer of ball games. He is a terrific athlete and in his high school days was quarterback for the football team at London South Collegiate. He also arranges ball games for the young people. I get lucky at the church baseball game and make a spectacular running catch, robbing Barry of a home run. I even manage to get a hit at bat and don't strike out. I have learned to throw sidearm so that people cannot see that I throw a ball like a girl. My biggest problem is to live up to my undeserved ballplayer reputation, but for the present my ego is intact.

Barry invites Margaret and me to his house for coffee after the Sunday evening service at Wortley Baptist. It's a set up, of which I am unaware. As we walk along Grand Avenue, Barry starts to evangelize me. I am embarrassed when (of all things, right on the street) he opens his Bible in public to show me a Bible verse. I say nothing, envying the nearest bush where I could hide. I am grateful when he closes his Bible and puts it away. However, I never forget the verse; it is Psalm 84:11: "For the Lord God is a sun and a shield, the Lord will give grace and glory. No good thing will He withhold from him that walks uprightly." When we get to his house, around coffee and a sweet roll, Barry continues to buttonhole me. To avoid the issue, I submit and kneel, praying a prayer that Barry calls the sinner's prayer. He wrings from me a decision to become a Christian. Margaret is pleased. All this does not offend me because I just don't get it. It's all too new to understand.

The summer of 1948 is passed pleasantly. George McBride, however, sees that I am being influenced towards Christianity and tries one more time to convince me that Christianity is bogus. I even join in the pact to prove the impossibility of Christianity. So much for my prayer to become a Christian. When George and I are together, we reinforce one another's unbelief. I am an enthusiastic atheist and skeptic. However, for me, my lack of faith makes for a poor atheist. Secretly, I suspect there just might be a God after all. All this dialogue has created in me a new curiosity; I want to read the Bible for myself. I will make my own decision based on the evidence. That will come later when I start to read the Bible in earnest. In a few weeks, I will have moved again to Sadler's boarding house. It's the cheapest bed I can find, and at nights when I finish my last cigarette, I read the Bible. The attic at 250 Wortley Road becomes my shrine. It is there that I finally feel the presence of God while reading Scripture. Now I am seriously considering what it takes to become a Christian. As an outsider, I have opened a door and am peering into a world as of yet unexplored. Behind the searching mind there is a repository of Bible stories that Grandma read to me as a child. Her patience with this spoiled kid is starting to pay off. But first, let me tell you about Sadler's boarding house.

The Sadler family had made a deal to purchase a run down-mansion on Wortley Road in London. It was perfect for a boarding house, with rooms left over to rent, plus another two apartments. Art Sadler had married hardworking Margaret in Forest, Ontario, in 1928. Margaret was the optimist. Art was the pessimist. To illustrate my point, Art told me how he bought a car for $200.00 which quit on him one week later. Discouraged, he sold it for $50.00 without even checking with a mechanic to see if it could be fixed. Turned out that all it needed was a universal joint which the new owner purchased for $2.00 So Art had to watch his neighbour drive a car which Art had subsidized to the tune of $150.00. Pessimism is expensive. To Margaret goes the credit for the vision of a boarding house.

Art had felt a call to the ministry when he was young but failed to respond. Like Jonah of Bible fame, another great pessimist, he eventually fulfilled his call. Meantime, he joined the army and did a stint overseas during World War II. Like other young men at the time, he had seen war and had been to France, Belgium, and Holland. He had returned to Canada where he renewed his determination to enter the ministry. He took the shortest route by going to London Bible School. Ultimately, he became a lay preacher in a country circuit of two Baptist churches that he served for a lifetime, working an additional forty hours a week at a London factory.

Art and Margaret had a son my age that everyone called "Beak." One meeting with "Beak" was all it took to know how Ron Sadler got his nickname. He was the only kid I ever met whose nose entered the room before he did. It served him well and must have been connected to an oversized pair of lungs, because Ron was a chain-smoking, nonstop talker, who regaled me with his tall stories for the next three years, while we shared accommodation at his mother's boarding house.

Sadler's boarding house, 250 Wortley Road

So Art and Margaret Sadler have this place at 250 Wortley Road. Across the street is the London Normal School, where prospective school teachers train one year for their teaching certificate. Six of these students (all girls) board with Mrs.Sadler. With no bedrooms left over, Ron Sadler sleeps in the attic. I need a boarding house cheap. For $8.00 a week, I get the adjacent cot with Ron, my meals, and my laundry. My attic room is hot in the summer, and cold in the winter, with a little wind tossed in to guarantee all the fresh air a fellow needs to stay healthy. I even see a little snow under my bed when conditions are right. It is enough.

After supper, I bike over to see my girlfriend Margaret. After my one and only kiss, I ride home and do my Bible reading. I'm in Genesis and racing along because I love history, and this book is about the origins of the Hebrew people. I am impressed by the truthfulness of the Bible. I draw the logical conclusions and accept the veracity of the Old Testament. It is a short jump to draw a similar conclusion about the New. It is here in my attic room one late night in August that I experience the warmth of my faith in Jesus Christ. I make my decision.
"I believe!"
I am no longer an outsider. I have stepped into a brand new world. It is the Christian world I spoke of in my introduction. For the first

time in my life, I understand who my Grandmother really is. Someday in heaven, she will have to introduce herself to me, because in my mind, Grandma was born old and never changed. With resurrection changes, I'll bet she's a beauty.

Barry Moore, your Bible-punching ways produced results after all. It's just that I am a slow learner. Soon, I am vocal about my faith, and there's no zeal like the newly converted. I quickly manage to alienate the girls who board at the Sadlers'. However, Margery Dorpaal, who also is a seasoned Christian, takes me aside and tells me to "cool it." Well do I remember the spirited conversations around Mrs. Sadler's table at dinner. I get a crash course on how to relate to knowledgeable girls who will one day be numbered amongst the teaching staff of the Ontario public school system. I must say it was fun. I get an understanding of life, which is a little more in keeping with normal living. It is a healthy, mind-stretching experience. But once again, I have raced ahead of my story.

To return to my narrative, it is a few days before the new girls will arrive, and I'm riding my bike to Eaton's in downtown London to buy the sweater I will be needing for school. I take the Ridout Bridge. There is a shortcut, but the path is gravel. I'm going too fast. I start braking at the bottom of the hill, but it is too late. Down I go, slipping and crashing my bike as I grind to a stop. I've skinned my knee and my trousers have a one-inch tear. I'm angry. My normal response is to resort to profanity. The words die in my throat. I reason, "How can I take the name of Christ in vain, if I am his follower?" The next revelation is this: "I must be a Christian or I wouldn't feel this way."

I notice something else. I'm not mad. I come to one of many life-altering decisions. The fire of anger is fueled by profanity. I gain control of my temper and my profanity. I am experiencing the first profound change in my personality. I have conquered my tongue. The saboteurs of personality fall away like spent rocket boosters for which I have no further use. My diction and use of language improves. "Wait until I tell Grandma this. All those rebukes for my swearing have finally started to reap a dividend. But Grandma is in Stratford, first, I'll tell Mom!"

I pay Mother a visit in her single room where she now lives. I tell her about my decision to be a different person and go to church. She is unresponsive. She is a sad person who has no friends. Her sole companion is the radio I bought for her. I tell her the news that I have become a Christian. She commends me for my decision. It is a commendation spoken without enthusiasm. Mother is on the road to becoming a recluse. Eventually she will understand it and genuinely approve. It just takes more time.

I have this burning desire to tell Grandma that I am now a Christian. Hitchhiking to Stratford is easy and I show up at 475 Albert Street where she lives with Uncle Gord and Aunt Elsie. I am warmly greeted. After the usual pleasantries, I deliver my declaration with enthusiasm. It is the last thing they are expecting from me. After an awkward silence, Gordon expresses his disappointment and says so.

Elsie, who always tries to be positive about everything, says, "As long as you're happy about it, I guess its okay. My parents were Jehovah Witnesses, and it brought so much controversy, I never wanted to have much to do with religion."

It is Grandma's reaction that matters to me and she shows her approval in her face. Her prayers for me that were unknown to this carefree kid have been answered. I remind her how many times she quoted, "Thou shalt not take the name of the Lord thy God in vain." She grins back at me with such a pleased look on her face that I glow with joy. The bond between Grandma and me has always been strong. This special day makes it even stronger. In the eight years that remain in her life, I am to become her pillar of strength to encourage her in her own trials that unavoidably come with old age. Eventually, she will have the special joy of seeing me enter the ministry and to know that she has contributed to my life. I am also able to assure her on that very special day of August 29, 1948, that I will be keeping an eye on Mother, supporting her in her struggles as best as an immature sixteen-year-old son can do. After lunch, I say a fond farewell and hitchhike back to London. Sunday I attend church with Margaret, knowing that I have begun an adventure that will shape the rest of my life for the better.

Monday is Labour Day; our Young People's meeting is held outdoors on the lawn. I decide at that meeting that I will become a minister. The call that Jesus gave to Peter 2000 years ago comes home to me.

"Follow me and I will make you to become Fishers of men."

I want to preach the gospel too. I want to become a minister. Margaret is pleased and asks me if I would like to go to a prayer meeting on Wednesday night. I am curious and agree. A Scottish layman, Bill Phillip, who sometime preaches is the speaker. He leads the meeting. His Scottish brogue is unmistakable; there is no doubt of his country of origin. Most of the people are elderly, but I am favourably impressed by their sincerity. Margaret, on the other hand, is embarrassed that she suggested coming at all. She is sure that I am offended by the bad singing and says so – but I disagree,

"I liked the sincerity of the prayers." I tell her, "So you don't need to apologize for anything tonight." She is pleasantly surprised. Her qualms about the meeting subside. I am comfortable with my newfound faith. I am comfortable with elderly Christians even though I am only a teenager. I am on a faith journey exploring every Christian venue that is offered and thoroughly enjoying the trip.

-oOo-

Fast forward twenty-eight years. I am now the pastor of Stanley Avenue Baptist Church, in Hamilton, Ontario. Frieda Gergaitus has come out of a tragic divorce and is seeking comfort somewhere. Because her church frowns on divorce, she accepts an invitation from a neighbour friend to come to ours. Joy Clark (more about her in a later chapter) was that comforter. Frieda very quickly commits her life to Christ and is a wonderful example of the power of a transformed life. Her friend John Whittaker has noticed the difference. John eventually becomes one of the three top executives at Westinghouse, supervising the creation of electricity producing turbines at $28 million a pop. John is intrigued with Frieda's story and asks how a very sad Frieda is now exuding such joy. A busy man, John cannot go to church on a Sunday but asks for an alternative. The only alternative Frieda can think of is the midweek prayer meeting which very much resembles that memorable prayer meeting that made such a lasting impression on me. When prayers have ended, surprising us all, John stands up and asks for permission to speak. I can't give you word for word what he said, but it went something like this,

"I have never been to such a remarkable church gathering as this. I can't get over the sincerity of ordinary people like this praying to God. I don't know what you people have, but I admire it and I think I want to be the kind of people you are."

With curiosity and desire like that, John gave his heart to Christ that night and has never looked back. That evening in 1976 is one of the most treasured occasions in my entire ministry.

-oOo-

Margaret and I have agreed that from now on we are "going steady". Infatuation is a lovely thing. It attracts and imagines that that special other person is perfect. As of yet, I was blind to the differences of viewpoint that made us incompatible for the long haul. For the time being, Margaret filled a deep need in my life and I will be forever grateful that in the providence of God our paths crossed for my good. Eventually we broke up. It was not without tears, but I knew we were in personality too far removed from each other to continue a relationship that just wouldn't last.

-oOo-

Joan Amy 1944   *Reginald (Rex) Amy 1945*

Sixteen-year-old Joan Amy is looking into the mirror and putting on her lipstick. It is a warm spring day in 1945. Joan has put on her best dress and is excited about Rex Amy's homecoming. Her soldier brother is back from the war, and they are going out for a walk. Rex has survived a horrendous Nazi air raid. This is the second time he has cheated death. Rex is one of three Amy brothers who were overseas in the Canadian Army. Rex (Reginald) has recovered from his war wounds and has been discharged home. Waterloo is proud of its army sons. The war is winding down to Victory; the army boys are hometown heroes. There aren't many of them just yet. Only those like Rex, who were wounded and discharged, are to be seen. They are a walking badge of respect, and Joan is proud to have her brother by her side. Her friends don't know the handsome Rex is her brother. Joan takes her time to tell them. Let them think what they will.

A fresh wind is blowing. Daffodils and forsythia are blooming. The grass has just turned green. Birds are singing. The day matches the jubilant mood of the sweet sixteen-year-old teenager who is admiring her good-looking brother. Rex in his uniform and Joan in her best, are walking down King Street, Waterloo. Admiring glances from those who are passing by enhance the walk. Joan Amy couldn't be happier to have her uniformed brother by her side. They are making their way Waterloo's Harmony Lunch Restaurant. Rex orders hamburgers. This is his special treat for his now grown-up sister (who was only twelve when he went off to war). It's been four years since Rex has had one of Harmony's famous hamburgers. They share a delicious lunch together. When they finish their meal, they reemerge on the street. As they return home to 59 Menno Street, Joan enjoys the promenade all over again. It has been a very satisfying day. This beautiful teenage girl will figure largely in my life in days to come.

Chapter 3
London South Collegiate

Tuesday, September 7, 1948. Today I register at London South as a new student. I have a flashback to those dismal days when I had allowed myself to be talked into moving to Calgary because Mother thought she just had to move back to Alberta where she remembered childhood happiness. How different this is from Calgary, where two years earlier I felt so strange and alienated. The difference is community. In Calgary, during the brief time I lived there away from my home in Stratford, I felt alone. Separated from familiar surroundings and without a friend, I was overwhelmed by Calgary. I was homesick for Stratford. In those days, I rejected what in a better frame of mind I might have accepted as probably a good high school. At London South, I already had faces to recognize – friends from Wortley Baptist to greet, and share my adjustment. Looking back, I see how helpful it is to belong to a people with whom one can have identity. No wonder immigrants from foreign countries seek their own. To live without community is a recipe for lostness. I am comfortable at London South, I even feel like I belong.

I am facing my first challenge. I have enough money to pay my room and board for two weeks but no money to purchase textbooks. This is that era of the past when it was the student's responsibility to find the cash to buy textbooks. Wednesday, the kids are at school with their textbooks, but I can only make notes. I go to prayer meeting that night and ask my new friends I have met to pray for how I might solve my problem. I even put forward an idea for how to get an answer to my prayers.

"Is there anybody in our church a year ahead of me who would loan me their grade twelve text books?" I ask.

The Alfords were there and had a daughter in grade thirteen with whom they shared my need. Althea Alford, a beautifully spirited girl, now comes to my rescue. She is a good student and a diligent Christian. She is happy to loan me her books. She is a clean meticulous book lover who has kept all her textbooks from high school. Thanks to Althea, I have my textbooks that are as good as new. I promise to return them unmarked. The first of many miracles has just taken place.

My next hurdle is finances. Within ten days, I will be out of money. The moment of reality strikes down my defenses. I will have to get a job and quit school. It is a sinking feeling to abandon my life's dream for an education, but with no alternative in sight (and in counsel with no one) I apply at the Empire Brass Company for a factory job. I am hired at sixty-six cents an hour starting in two days. I'll be making $26.40 a week. I return to my boarding house depressed and resigned to my fate. After a quiet supper, in despair, I ride my bike over to the Moores'. I share my decision with Barry Moore, who has become something of a role model and mentor. I can still hear his surprise and admonition.

"God didn't save you and call you to the ministry to work at Empire Brass!" Barry declares. "Where's your faith? Get off your butt and get a part-time job. Pray for guidance and your needs will be supplied." He remonstrates with me. "Rake leaves! Dig gardens! Get a weekend job. Do anything, but don't quit school. God will get you through!"

These inspiring words challenged me. An epiphany of hope! "My God shall supply all your needs according to his riches in glory." That's what Barry said. I take heart and believe him because that's what the Bible says. Our meeting is brief.

"I gotta go and tell the Sadlers what you said." I am ecstatic with new joy. Waving Barry goodbye, I ride back to my boarding house and share my new enthusiasm with my landlady, who says, "Well, I suppose you can try something else, just so long as you pay your board."

Fired with new zeal, I reply, "I will. God will see me through this; I just have to find a way."

With that, I say my prayers and go to bed. I already know exactly who will help me. It's the Thursday of my second week at London South. I won't be at school today. I am going to hitchhike to Tillsonburg. Uncle Norm will lend me $50.00, which of course I will repay. I will ask him for this money to keep me going.

I can still remember the day. I awake to a warm, sunny September morning. The leaves are just starting to turn to an autumn gold. In no time I have hitched a ride, and by 11:30 AM the familiar streets of Tillsonburg greet me. I arrive in time to have lunch with Uncle Norm and Aunt Jean. My surprise visit doesn't deter Jean. She invites me for their noon meal where I explain my mission, fully expecting a positive reply.

Uncle Norm says to me, "Bruce, I could lend you the money, but what will you do when that runs out?"

"Well, I hadn't thought of that, but something will turn up," I reply.

"Sorry, Bruce, but I can't help you. Here's two dollars just to let you know that we care about you,"

Uncle Norman is kind but firm. For my education, I have to go it alone. Norman has made me face reality and it's embarrassing, but I soon get over that. Already I'm formulating an idea.

I'm grateful for the two dollars, and understand the problem. Undaunted, I bid them farewell and hitchhike back to London. I have an alternative plan. (Who knows, maybe Gabriel had something to do with it. I believe in guardian angels!) I go to the office of the London Free Press and submit an ad under the heading, "Employment Wanted". The ad costs $1.80 and reads, "Ambitious studeent desires to work his way through high school. Phone 53869" which is my landlady's phone number. I have twenty cents left. I blow fifteen cents on a butterscotch Sundae. I don't remember what I did with the nickel. Friday morning I'm back at high school, brimming with confidence, and quite oblivious of my omission to tell Mrs. Sadler about the ad. I have begun an entrepreneurial journey that in sixty years will take me to the book publishing business.

The next day, when I return to Sadlers' after school, a frustrated Margaret says to me, "I have had some interesting phone calls to ask you about." Looking me straight in the eye, with firm resolve, she says to me,

"I know you told me that you are going back to school, but you didn't say a word to your boss at Empire Brass. He called this morning, and he wasn't very happy that you didn't show up for work."

"Oh, oh!" I reply. "I forgot."

"By the way, did you put an ad for employment in the paper using my phone number and didn't tell me?"

"I guess I forgot that as well, Mrs. Sadler. I'm sorry."

I am learning that resting in the Lord's provision can be so relaxing, one can assume a little too much. I am also learning the hard way that to keep all this to myself is a secret that can be counterproductive.

"Well, Bruce Woods," says my landlady, "the next time you do something like that, I want to know about it first."

I'm sheepish and whisper, "Sorry, I should have told you."

"I should think so." says Mrs. Sadler, "Now here are three numbers you can call." Suddenly, I get excited as Margaret hands me the scratch pad. I phone them and 'Voila!' just like that, I have three jobs. The first and second are raking leaves, for which I charge seventy cents an hour. The third job is painting. Mr. Jacobs owns three houses. They all need painting. He could do better by getting an experienced painter, but he hires me at seventy cents an hour because he wants to help me. Mr. Jacobs is one of those rare persons who is more interested in helping a teenager who needs a job than getting a professional who would have served him better. I am grateful and make $11.00 a week. One week's work stretches out to another, and in the end, this will sustain me till mid-December. I pay eight dollars for board. A dollar goes for my tithe which I give to my church. (I had just heard a sermon on tithing.) Ten cents is for Sunday School. With the balance, I buy my clothes and sundries. I soon discover that a leftover dollar and ninety cents isn't enough. I take on another part time job at the A & P, bagging groceries on Saturdays. Dragging myself home after six o'clock, I eat alone (I am late). Mrs. Sadler is prompt, and supper was served at 5:30 PM. By seven o'clock, exhausted, I tumble into bed and sleep for thirteen hours. I have learned my lesson: one part time job is enough. I have schoolwork to do with precious little time for recreation. I drop the second job. Poverty is still my challenge, and I'm about to face my next test.

It's Sunday, September 19, and there's been a change in the weather. I have been a Christian for all of four weeks and attend church dressed in a white shirt, tie, and my blue pants. No sooner am I seated when I notice that everybody is wearing a suit jacket. Vainly, I look to see if somebody is dressed as plainly as I am. Nope! I am the only one without a suit jacket, and I can't afford to remedy the situation. There is no vanity like that of the impoverished underdog. It is a sin to be poor (or so I imagine), so I say to Barry Moore, "I'm not coming back to church."

"Why not?" exclaims Barry.

"Look at me," I say. "I'm the only guy in church that isn't properly dressed."

"What do you mean?" he says. "You look okay to me."

I explain to him my predicament and Barry replies, "I can fix that."

"How?" I plead.

"Come over to my place. I've got a jacket I don't wear anymore. You can have that."

I am pleased at my good fortune and accept Barry's jacket. It fits perfectly and is brown bordering on orange. The next Sunday, I wear my orangey-brown out-of-style jacket with my blue pants, pleased that I can sit in church without attracting any undue attention. I improved my lot considerably one year later when I bought a light green jacket which I wore with black trousers, imagining myself to be the best dressed dude in the church.

The next two months will teach me how to pray for things I need even though I don't have the money and to experience God's provision. God is watching 'From a distance.' And Bette Midler hasn't even been born. On one occasion, I have two dollars for the rubbers (galosh-style footwear) I need to wear to school over the only shoes I own. The need is acute because I've worn a hole in the only shoes I possess, and on rainy days, my feet get wet. I will do this on Thursday. Wednesday night I'm in church because I want to hear a missionary from Africa who is sharing his vision for Nigeria. When the offering came round, I put the only two dollars I have into the plate and prayed, "Lord, you know I can't afford to do this, but I'm trusting You for my footwear." By the next Saturday, God had provided me with a babysitting job. I'm of the opinion that most Christians, including me, become too measured when it comes to giving. It was great to serve God with such reckless abandon. No wonder new converts get so many of their prayers answered.

Even though I'm busy, I decide to pay Mom a visit in her rented room. When I arrive, she looks forlorn but is glad to see her son. She informs me of things all too familiar, and all too false.

"The people in Stratford that ruined my life there have spread their lies to the roomers here where I live," Mother tells me.

Vainly I protest. I try to explain that her logic is utterly impossible. But her mind is made up, and she says she must move to flee her persecutors.

Bruce Woods, 17 years old

During the next two years, she will move some eighteen times for exactly the same reason. Sometimes she doesn't even inform me where she is living. There are times I lose track of her, and then she reemerges in a new location. She is frightened and alone. I try my best to comfort her, but it is impossible to have a sensible conversation about her self-imposed exile. Exasperated, I change the subject and keep her informed of the things that are happening in my life.

Chapter 4
The Coat

Hindsight is a marvelous teacher. I now race ahead of my story to illustrate one of the most significant experiences of my life. It is a story that requires me to leap fourteen years into the future in order to redeem the crisis that nearly overwhelmed me four months into my new Christian life. Six weeks after I turned seventeen (on Hallowen, my birthday is October 31)

It seemed like everything went wrong all at once.

-oOo-

It is the year 1962, and the phone is ringing at the senior Bruce Woods house in Toronto. He has a son living in Georgetown by the same name (me) who is now a pastor, but Bruce Woods senior is too preoccupied with his troubles to pursue any contact.

"Bruce, I haven't seen you and Phyllis for a year. What are you doing with yourself these days?" says Wray Woods, his brother.

"Well, I guess you've heard about the car accident."

"I did, and that's why I'm phoning to find out how your wife is doing."

"Recovering slowly. She really got banged up in the accident; it was a head on collision. It will be a year before she's back to normal."

"And how are your children handling all this?"

"Well, naturally Patrica was really upset; Michael's okay as long as he has a car to tear apart. He's into stock car racing these days. Tony took it the hardest, but she's only fifteen."

"What about Bruce Junior? Does he know?"

"I don't think he knows; I haven't told him. I hardly ever see him."

"Do you even know where he is?"

"Well, Wray, as a matter of fact, he has graduated from an American seminary somewhere, and has a church in Georgetown."

"Really! For a non-church-goer like you, to produce a son in the ministry is quite an achievement. There must be a recessive gene somewhere in previous generations that made its appearance after a hundred-year hiatus. Or does the explanation lie elsewhere? Ethel, perhaps?"

"More likely it's Ethel; there's not much church in our family."

"Hold on there Bruce; you know I'm a faithful Anglican."

Bruce rolls his eyes and says, "Yeah, I know, but you're another exception that proves the rule."

"I had heard he was in a church somewhere. Stewart and I were just talking about him the other day. I think we ought to reconnect with him. I know I would. Maybe we could drop in on a church service unannounced and hear him preach. If that could be arranged, would you like to join us? "

"No thanks, Wray; I'd be afraid the building would fall down if I went to church. I can't even remember the last time I've been in church, it's so long ago."

"Not even to hear your own son preach?"

"Ethel's son."

"Your son, too. " These things take more than one person, you know."

"Yeah, I suppose so."

"Where is he?

"Georgetown; I believe it is a Baptist Church on Maple Avenue. The reason I know that is because it is called Maple Avenue Baptist Church."

"He must have invited you to visit some Sunday for you to know all this."

"He did, but I have no intention of being a hypocrite by attending church even if my own son is preaching."

"Well, since our church gladly welcomes hypocrites, I have no such compunction. I want to hear your son preach and who knows, maybe even Jim will come along. Sure you don't want to change your mind?"

"Absolutely not!"

"Very well then; thanks for the information. Us hypocrites will go to hear him preach and bring you back a report."

"Thanks. I'll be glad to settle for a report."

"Bye for now."

"Bye and give our regards to Rene."

"Glad to."

"By the way, perhaps this is as good a time to drop the bomb as any."

"What do you mean by that?" exclaims Wray

"I've got cancer."

"You've got to be kidding."

"You don't kid about cancer. I've got it and I've got it in the lower bowel."

"Bruce, that's the worst news I've heard since I don't know when."

"Well, I couldn't believe it when I heard, but I've seen the charts and it's serious."

"How serious is serious?"

"It is inoperable. I've got to undergo chemotherapy with no promise of the results."

"Well, Bruce, I know you don't set much stock in prayer, but I'm going to be praying that by God's grace you will recover."

"Thanks, it's nice to know that you care. By the way, if you do decide to pay my son a visit in his church, I want no mention of this topic with him."

"Sure, Bruce; I understand."

-oOo-

Backtrack fourteen years and my crises. In 1947, a year before our family fell apart, Mother had purchased a winter coat for me. It served me well in 1947/48. It still fit me when the cold weather arrived the following winter. I would wear it to school. When I rode my bicycle to work, I would wear it again, carefully removing it, while I put on my work clothes to paint Mr. Jacobs' houses. Friday, December l0, 1948, was cold and blustery. No time to be painting houses, but I only had an hour's work left. Dutifully, in wretched conditions, I completed painting the exterior of Mr. Jacobs' house, knowing that from now on I would be unemployed. It was a miserable day with wind and sleet. I was so cold that I put on my winter jacket over my work clothes to keep warm. After I cleaned up, to my horror I discovered I had paint drops all over my winter jacket. My coat was ruined! Why didn't I think to wear my coat under my work clothes!

Now I had two problems: first, how to clean my coat, and second, since I am now out of work, how was I going to pay my board. I remember so well the ride back to my boarding house. Facing the wind and riding my bike through snowy streets, and looking into the front windows of many houses, I saw the warm glow of lights that was home for somebody. I had no home. How I longed to be somebody else. The kids at school didn't have to struggle like this. They could play soccer or hockey with friends after school. I had to work. With a ruined coat, I had wiped out two weeks of wages, or so I thought. I never felt so miserable. I felt so sorry for myself that I was crying. I thought at this rate, I'll never make it through high school, let alone university. Pessimism had vanquished faith. Fortunately, the malaise was temporary. The dry cleaners were able to rescue my coat. I wore it another year before it gave out. How I made it through the long, long winter I will relate in chapter 10.

-o0o-

The coat episode was my lowest point since I began my adventure between two worlds. I have used that story to encourage many a weary pilgrim who has despaired of facing the trials of life. However, more often I have used the coat story to inspire. Fourteen years after my coat incident, I am the pastor of Maple Avenue Baptist Church in Georgetown, Ontario. It is September. The service, which begins at 11 AM, has an interesting distraction for me. There in our small congregation are four distinguished visitors. Three fine-looking men are sitting near the front. One of them also has his wife along. I immediately think, "This is a well-heeled American search committee from a big church south of the border checking me out for a possible call." I had only been at my church for three years. I thought, "No matter how attractive the offer, in good conscience, there is no way I could leave my congregation for some fancy American church, no matter how appealing the opportunity."

I didn't have to face that kind of a decision. After the service, our distinguished visitors introduced themselves to me. They were my uncles – Jim Woods, a sales rep for Canada's national magazine, Macleans; Stewart Woods, vice-president of the Toronto Star; and Wray Woods, sales manager for Neilson's Ice Cream Company, along with his wife, Irene. I had met them nineteen years earlier, but that memory had been erased by the passing of time. When the service concluded, my favourite deacon Henry Sienko asked me who the visitors were,
"I don't know but they are staying put. I will let you know as soon as they identify themselves."

At last the church had cleared, and my distinguished guests approached me, grinning from ear to ear.

"That was a terrific sermon you preached; I thoroughly enjoyed it. Let me introduce my wife Irene Woods, I'm your uncle Wray Woods and these other two ruffians are your uncles Jim and Stewart. We could have told you we were coming, but we wanted to surprise you. Now, as soon as you recover from the shock, we would like to take you and your wife out for lunch."

By now, my wife, Joan simply said, "It's a lovely idea but what are we going to do with three children! I have a better idea. Let's all go over to the parsonage. We can have lunch ready in no time. I have enough for all."

With eggs in the fridge and tinned salmon on the shelf, we proved the point so often made: "It's not the food; its the company."

Later in the conversation, my Uncle Wray says to me, "In your sermon you alluded to the hard times you had working your way through high school. Believe me, when you came to the coat incident, I had tears in my eyes. If I had known then how strapped you were for a roof over your head, I would have adopted you, and you wouldn't have had a thing to worry about right through university and graduation."

To which I replied, "And in those days, I would have accepted; but if all that had happened, I would have been deprived of one of the greatest adventures in faith and answered prayer that I could have imagined. And in the bargain, I would have been deprived of God's great school of faith and trust. So thank you so much, Wray, but I guess I was better off just the way it was."

My Uncle Wray agreed, for he, too, as already mentioned had become a committed Anglican Christian and had his own wonderful pilgrimage which he later shared with me over a business lunch in Toronto. After that significant encounter, we became very close because Wray, like me, was a zealous Christian. He never forgot the "coat" incident and made up in later life what he was not able to do for me when I was starting out. For example, when our family had grown to six and we were strapped financially to buy a car, he arranged for me to pick up a used Buick in good condition. Later, when I tried to make a payment at the bank, the loan officer said,

"According to our records, that account has been paid in full." The

God of miracles buried a coat when I was a teenager and resurrected it into a car fourteen years later.

Chapter 5
My New Family

When I started to attend Wortley Road Baptist church, I became a member of an extended family so gradually that I was unaware of it, much the way a child grows up at home and takes siblings for granted as though they were always there. At the top of the pecking order was our pastor, John R. Dunkin. I admired him so much that I was sure he could do no wrong and that every word he spoke was gospel. I always told him I enjoyed his sermons even if I didn't understand them.

Wortley Road Baptist　　　　　　*John R. Dunkin 1948*

These were days when it was good to be right. All others – well, you can guess for yourself. Don Hansford, who became a United Church minister was one of the errant. In vain did I try to persuade him to become a Baptist. Had I succeeded, all the dear United Church folk he served would not have had his godly example. So that's one debate that I'm now glad I lost. Those were the days of strong opinions on things that didn't matter, such as when Eva Murray was forced by our pastor to cancel a joint meeting with the young people of the Hamilton Road Brethren Assembly. John Dunkin then unsuccessfully explained to Eva how important it was to be a separatist. By this he meant separate from not only the world, but from other Christians with whom we differed. That included minutia on many topics and John Dunkin's word was law. Amazingly, we just went along with it. So even before I had studied the Bible for myself, I was a Fundamentalist Pre-Millennial Dispensationalist, separated from the world and not associating with the like of other denominations, and especially those other Baptists from (ugh) the Baptist Convention of Ontario and Quebec. You see, it wasn't good enough to be a Baptist. One had to be a member of an exclusive Baptist church, just like us.

We were separated from the world. Separation meant that we didn't dance, go to movies, drink alcoholic beverages, smoke, or play cards. For the girls, it meant one thing more, no lipstick. Friends around the workplace called these girls "paleface". These people who were "separated" from the world came mainly from Baptist and Pentecostal churches with a smattering from other smaller denominations with names like Nazarene, Free Methodist, Brethren, and Associated Gospel Churches. (Already I was questioning my pastor's rigid views, but only a little. I was on the road to what the old-timers would feel was compromise). However, back in 1948, I reveled in the fact that we were different and exploited our advantage at every evangelistic opportunity that came my way. It was great to belong to something that was such a worthy cause. This was taught on every occasion right from Sunday School up. For example, one little tyke was   talking to his friend whose Grandma had just died.

"If your Grandma didn't believe in Jesus, then she didn't go to heaven." says this four-year-old to his friend.

"How do you know that?" says his startled playmate.

"The apostles said so."

"What's an apostle?"

"I don't know, but you can find out at our church."

"Where is your church?"

"I don't know, but if you ask your mom to phone my mom, she can tell you."

Now if you can overlook this little bit of irreverence, let me affirm here and now that I believe that Christ is the Saviour of the world and my heart's desire is that everyone would come to this understanding. It will transform your life. However, over the years, I have mellowed a bit. It's not that I have changed my views. However, I am a little more discreet in sharing them with others, and I am willing to believe that if a man lives up to the light that he has, I hope to see him in heaven.

Living up to high standards is not without its benefits. For this reason, I quit smoking. At least I thought I did. That little monster proved harder to kill than I thought, although eventually I managed to win. My family on both sides thought I would get over my religious zeal, and so they were willing to wait it out. In the meantime, both sides agreed I was better off without my cigarettes. Years later, I can safely conclude I made a better go at life than many of my skeptical in-laws. Now that I've become a grandfather of ten and enjoy the "Amy Reunions" (my wife's side of the family; the Woods clan is so splintered with divorces that it's impossible to have reunions), I can only say we must have done something right to enjoy such family stability.

Getting back to my addiction to cigarettes. I decided to limit my smoking to three cigarettes a day the first week. The second week it was two. The toughest was week number three. I would light up and take a few drags, butt the thing out, and relight it a little later. This way I lasted the day. Week number four, it was cold turkey. I suffered through a tormented week but noticed after seven days that my cravings started to diminish. Five weeks later, I told George McBride that I had quit for good. I should have known better than to boast; George challenged me, "You're still addicted, and if you took one drag of a cigarette you would be finished."

"No way!" says I, "and I'll prove it. Gimme a cigarette."

That was a challenge I should have dismissed, but I wanted to prove to George that the power of God was sufficient for everything, including not smoking cigarettes. That night I finished off five and found myself as addicted as ever. Lesson learned. We do not prove the power of God by our human resources. Give the Holy Spirit something to do. He's been taking care of the reputation of the Church long before I came on the scene, and he'll manage things quite well after I'm gone. Believers are only junior partners in an eternal arrangement with our Lord, so leave the convincing up to God.

Getting back to our rather austere Baptist way of life, I have a great many role models to be thankful for. First, there were the deacons, like godly old Mr. Jim Phillip (the one that had led the prayer meeting). Then there was Dudley Collins, a salesman for Ford who was top performer for all of Canada in 1950; Ken Brown, principal of Ealing Public School; Robert McRonald, Fire Chief of the London force; Art McKenzie, our Sunday School Superintendent, who later became a successful real estate salesman; and Lloyd Alford, who eventually developed his auto parts business into a Canadian Tire franchise. Lloyd quarreled with John Dunkin, and in protest, went over to Adelaide Baptist for a while. However, he mended his fences and returned to Wortley after Pastor Dunkin moved on to another posting. Other godly examples were Gordon Duke, who sadly fell for a Ponzi scheme and lost all his hard-earned money made in the insurance business. (Fifty years later, I would lose $64,000 in exactly the same way. Fortunately for me, that only represented 25% of my assets. How I turned that loss to a gain will come later.) Others who set a good example were guys like Bill Pollard of London Life; Gordon McKay, a terrific chalk artist who did his work all over the area; and an array of wonderful people whose names are now lost to my memory. For quality people, Wortley Road Baptist was an inspiration.

My crowd was teens like myself but included people from other churches such as Wes Suchard, who became a chartered accountant and made a lot of money. He and his wife Sally (Stacey) have been exemplary in the downtown London Mission Services, not to speak of the business community, where Wes and his friend Don Hill still lead a downtown Bible study for business people. Wes illustrates God's patience with us. Wes sowed a lot of wild oats but successfully prayed for a crop failure. Well do I remember a day when Wes expressed his displeasure at his autocratic father by driving his dad's car at seventy miles an hour, heading west on Riverside Drive. We narrowly missed a head-on collision by inches. Don Hill was another rebel just like Wes. One day he heard God saying, "The wages of sin is death."
 Don agreed and decided to quit before payday.

Then there were studious Bill Foster and his piano-playing sister, Marie; they both went into full-time ministry – Bill as a professor of Biblical studies at London Bible Institute, and Marie as an American pastor's wife. My personal buddies were Don Fitchett, who became a preacher of some renown, and Gerry Rowe, who worked for the municipality. Don came to Christ through Gerry and me. I shall never forget the night that he and Rusty Baker came to Central Baptist Church to scoff. Afterwards we came back to Wortley Baptist, before the church was locked up. Marie was playing the piano. Rusty sat in the front row, while Don walked up to the pulpit and said, "Wouldn't it be wonderful to be a preacher, and sway the people to Christ."

Rusty gasped and protested, "Fitchett, you've gone over to the enemy."

From that time on, Gerry, Don, and I were inseparable. Gerry was, as I explained, a civil servant who worked for the city of London and a lay preacher of distinction. In many ways Gerry and I were to become inseparable friends, so I will enlarge on how this came about in chapter seven. There were others like the inimitable Barry Moore, who left teaching school to become an international evangelist. He was always on top of his game, whether he was quarterback of the London South football squad, throwing forward passes to Art McKenzie, or preaching a powerful sermon to an audience in faraway Ukraine.

Then there were friends: Ian McRonald, who tragically died before he was thirty when he was run over by a streetcar in Toronto; Ross Millar, who became sales manager of D.H. Howden & Co., a hardware distributor; Paul Postian of the famous carpet importers, who accepted Christ but was not allowed to attend our church. He was unable to break loose from the Armenian Church until after he was married. These were a few of a wider circle of friends that included kids from Central Baptist and the Hamilton Road Brethren Assembly. When I left Stratford, I had a hundred kids that I knew by first names, none of them Christians as far as I knew. (Later I discovered several that were, but weren't telling.) After moving to London, I quickly replaced my old friends with new ones. They helped to make my life meaningful. I didn't quite know what God had in store for me, but I was sure He had a plan for my life that included having to work my way though high school. However, after five weeks of this, I freely admit I found myself wishing my life were easier like that of the teens I hung out with at the church.

Chapter 6
It's a Wonderful Life

Thanksgiving Monday, 1948, came as a welcome reprieve. The kids of the church had decided to have a game of touch football at the Normal School playground. It was a balmy day but overcast. Eventually, it rained, but not till long after the game was over and, our fun was delicious. I remember thinking how good it was to be out-of-doors and just have some recreational fun. I had taken this for granted for sixteen years. I suppose I had thought in previous times that life would always be like that with no responsibilities. Now I had learned differently. For a brief time, I started feeling sorry for myself and was not a little envious of my friends who had no such strictures to contend with. My self-pity didn't last long. The truth was I had a wonderful life. Living at the Sadlers' with their son Ron and six girls who were preparing for their careers in teaching was fun. Because the Normal school was just across the road, the girls always came back for lunch as did I. The lively conversations around that table were rich in lessons on life and always included at least one joker who kept us chuckling.

In 1948, the word for "cool" was "indeed". That word came in quickly and swept through the rank and file of the high school. Even the guys on the football team were using it. Everything that elicited a response ended with the word "indeed." Naturally, I brought the word back to the boarding house and, like an unwanted virus, found myself scorned for using such an ungainly behest. Ganging up on me, the girls were soon trying to disabuse me of its use. We sure had fun with that one. Like the common cold, the overuse of a word can peter out. The word "indeed" came and went like the epithet "Kilroy was here". Boy, did everybody ever get into that one. In those days everybody's favourite comic strip was "L'il Abner" Al Capp, kept North America laughing; his daily comic strip was always a topic for conversation. One day he added mystery to his comics by the graffiti "Kilroy was here" with people responding with alarm. An international phenomenon was born. His readers responded. The epithet was popping up everywhere on school chalkboards and even on the street. Finally, after a year of teasing us, Al Capp revealed his identity. Kilroy turned out to be an undertaker. Yes, life was busy and, at times, even burdensome: but for me, with only a few notable exceptions, mine was a rewarding experience with new adventures ever keeping me fascinated with the joy of living.

Chapter 7
Friendships

Gerry sits on the bench as though he had little enthusiasm for gym class. I share his apathy. Neither of us fits the category of "jock". We take gym because there is no way to avoid it. Soon we are talking.

"You don't talk like the other guys in my class," opines Gerry.

"I don't?"

"Nope. It makes me kinda wonder," stammers Gerry, "if you are the kind of guy that goes to church."

"As a matter of fact, I do."

"Which one?"

"Wortley Road Baptist church."

"So you are a Christian?"

"As a matter of fact, I am."

"So am I."

This is how Gerry and I met and found an instant friendship. I could talk with Gerry about serious things. Russia had just exploded the first atomic bomb and the scare of nuclear war was a common topic. Meaningful conversations with teenagers about eternal questions is off the radar screen of the kids in our school. Where did I come from? Where am I going? Does God have a plan for my life? What happens to me after I die? With Gerry, we could discuss these things for hours. Gerry had become a Christian by attending the Hamilton Road Brethren Gospel Hall the same summer I had started attending the Baptist church. Our experience was the same. Our circumstances were quite different. Gerry's parents did not approve of his Christianity and forbade him from attending church. At sixteen years of age, that's hard to do. Gerry simply ignored his parents and went to church anyway. There were frequent arguments and Gerry often left the kitchen table with supper unfinished. They seemed to be an abrasive family. Gerry and his parents never seemed to get along.

Me and my two preacher buddies,
Don Fitchett and Gerry Rowe

I could never quite figure out Gerry's parents. For all their arguments, Jerry could have the family Chevrolet anytime he wanted it. The result was fantastic. We had wheels. Every time we needed mobility, it was Gerry to the rescue. First came the litany of complaints about his unreasonable parents; then came the privilege of the car. I never could add it up. Now, Gerry had been a loner in his church, because most of the youth were in their twenties, whereas Wortley Baptist had a wonderful array of teens. Soon Gerry was attending our church and meeting the kids. The first was Ian MacRonald. Ian was a gangly six-footer plus and had a nice singing voice. Often he would sing duets with Sally Stacey which made all the seniors sure that they would make a lovely couple. That was simply not to be. Sally liked Wes Suchard who also came from the Gospel Hall. Wes, like Gerry also had conflicts with his parents and the same automobile privileges as Gerry. No wonder they got along. If Gerry for some reason couldn't access the family car then we'd just call on Wes. Wes was a six-footer plus and seemed to be very much a ladies' man. Sally had a lot of competitors. In the end her sensible level-headed Christianity won the day. Wes and Sally married. Sally was the president of our Young People's group.

Ross Millar was another one of the gang. Athletic and popular with the high school kids, Ross had not had it easy. His father had been the pastor of our church when he suddenly had a heart attack and died.

Ross was only eleven at the time. Marie Foster was our pianist at Young Peoples and could play any song after hearing it only once. Wow, what a gifted girl.

We also had imports from Central Baptist Church, because our Young People's group had guys. There were the Bodenham sisters, three of them. Ivy liked Bill Carey, and the feeling was mutual. Then there was Betty Logsdon, who it turned out, had taken a fancy to me. I was friends with them all, and confess that with the loss of my family home, a transformation had taken place in me. In Stratford, as long as I had the security of my house and all my guy friends, trying to fall for a girl was a chore. Just no chemistry. Now that I was a boarder in a household not my own, I find myself falling for every girl that comes along. First, there was Marjorie Dorpaal. Older than me by a year, she was one of Mrs. Sadler's boarders. She was a beautiful girl, nursing a heartbreak because her boyfriend from Windsor dumped her after a two-year courtship. I wound up being her listening ear while she relived her courtship with Dave. By the hour, she poured out her heart, and I just listened until the other girls remonstrated with me.

"She's just got to get over it, and she isn't getting any help by rehearsing her memories you."

Gee, I wasn't interested either in her boyfriend stories. I was just waiting for her to get over it so that she would consider me. That thought never seemed to occur to Marjorie, so I gave it up for a bad job. Besides, I was getting interested in Charleen McClure. Charleen didn't board with Mrs. Sadler. She had secured a lovely room above the funeral parlour down the street (obviously her parents had money). She only took meals with Mrs. Sadler because the funeral home would not permit meals to be cooked in their two-room apartment. I finally asked her out for a date. It had to be something that was free (remember, I'm a poverty-stricken student). I asked her to come with me to a Youth For Christ rally.

The YFC rally was typical for the times. Barry Moore led the singing and we (a crowd of both youth and older church members) joined in with enthusiasm. At some point we learned a new chorus. One I remember had lyrics to inspire anyone in 1948.

After all He's done for me. After all He's done for me.

How can I do less than give Him my best and live for Him completely

After all He's done for me.

Oh – Oh He's done so much for me

Oh – Oh He's done so much for me

If I should try for all eternity,

I could never never tell you what He's done for me.

During the announcements, Barry and his co-chair Desmond Tyrrel have a stunt arranged. Barry leads the way.

"Des, I really like your tie." Des responds. "You really like it that much!"

"I sure do. I wish I had one exactly like it."

"You don't have to go out and buy one like mine. I'll lend you this tie anytime."

Barry gets excited and replies, "You really mean it?"

"Of course I mean it."

"You mean right now?"

"Sure." says Des, "You can have it right now."

With this assurance, Barry whips out the scissors and cuts off the tie below the knot. Des never blinks an eye, and now he's looking at Barry's tie and says, "I really like your tie too." Of course, by now the audience is laughing and wondering what's next.

Barry replies, "Des, for a friend like you, I would give you my tie anytime."

"Thanks," says Des, and promptly takes the same scissors and cuts off Barry's tie.

"You're welcome, Des, because you are my best friend."

The audience is awestruck. We don't know whether to laugh or protest. The only thing this penny pinching teenager can think is, "Wow, what an extravagant hi-jink to please an audience." But I laugh with the others. Next, we hear a rousing sermon by an evangelist I've long since forgotten. They conclude the meeting with a hymn of invitation for people to come forward for salvation. I think the meeting was wonderful, but I can see that Charleen is bored.

On the way home, I courageously take her hand. Instead of the response I was looking for, Charleen just turns to me and says, "Bruce,

I'm sorry, but please don't hold my hand."

"Of course, I understand perfectly," I stammer.

Wow, was it ever tough making conversation after that. I got the message loud and clear. It was a bit awkward over meals avoiding eye contact; that was the last of any dates with Charleen.

With this not-too-subtle rebuke in my mind, I turn my thoughts to Stratford and all the girls I had tried to fall for. I pick out Pat Wilkes. Surely she would be a great girlfriend. Right away, I know what I will do: I will hitchhike to Stratford, stay overnight with Aunt Elsie, and see if Pat will go skating with me. In those days it only cost a dime for public skating in the Stratford Arena. I examine my resources. I can afford twenty cents. With my shoes polished so you could see your face in them, I make it to Stratford in one hour flat, arriving at five o'clock. After supper is finished, and with my mission explained to Aunt Elsie, I phone Pat Wilkes right away and ask her to go skating with me.

"Sorry, Bruce, but I have other plans for tonight; thanks, but no thanks."

"No problem; just cancel those plans and come skating with me."

Elsie is now choking back her laughter as she listens to me talk.

"Sorry, Bruce, but my plans can't be changed," says Pat Wilkes.

"Do you know that I hitchhiked all the way from London just to ask you out skating? I've been thinking about this all week; please change your mind. (Now I'm getting desperate).

"Nice of you to think of me that way, but I'm sorry and I don't intend to change my plans."

"Well, if that's the case, would you go skating with me if I came to Stratford some other time?"

"I don't know about that until the time comes, so I can't give you an answer just now and really Bruce, I have to go, so we'll have to end this conversation right now."

It was then that I remembered how I used to tease Pat and wished I could live that one over again. Deflated, I finally give in and rasp, "Sure was nice to talk to you. Stratford girls are so much better than the ones in London."

"Oh, Bruce, you're just saying that, but really I have to go now."

"Yeah, well, okay. Sure was nice to talk to you," I lied. Shattered, I hang up the phone, look at Elsie, and whimper, "She turned me down."

Now Elsie is laughing till the tears roll down her cheeks. Uncle Gordon comes inside from talking to the neighbour.

"Gordon, did you ever miss all the fun; I wish you could have heard this nephew of yours pleading with a girl to go skating with him.:" Meantime, my face is getting redder by the minute, and now, after my humiliation, Elsie is just making things worse. She did comment on how shiny my shoes looked but that was poor compensation for my shattered ego. I hitchhiked home that same night, turned into bed like a wounded puppy dog, and did a Scarlett O'Hara.

"Oh, well, I won't think about that just now. I'll think about that tomorrow."

Chapter 8
The Sunday School Teacher

It was a startling announcement that the oldtimers saw as decadence. "It's true," the deacons confirmed the report, "Sunday School is no longer to be conducted at 3 P.M., it will start at 9:45 A.M. with fifteen minutes recess to church time which was universally observed at 11 A.M.. That fateful Sunday in 1949 was backed up by a pulpit announcement by Pastor John R. Dunkin.

"Studies show that churches that move the Sunday school hour to a time before morning service increase by 10%. We are just keeping up with the times," opined Pastor Duncan. It was settled just like that and the oldsters were sure that the devil would find bad things for the young people to do with all the free time on a Sunday afternoon. The results soon silenced the naysayers. Our Sunday school increased by 10% with the move, and in the same year the scenerio was repeated all over North America and the world. Robert Raikes would not have approved. The Sunday School movement originated in Gloucester, England with two hours of instruction every Sunday afternoon. The goal was to educate the poor to read and write. The textbook was the Bible. The byproduct was a Christian populace that would evangelize the world. When publice schools were established for all children and made compulsory. The Sunday school was shortened to one hour and everybody attended from young to old. The state would educate the young; the church would care for their souls. Since most of the teachers were Christian, it was like government sponsored Christianity. No one forsaw that the day would come when the schools would become completely secular.

In 1948, when I became a Christian, I attended the youth class and Richard Horner was our teacher. In 1949 like all the others we switched to the morning time of 9:45. The hour began with children's choruses that were sung by all. That's where I learned to sing such songs as Climb Climb up Sunshine Mountain, Wide Wide as the Ocean, I've got the Joy Joy Joy Joy Down in my heart and the ubiquitous Jesus Loves me This I know. Next, came the celebration of birthdays when anybody with a birthday walked to the front to put their pennies (one for each year) in the lighthouse that lit up with every dropping penny. The money was for the missionaries. Then we sang happy birthday to all who were celebrated in this fashion. At last we sang a hymn and broke up into classes that were geared to age. The adults remained in the auditorium. In 1950, I was thrilled when Art Mckenzie asked me to teach a class of five ten year old boys. My first opportunity to teach the Bible to others had arrived. Art gave me a Sunday school manual that outlined the lesson. Like thousands of others before me, I became an expert on the lesson to be taught that Saturday night before Sunday. I often wonder who learned more, the teacher or the pupils.

I started with five boys, after a year I had ten. Pastor Dunkin noted the increase and commended me. How that happened can be illustrated by the Heslop brothers. I was selling Fuller Brushes door to door for my livelihood when I was eighteen. One snowy day in November, I was shocked when snowball thrown by this kid hit me squarely in the chest and spattered by face. Angry, I called out, "Who threw that snowball?"

Jack Heslop looked guilty and scared. The kids he was playing with spilled the beans and soon I had apprehended the offender. I marched him to the front door of his house to remonstrate with his mother, when suddenly I thought, "I've got a prospect for Sunday School." By the time his mother answered the door, my temperment had changed and I sweetly said,
"Your son and I have just had a meeting over a snowball, but that's not what I want to talk about. I'm a Sunday school teacher and I wondered if your son would like to be a member of my class?" Quick thinking to be sure. Surprized but pleased his mother thought it was a good idea and wondered if his younger brother Richard could also attend. Technically, Richard was a year too young (should be in the class before mine), but I saw the wisdom of two brothers staying together. Art McKenzie agreed and now I had seven. I took those boys tobogganing and did other fun things together with my guys. That's how I grew that class to ten. Imagine, this spoiled kid who used to cuss and tell dirty stories, teaching a Sunday school class.

The Sunday school movement was strong in 1950, millions of kids participated across Canada. If they didn't take in the lesson for daydreaming (like all too many did) they had the Sunday school paper to take home with an appropiate story with moral undertones to digest.

I wonder if most of those papers were read by parents rather than the kids. I know the two years of my life as a kid, when I attended Sunday school, I never read them. In 1950, this mass distribution of Christian literature was a booming business. The Canadian world was everywhere infiltrated by the church. The oldsters of any congregatiion would tell of hundreds of kids crowded together every Sunday in every church learning the stories of the Bible. Then came organized sports, television and now computors. The powerful Sunday school movement is now only a memory.

The absence of the Sunday school is showing up in our culture. Kids of a bygone age were by training a generation of joiners. Cub Scouts and Girl Guides was a powerful movement and benefited from the plethora of kids who earned their badges and matured in the art of inquiry, (but always in a climate of morality and ethics). As they matured they joined Kiwanis, Optimist, Rotary, and Toastmasters International. Today the Club movement is in decline. Go to a Lion's club meeting and one is struck by the aging of the members, and the lament that the young people are not taking up the challenge. Fifty years ago the tens of thousands of Sunday School teachers labouring over their lesson created a thinking class of adults that loved to go to a lecture and learn something new. The absence of that breed of thinkers has dried up the pool of joiners who nourished the club movement. The information age has increased our knowledge but bypassed the invaluable societal joys of fraternity. We have become a solitary generation with a shrinking circle of associates and friends. As a now retired pastor who has visited many oldsters, they all complain of the loneliness of life. Small wonder. The rich world of associations over a worthy cause has impoverished our lifestyle. With money to burn we are the only ones at the fireplace, with only the occasional stranger to break the monotany. The only solution is to go the pub to drink. The other alternative that I recommend is, go back to church.

Chapter 9
Best Romance Story out of the West

In September, 1966, after two months of negotiations, I accepted a call to Ruth Morton Baptist Church, Vancouver, British Columbia. I remember the first time I heard of the church. Somebody called it the flagship of the Baptist churches in British Columbia. "Ruthmorton like Throckmorton," I thought. The difference never occurred to me until years later, when I learned that Ruth Morton Baptist got its name from a woman. I was not impressed. It may at one time have been a flagship, but through the years with the removal of its young people to the suburbs, the flagship was listing badly and in need of repair. I was sure I could restore its former glory and rebuild its congregation. The experience proved memorable: not for what I did for the church, but for what the church did for me.

When one writes a memoir, provided one tells all, the reader discovers the private life that has been hidden from view for years. By now, my reader knows that I am a hopeless romantic. This is not without its advantages. The romance I now describe is of another adventure-seeking guy just like me. His name was John Morton. I am now the pastor of the church that was named after his wife. Imagine a love story better than this. Ruth Morton Baptist Church is Canada's own Taj Mahal. Let me tell you the story as I did for Radio CBC back in Vancouver in 1971, when the province of British Columbia was celebrating its centennial.

John Morton   Ruth Morton 1892
Courtesy archives Vancouver Public Library

Ruth Morton Baptist Church as it stands today
Corner of 27th Street East and Prince Albert

Sunday, June 27, 1971

"The other day I was driving along Denman Street where it overlooks English Bay. Glancing east for oncoming traffic, I noticed a street sign – Morton Avenue. The street is only one block long. The pioneer who gave it its name was John Morton. I'm afraid a lot of Vancouverites don't realize how important a fellow Mr. Morton was in the old days. But for those who have read their history, they would know he was the first white settler to come to these parts with the intent to stay.

Others had been at the Burrard Inlet before him for exploration and survey, but to Morton belongs the distinction of being the first settler. Actually, there were three that came together. Samuel Brighouse and William Hailstone were with him. Morton came first in June, and then in October. The three came again, this time to decide what land they would claim for their own.

Grasp this staggering thought! Take up all the waterfront between Stanley Park and Burrard Street; picture all those modern skyscrapers; add to them a host of luxurious hotels and throw in hundreds of magnificent apartment buildings. In short, the 550 acres that make up Vancouver's fabled west end. The richest slice of real estate east of Toronto's Golden Mile. John Morton and his two friends owned all that land.

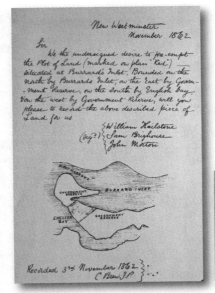

John Morton was one of the impoverished sons of the Morton family. Years later, when John Morton was a successful businessman, he was able to return and was lauded by his peers for his accomplishments

When I came to Vancouver, the name John Morton meant nothing to me. In this I suppose I had a great deal in common with most Vancouverites. I knew that there was a church called Ruth Morton Memorial Baptist Church. I knew that to be the minister of such an historic church was something of an honour, but I had no idea who Ruth or John Morton were apart from being of husband and wife and obviously very endeared to one another.

Shortly after I arrived, I was given further details of how Morton had fulfilled a desire to build a church that would be a lasting contribution to the community he helped to create and a tribute to his beloved wife. The church that bears the Morton name has a very prominent stained glass window facing north. On the glass is an inscription that reads

"This church was built by funds set apart during his lifetime by the late John Morton and afterwards added to by his wife, Ruth Morton, and as a tribute of his regard for her is called the Ruth Morton Memorial Baptist Church."

I have stood by that window many times gazing into the colours of that work of art and wondered at such devotion – and pondered – what kind of a man John Morton really was. I decided to find out, and what I discovered is one of the most fascinating stories to come out of the west.

John Morton was the son of a Yorkshire potter. Into this family of brick makers living in the village of Saledine Nook, there were born eight children. Sounds like a charming place to live, doesn't it!

When John grew up, he heard about the fabulous gold strikes on the Fraser River and in the Cariboo. He and his cousin William Hailstone voyaged to New York on the famous paddle wheeler the Great Eastern that laid the first Atlantic cable. On board ship, they met Sam Brighouse and struck up a friendship that kept the partners together for half a century.

They arrived in New Westminster on June 25, 1862, and immediately made preparations for the goldfields. Meanwhile, Morton wanted to see the sights and went for a walk down Columbia Street. Passing by a shoe merchant's shop, he chanced to see a lump of coal prominently displayed in the shop window. Having served his apprenticeship as a brick maker in England, Morton knew that coal and potter's clay usually went together. Discover the source of the coal and you get the clay one requires for making bricks. Reasoning that a pioneer community would need a large supply of bricks for building, he determined to get in on the ground floor and make some money.

Discovering the location of that coal specimen required both finding the Indian that had brought it to the store and a canoe trip along the Burrard Inlet to the mineral source. They must have made quite a pair, the Indian guide and the Yorkshire man. Neither could speak the other's language, but somehow, they managed.

The Indian led Morton to the foot of present-day Granville Street, but Morton wasn't impressed with the coal seam or the hoped-for potter's clay. Yet, for all the poor grade coal, the name stuck, and today the western extremity of Burrard Inlet between Stanley Park and the fashionable West End is known by the ubiquitous name, "Coal Harbour."

Morton's disappointment in failing to find potter's clay was soon forgotten. He had become totally absorbed in the magnificent scenery, the untouched virgin forest, the azure sky, the blue waters of the inlet, and the snowcapped mountains. Somehow, right then and there, Morton knew this was where he would invest a lifetime.

The Indian guide wanted to show him more, and so they made for the narrows. It is still an exciting canoe trip, but make sure it's a calm day and stay away from the large ships. A hundred and forty years ago, it couldn't have been more sensational, because as they rounded Brockton Point, they ran head on into two thousand Indians preparing for war. The Squamish Indians had banded together to repulse an expected invasion of the dreaded Haidas from the north. For Morton, this was a moment of high tension, but fear soon gave way to relief when the warriors proved friendly. Rounding the narrows the pair paddled silently by Second Beach and onto the tranquil waters of English Bay. The Indian caught fish while Morton swam and sunned in the unparalleled splendour of the white sands of English Bay.

When Morton returned and shared his discovery with his astonished friends at New Westminster; he temporarily put the matter out of his mind. For the time being, Morton and company would give their attention to gold.

It was the lure of the goldfields that had attracted these men and many others from all over the world to British Columbia. New Westminster was the jumping-off spot for the Cariboo and – as of yet – the three Yorkshiremen were hoping to strike it rich in gold. It was a grueling 350 miles inland to the Cariboo, and then, as with so many others, a disappointing summer. Thousands came, but very few went away wealthy. The only stroke of luck that Morton had was on the way up, when the owner of a mule team, having just shod his beasts, had two dozen nails left over. Not wishing to pack the horseshoe nails, he gave them to Morton, who in turn sold them to a needy customer at four dollars apiece.

One morning in September, Morton awoke to find the ground covered with snow. His two sleeping companions looked like two mounds in a graveyard. That was enough! The Yorkshire trio cleared out. Returning to New Westminster over that impossible trail must have been doubly hard. They were empty handed and the prospects of a long, hard winter lay ahead. It was then that Morton remembered the coal seam. Perhaps he had dismissed the idea too lightly. Perhaps they might return and explore the area further – and that's exactly what they did. Returning to Coal Harbour in October they discovered an excellent supply of top grade potter's clay suitable for making bricks. Their minds made up, they would preempt the land now known as Vancouver's West End and go into the brick business.

When New Westminster found out that Morton, Brighouse, and Hailstone had preempted 550 acres of timberland so far removed from the existing settlement, they laughed and dubbed them "the three English Greenhorns". Undaunted by the derision, the men were soon building a shack, Vancouver's first house. Later, Brighouse brought in the stove that would serve as a kiln, packing it piece by piece on his back all the way from New Westminster. In the end, the brick kilns failed, and the vision which had led Morton and his friends to preempt the land never produced the anticipated pottery. Obviously, the real wealth was in the land itself. As this became increasingly apparent, it was the "Three English Greenhorns" turn to laugh while all New Westminster envied – and all through the vision inspired by a lump of coal.

Morton and his two friends didn't realize their wealth right away. It takes time for property to increase in value. For years he was a rich pauper with plenty of land which nobody wanted to buy. In the meantime, he worked where he could to keep body and soul together. He dug ditches, peddled milk, sold vegetables, worked as a logger, and built roads.

After fifteen years, Morton got the chance to return to England. Back home at Salendine Nook, he was lionized and lauded by his family and friends. Romance bloomed, and he married pretty Jane Ann Bailey, the daughter of Blackpool's mayor, who bore him a daughter named Elizabeth.

Returning to British Columbia, Morton heard the exciting news that the CPR. was coming all the way to Vancouver. With his large holdings in the West End, the prospect of wealth was inevitable. To add to Morton's joy, his wife was expecting again and bore him a fine son named Joseph. But Jane Ann was mortally ill. She died two days after the child was born. The grieving Morton placed his infant son with friends and his daughter at St. Anne's Convent in New Westminster.

In spite of death and tragedy, life must go on, and to Morton's credit, he took up farming near Mission. There he met Mrs. Mary Ann Trethewey who operated a trade-in store. Mrs. Trethewey was a born matchmaker who had played cupid on more than one occasion. When she found out about Morton and his motherless children, she lost no time writing Ruth Mount, an old country family friend who was now living in Iowa. At Mrs. Trethewey's arrangement, John and Ruth were introduced, and it was love at first sight. Elizabeth and Joseph had a mother.

It was a strange honeymoon. Taking the stage to Vancouver from the New Westminster church, Morton had wanted to show Ruth the white sands of English Bay. An old rowboat secured from Gassy Jack proved leaky. The newlyweds had to content themselves with sitting on the sand watching a pig root for clams, followed by a hungry crow picking up the scraps.

Life on the farm at Mission wasn't easy. The reality of pioneer conditions is reflected in a comment made by Elizabeth Morton who, recalling those days, remembered the frugal life and the hard work, but especially the hard work. At last, in 1887 the first trains of the C.P.R. began to run. The land boom was on. Morton's property increased in value and affluence came at last. For those who could afford it, a child's education in England was a must. Proof that John was doing well was evident in the fact that both Elizabeth and Joseph enjoyed a British education under the watchful eye of Ruth, who accompanied them for their four-year term.

Note: *The CPR exacted a high price for running the railroad to Coal Harbour. The three greenhorns were left with 1/3 of their original land claim which was now more valuable due to the railroad. Morton opposed the arrangement reasoning that in time the CPR would come to them with more favourable terms. Hindsight proved him right, but Christian gentleman that he was, in the end he capitulated to the pressure of his*

friends who for a little extra persuasion included a Baptist minister Rev.
Robert Lennie to argue the point. The greenhorns died wealthy. They would
have been wealthier still if they had listened to Morton.

Morton operated several business ventures, including a hotel. He
also built cottages on English Bay and had part interest in the old horse
show building in the west end. The venture that captures my fancy,
however, was his pony ranch which he operated on English Bay for
the delight of the youngsters.

Above all interests, Morton loved his church and could be counted
on for a generous gift every time a new Baptist church was opened.
When the First Baptist Church relocated in 1910 to Burrard Street, the
lot purchased was part of the original preemption that Morton had
staked out years before. It had since passed to new owners. Ironically,
the man to put up money for the lot he used to own was Morton, who
bought it for $1000 (see "From Milltown to Metropolis", by Alan
Morley, to whom I am indebted for all this information.)

Shortly before Morton died, at the prompting of his good friend,
Willard Litch, he set aside money for the building of a church in old
South Vancouver. Litch was the pastor of a struggling congregation
that needed a church building. It was his mind that the church would
be built where it stands today, on the corner of Prince Albert and East
Twenty-Seventh and that it should be called the John Morton Memorial
Baptist Church. Morton thanked Litch for the suggestion and agreed
to everything except the name, because he felt he wasn't worthy of the
honour. He did request, however, that it should be named after his
beloved wife; and so it remains to this day, the Ruth Morton Memorial
Baptist Church. Three weeks later, John Morton's death was
overshadowed with the sinking of the Titanic. That tragedy was such
news that Vancouver hardly noticed the passing of its first settler. The
Titanic sank on April 14, 1912, John Morton died four days later.

In this last act of Morton's life (and the money he put up for the
building of the church), he hardly intended a monument to perpetuate
his own name. He was too retiring a man for that; and yet, by this act
of devotion, he inadvertently gave cause to the church that would in the
end justly render tribute to the old pioneer himself. Endowing that

church was John Morton's last earthly enterprise.

In 1916, some fifty-four years after the coal incident that had led to so much, John's widow was attending the church that today still bears the Morton name. It was Thanksgiving Sunday, and the auditorium of the church was adorned with the traditional stalks of corn and display of vegetables. That Sunday morning a very unusual object was the centre of the décor. It was a hundred-pound lump of coal brought in by one of the members for the festive occasion. One wonders what passed through the mind of Mrs. Ruth Morton as she viewed that massive lump of coal prominently displayed in front of the communion table.

Ruth Morton outlived her husband by twenty -seven years. She became something of a legend, and was often referred to as Vancouver's grand old lady. Just how wonderful the love between these two Vancouver pioneers must have been is illustrated by something I found among Ruth Morton's letters. It is a line written some twenty years after the death of John. The words are from Tennyson and read; "O, for a touch of a vanished hand and the voice we loved that is still."

Time has taken them both from this earthly scene, but the church which still bears their name and memory will not forget them. Proof of this came in 1971, when the province of British Columbia celebrated its Centennial. With a history like this behind our church, we knew that we had to join in on the festivities. So we dreamed up a reenactment of John Morton's discovery of Coal Harbour, which was filmed by CBC and broadcast four times – three times in British Columbia and once all across Canada. The city of Vancouver got involved and gave us $500 toward our project. My son Mark played the part of the Indian guide, and church member Henry Fietje was John Morton. They camped overnight at the foot of Main Street by the CN steamships dock (the exact place where Morton camped overnight on his memorable first visit). Saturday, June 26, they visited all the places that Morton saw and ended up at English Bay, where they were met by Alderman Art Phillips (later Mayor Phillips). Festivities included lunch at the famous Three Greenhorns Restaurant; a parade on Fraser Street, and a concert in Kitsilano Park at night.

Sunday, June 27, 1971, was John Morton Sunday at our church. On hand for the occasion was Mrs. Viola Gleig, John and Ruth Morton's granddaughter. Joan Morton, a distant relative from England, flew over for the special occasion. My wife and I arrived in a horse and buggy driven by Henry Fietje. The church was packed with spectators, and CBC filmed the whole thing. Taking a leaf from the past, we made special arrangements to have a hundred pound lump of coal prominently displayed on the communion table. A few members of the Willard Litch family attended, but his son, who had moved to Ontario was missing. His letter was very interesting.

Erin, Ontario
June 25, 1971

Reverend B.A. Woods
Ruth Morton Memorial Baptist Church
Vancouver, British Columbia.

Dear Mr. Woods,

John and Ruth Morton, Willard Litch and numbers of others including the writer will be worshipping with you on Sunday, June 27, 1971 at eleven a.m. – even though not present. What a momentous and appropriate occasion to celebrate John Morton Day! He was truly Vancouver's Father and a devoted son of his Heavenly Father. What a fruitful combination it proved and what a man by whom to measure his successors!

Your brief script of the B.M.M.B. Celebration from Friday to Sunday of this week really grabs the imagination. The drama of these days will make Morton real to old timers and new timers alike. I congratulate you on your research and zeal in putting this lively account together. I like the relationship you have drawn with the church of John Morton's boyhood. All this adds up to realistic communication between – church and state - past and present – old world and new – economics and religion. You have presented the story with a good sense of the factual, the dramatic, the literary and the imaginative.

I look forward to joining your audience my next visit to the Coast. In the meantime my prayer my interest and a gift to further your labours.

Sincerely,
Richard Litch

CBC reenactment of the coming of John Morton to English Bay, 1971
Our son Mark Woods portrayed the Indian guide,
Henry Fietje played the part of John Morton

The float: Saturday afternoon parade to Ruth Morton Baptist Church

A somewhat fictional arrival of John Morton and his wife Ruth,
Sunday June 13, 1971

My wife Joan and I arriving at the Ruth Morton Baptist Church
The church was packed with visitors that day,
The service was filmed for television by CBC

Chapter 10
Crisscrossing Canada

When I accepted the call to Ruth Morton Baptist Church, Vancouver, I became the recipient of a generous church. Their policy with an incoming pastor was to loan $5000, interest free, so I could buy my own house. Six years later, the home we bought (after the resale in 1972) netted us a profit of $5000. Meanwhile, to get to Vancouver, we sold some of our furniture and packed the rest (including our prized Janssen piano) into a U-haul trailer. In those days I owned a 1960 black Buick that the neighbourhood kids called the Batmobile. Indeed, the Hollywood version for the Batman movie was modeled after that very car. It was now to be remodeled for our purposes. First, I removed the back of the rear seat to make room for a homemade foam mattress. Next, I removed a steel strut so that our son David could slide his head into the trunk and stretch out leaving room for Mark, our oldest, to sleep in a crouched position on a plywood (plus foam) bed. That bunk bed stretched from the front seat to the back window. Our daughter Debbie got the back seat. (Tangled legs between David and Debbie had to be negotiated between themselves). We still had Sara to bed down but at nine months and still nursing, she could fit into the front. (Can you imagine such an arrangement these days with seat belt laws?)

Obviously, our idea was to drive through the night, making extra time. We never tried it driving to Vancouver. It was the first week in November and winter had come early. The Prairies were adrift in snow. Our education of Canadiana is expanding. The following year, we attempted it on a return visit to Ontario, but in the summer. That expedition lasted for the first night. After 1500 miles, we stayed in a motel. Rested, we repeated the marathon for the next 1500 miles. This enabled us to travel east in two days. When I could stay awake no longer, Joan spelled me off for sleep. We found ourselves using this arrangement for the next three years for cross country junkets and summer vacations in the east at my mother-in-law's cottage at Sauble Beach. Homesickness (that unexpected visitor) never occurred to us when we accepted the call to Vancouver. That elusive stranger would determine our life for the next six years and preclude where we spent summer vacations. Reunited with old friends and family. cures the ailment temporarily and exacerbates the disease when parting inevitably must come. When Mark turned sixteen, we had three drivers and could cross the continent nonstop. Two days and we were home in Ontario. My apologies to loyal westerners. Beautiful as British Columbia is, we never could make the western adjustment.

Getting back to that first 3000-mile trip across Canada, we were well prepared. Breakfast was the Kellogg snack pack. One could open the package, pour in milk and sugar, and Voila, breakfast! Lunches were made by my wife (making up our sandwiches in the front seat) and duly passed to the kids one by one. They were mostly comprised of cold meat and bread with a little lettuce. We ate our evening meals in a restaurant. Well do I remember crossing the border at Detroit. David was tired and decided to take a nap. When the customs officer opened the trunk, there was David smiling up at the astonished man. Forty-two years have passed since those days.

We had not planned as well as we thought. I imagined the prairies as we would Ontario in November. In 1966, we drove into a howling blizzard with snow drifts everywhere by the roadside (and we're pulling a U-Haul trailer). To complicate our trip, I lost my wallet, leaving us with only $75.00 that fortunately was safe in Joan's purse. Pastor Walter Thompins of Westbourne Baptist Church, Calgary, loaned us $100.00 so we could make it to Vancouver. We had never met until he delivered the money. Even that was a story. We had reached our motel in Calgary and were out of cash, but it was Sunday. Walter (fortunately for us) had not yet left his home for the evening service. When I explained to him our predicament, he told his congregation and said he needed the evening offering to help out a pastor in distress who would repay as soon as he could. It was enough, and Walter and I became friends from that moment on.

It was a relief to make it to Revelstoke, where we were able to leave winter behind, but not before we had navigated the snows of the Roger's Pass. At last in the Rockies and with temperate weather, we were able to take in the grandeur of the panorama that unfolded before us.

Debbie, who was only eleven, said, "They are so beautiful and grand, it makes me want to cry."

"I know exactly what you mean; it affects me the same way." said her mother.

The feminine nature is different from the masculine. I learned from my wife and daughter new understanding that day. The final day was spent driving the Fraser Canyon. Spectacular scenes unfolded before us when suddenly the tell-tale evidence of a flat tire brought us to a screeching halt. Those were the days when the driving of old cars came in handy. I had no trouble changing the tire. I was dumbfounded, however, when I looked at the tread of the snow tires that were purchased new in Ontario. They were worn to the threads. True, they were retreads but nevertheless new when I bought them only three weeks before. Pulling that trailer over icy roads had done them in. We prayed that car into Vancouver, fearing that the other snow tire might not make it. We arrived Tuesday, November 8, in the rain. I was reminded of an earlier arrival back in 1947 with my mother when we met the same kind of weather. Suddenly, I was filled with foreboding and the thought crossed my mind, "I wonder if coming to Vancouver was such a good idea."

It rained nonstop for forty days. In desperation for some snow at Christmastime, my wife Joan bought an aerosol can of the fake stuff and coated the windows with white foam that only lasted for a day. Being easterners, Christmas without snow – ugh! When our congregation would ask how we liked] the west, faking it, we would say, "We are Vancouverites complete with web footing and all."

Sara [our youngest] in playpen with her cousin Scott at Sauble Beach, 1968.
That playpen was our extra luggage compartment on the roof racks
of our 1960 Buick

(Well, we tried but could never get Ontario out of our blood. Westerners who have tried the east should understand. After trying out employment in the east, they usually return to the west if they can). Why does the pastor and his family take their vacations back in Ontario when British Columbia is so beautiful? This was the question our astonished congregation would ask. I know that Vancouver has much to offer, but we hankered for the east. We tried to break the habit by taking one summer vacation in California and vowed we would never do that again. With that notable exception, we vacationed every summer in the east. We finally bought a cottage at Muskoka Baptist Conference, Huntsville, Ontario. The die was cast. The following year, I accepted a call to Stanley Avenue Baptist Church in Hamilton, Ontario, and have lived here ever since.

However for six years, we were Vancouverites. Ruth Morton Baptist was my church. The congregation would now experience the new pastor's vision for the future. A scale model of the newly remodeled Ruth Morton Church was personally prepared by me and presented to the deacons. To their credit they backed me enthusiastically. When we stripped the walls of the church for renewal, to the astonishment of all, we discovered dry rot. Had we not immediately remodeled, the church would have caved in. We averted a catastrophe that no one realized was silently eating at the foundations. The $50,000 cosmetic facelift would have cost three times that amount if we had not discovered the structural decay which we repaired at minimal cost. A Providential mercy! The new sanctuary proved to be a masterpiece. The church today stands as one of Vancouver's finest and is steeped in Canadian history.

Deacon James Scott, me, Manny Mix. Examining the model I made of how our auditorium would look after the renovations

Yes, I've had a wonderful life full of adventure, but in 1948, oblivious of what was waiting for me twenty-three years in the future, I was just trying to get through high school.

Chapter 11
Crisis Management from Above

From time to time, I visited Mother, who was increasingly hard to find. Paranoid and out of touch with reality, I could only show her loyalty and love. I was her only connectionresource to reality. With God's grace, she wobbled through life and even remarried. A farmer whose wife had died advertised for a housekeeper. By now Mother had been housekeeper for two elderly gentlemen. That's when a fifty-year-old farmer placed his ad for housekeeping help. Out of money and desperate for a roof over her head, mother answered the ad and got the job. Jim Langford married my mother in 1951. Grateful that she had security, I was able to get on with my life. But now I am four years ahead of my story.

1948 was a pivotal year in my life. It was pivotal for others as well. Newfoundland became the tenth province of Canada. It took fifty more years, but I finally got to tour that beautiful province. 1948 also saw the creation of the state of Israel. I got to visit that fabled nation in 1990. 1948 also saw what I call the great reversal. The Japanese citizens of Canada got the right to vote. I have a lot to say about the daughter of one significant Japanese citizen, but I will reserve my comments until we get to the Terry Fox Story.

On December 29, 1948, I was telling Bill Carey, a friend, my dilemma.

"I'm out of a job and I'm out of money; like it or not, I must quit school and find a job."

When Bill's mother found this out, she came to my rescue. The Careys had moved to Canada from the United States when Bill's dad had become music teacher at London Bible Institute. The move had been at great personal cost. He had been a tenured music teacher in a New Jersey high school. Now, on half the salary they had enjoyed in New Jersey, having felt the call to teach music in a place that prepared men and women for ministry, the Careys had come to London. Mrs. Carey's missionary vision came to my rescue just in time. Four months after their arrival and right after New Year's, I moved into the Carey residence. It was a sacrificial act that the Careys could not afford.

Dixon Glass of Central Baptist Church took note and supplied a little grocery money to the Careys to help. But once again, I am ahead of my story. I have not told you of my decision to stop being a Christian.

Christmas 1948 was a far cry from the celebrations Mother and I had known through the years. We ate a few pork chops together in Mother's one-room apartment on the 23rd. So to begin with, it's not even the right day. I'm not prone to depression, but that particular Christmas was an exception. I was discouraged about my inability to quit smoking, which was also affecting my Christian zeal. I had determined to go to Stratford for Christmas. I was discouraged with London and told Mother that I would hitchhike to Stratford for a little excitement. On Christmas Eve, I arrived unannounced at Gord and Elsie's house. I had decided to look up a few of my old friends and see if there were any parties going on. I wound up at Robert Herlick's house on Brunswick Street with a few others who were dancing to the latest recordings and drinking Coca-cola. We were smoking cigarettes and I was talking nonsense, just like the good old days. Back in my element, I am pretending to have a good time. "Living the Christian life is too hard," I reasoned. "I have to quit school and get a job." I looked at my former friends and thought, "They don't go to church and neither will I." I resolved within myself to quit the Christian life. That's when the Holy Spirit moved in, using the most untoward circumstances. Robert's older brother, with his girlfriend and two other couples, crashed our party at midnight. They were so drunk that one of them came through the door crawling on hands and knees. I never felt so out of place in all my life.
"Gotta go!" I exhaled, "Gord and Elsie are expecting me."

What a relief to get out of that house. Midnight in Stratford with new-fallen snow was idyllic. Christmas Eve 1948 was a spectacular sight. The fresh-fallen snow covered everything with a blanket of white. The stars were never brighter. It was cold and I could hear the snow crunching under my feet as I made my way down Brunswick Street. The Milky Way filled the sky and bright stars shone in their pristine beauty. In today's world, what I saw that night is only possible if one goes to a planetarium show. (Progress and light pollution have obscured the skies.) I picked out the brightest star I could find and thought of the Christmas story. "It must have been a star like that that led the wise men to Bethlehem," I mused. Suddenly, a flood of memories crossed my mind. The Christmas carols we used to sing around the piano in past years. I thought of all the Christian kids I had met who were so different from the gang at the Herlicks' house!

"Is this what I want? I don't think so!" Looking beyond the brightest star, I prayed. "Lord, I don't want to go back to the empty life. There's only one way to live and that's a life lived for Jesus Christ." Suddenly I found myself praying as I walked,

"Lord, I was so discouraged that I was ready to quit the Christian life, but I know that's not what I really want. From now on, I want to live for you and never turn back. God helping me, this is my vow."

I guess I really am a citizen of two worlds, and do you know what? I can't go back to a one world life.

I arrived at my Uncle Gordon's house sometime before 1:00 AM. Gordon was finishing off his fourth beer, and Aunt Elsie was getting uneasy. Uncle Gord loved to get drunk. His problem was he just couldn't hold it.

"Hey, Brucie, it's Christmas! How about having a beer; there's nothing against having a beer in the Bible – why, Jesus even made the stuff."

(I suppose this was a reference to the miracle story of when Jesus turned the water into wine). Selective knowledge to be sure, but I was still a weak Christian. Promptly forgetting my prayer vow, I accepted the offer. I never really liked the taste of beer, but I didn't want to let on to the contrary. I even faked a little, pretending to be tipsy when I wasn't. I was able to deceive those that were well soused, but Elsie knew I was just putting on. A seasoned veteran of this kind of thing, she knew better and called my bluff the following day. At 2:30 AM, Gordon, who was now getting pretty sick, threw up and made a proper fool of himself. I can still see how angry Elsie was as she cleaned up the mess.

"Why do you do this? You know damned well you get sick every time you drink too much. I don't know when you're going to learn."

Gordon's exhibition broke up the party and the house emptied out in five minutes with Uncle Gordon profusely apologizing to his guests, and especially to Elsie. Meantime, I got to sleep on the floor beside

Grandma's bed. Dear Grandma had blissfully slept through the entire episode. Amazingly enough, Christmas morning everyone seemed to have gotten over it, so we had turkey dinner and all the Christmas trimmings. How different that Christmas was from the ones I remembered when mother would spoil me with every lavish gift she could afford. I watched my cousins Bobby and Cheryl as they excitingly opened their gifts which were so much more modest than the ones I used to receive, and vicariously relived the past through their tender years. I was learning new lessons on what really matters at Christmas.

My plans included hitchhiking to Toronto. After Christmas dinner, I was off to the big city where I intended to pay my father a visit. I had written my father a letter so that he and Phyllis would know I was coming. If hitchhiking on Christmas day after dark is a non-starter for our generation, that thought never crossed my mind sixty years ago. (During the war years, hitchhiking was a national phenomenon and continued to be an acceptable mode of travel for at least a decade after.) I arrived at Dad's house at 15 Bedford Park before midnight and spent the next two days with dad and my stepmother Phyllis. With the advantage of maturity and age, I now understand the conversations we had when I niavely answered their questions, without so much as a thought.

"How is your mother? How can she survive when she has no money?"
I told them everything, holding back no information about her mental illness. In retrospect, I know Mother would have been devastated with my disclosures. Fortunately, she never found out, and I never revealed anything to her that would have wounded her. I can still hear Dad's reply
"That's too bad."

I candidly told them everything they asked without a qualm. Today I wonder if retiring that first night, Phyllis didn't say to my father, "Well, after hearing all that don't you feel a little bit guilty?" If only I could ask the kind of questions I would now like to ask. But maybe I wouldn't; divorce is a touchy subject that opens up old wounds that are hard to heal.
It's December 28 and I am now back in London, having hitchhiked

home. Home? My boarding house was my home, and I had no money to pay my landlady. All I could do was pray. I did pray.

"Lord, help me to finish grade twelve." From that prayer onward, I have never looked back. Even as I prayed that prayer, powerful forces were at work that would pick me up and carry me through to the goal that would give meaning and purpose to my life. I have already alluded to this. Amazingly, God would use such ordinary people to help.

Early in December, I had met Betty Logsdon, whose father was Franklin Logsdon, the pastor of Central Baptist Church. She had already caught my eye (or was it the other way round?) Since Margaret Dennett and I had parted ways (we were still friends but badly mismatched in our interests), Betty proposed that Ian McRonald and I join her and Ruth Horner to form a quartet. We would audition at the Watchnight service at Central Baptist Church on New Year's Eve.

"A set-up if I ever saw one," said Alice Carey.

When I heard that, I was indeed deflated. I thought it was my undiscovered singing talent that commended me to the platform of success. Here, all the time, it was Betty Logsdon's influence pulling strings behind the scenes. We sang, "All that thrills my Soul is Jesus." At the time, I was still smoking. Given the impeccable standards we lived by in those days, that should have disqualified me from platform participation, but Betty bent the rules, or maybe she just didn't tell her dad about my abominable habit. Her faith was rewarded. January 1, 1950, I quit smoking. The Holy Spirit simply did a miracle for me and took away my craving for nicotine.

Imagine! I was singing at the Watchnight service on December 31 at the alien Central Baptist Church. I had never been to a single service before. This was a real dilemma for me, because I was smitten with loyalty to Rev. John Dunkin who also expected me to be at the Wortley Road. Baptist Watchnight, too. It's what one might call a conflict of interests. Girl power won the day. However, just in case somebody might get the wrong idea, before we were to sing, I informed the audience that I was, "Bruce Woods from Wortley Road Baptist Church." (The audience caught the implication and laughed.) My Wortley loyalty wavered after the New Year's party at Betty's house following the Watchnight Service. Although, I never missed a Sunday morning service at Wortley, I attended Central Baptist at night. I was especially attracted to Dr. Logsdon's preaching. However, a very pretty Betty Logsdon, with flowing black hair to her waist, helped, especially because she played the piano and she was good. Soon, I was to be invited home after every evening service for an after-church snack with Betty and her parents. I had taken a tumble for Betty Logsdon. I had imagined that I had me a prize. Alas, I was soon to learn that others were also after the prize.

Fran Carpenter, our Young People's president, has just announced a sermon contest. Prize money is $5.00. I am so excited that I cannot wait to tell the Logsdons. I intend to win the contest and collect that prize money doing the thing I hope to spend a lifetime at – preaching the gospel. Already I am hard at work preparing my oration. I think about public speaking as my forte. There are three others who wish to compete. I am sure I can beat them all. A dark horse candidate from Central Baptist hears about the contest. Betty has told Bruce Lockerbie about the event, and he asks for permission to compete. Fran tells him the contest is open to any who wish to apply. Even though Bruce Lockerbie has a preacher father who can coach him, my confidence knows no bounds. I am sure to win.

"Bring on the competition. I am ready." After hearing three poorly constructed sermons by the others, I can taste the prize money. The fourth week, Bruce Lockerbie delivers a twenty-minute sermon that is well organized around three points. The kids are impressed. I am not intimidated. I have poured into my sermon everything I have learned over the last six months. The fifth and last week has arrived and I give it everything I have. My sermon comes out like buckshot and touches on just about everything from Genesis to Revelation. It covers the whole Bible in twenty minutes flat, and when I am finished, I take my seat, awaiting the vote with happy anticipation. Fran counts the votes.

"And the winner is Bruce Lockerbie!"

The kids all clap and my competitor takes home the prize money.
I am devastated! There must be some mistake. "That's the problem with these shallow Christian kids," I think, "How do they know a good sermon when they hear it." Betty Logsdon and I go for

a walk after the meeting while I try to regain my composure.

"Was his sermon really that much better than mine?" I query.

Betty lets me down gently. She has grown up listening to her father preach for sixteen years. She explains why my sermon failed the test and encourages me to try harder next time. Older and wiser, as I now look back, there is no doubt about who should have won. Bruce Lockerbie went on to write many books and is today regarded as one of North America's finest preachers. I was up against the best. No wonder I lost.

With the coming of March, my next crisis looms. The burden of caring for Alice Carey's mother has fallen squarely on her daughter. The Careys requires a spare bedroom, mine. Again, Dixon Glass to the rescue. He approaches the Christian Businessmen Committee to finance my needs to get me through school. For two months, I board at the loneliest spot in London. A place near Central Baptist is found for me. My landlady gives me room and board, but I am banished to my bedroom except for meals. That was the loneliest two months I ever remembered. Thank goodness for the Easter break when I was able to work for a week with Ross Gilmore who ran a painting business. That's where I met George Maracle a first nation's Indian who was one of the handsomest men I've ever met. Muscular and tall, he seemed to be good at everything and, as a Christian, greatly encouraged me to persevere. He also taught me how to paint a door without leaving brushmarks.

With the coming of May, the students from LBI vacated the dorm for summer employment. What a relief it was, when London Bible Institute gave me a room after the students had vacated the dorm. I thoroughly enjoyed meeting a few lingering students who had city employment. May was indeed my liberation month. May was also heartbreak month.

Betty Logsdon takes a shine to classmate Paul Scragg and I am out in the cold. Faithfully on Sundays, I now attend both morning and evening service at Wortley Baptist. I now explain to those worthy people that having tried another Baptist church, I know Wortley is still the best.

By June 1st, the money provided for me by the Christian Business Committee runs out. Mom and Pop Gartley come to the rescue. Betty Logsdon had introduced me to these wonderful people who were trophies of grace. They had become Christians late in life but were full of the zeal of the Lord. This poses both a solution and a problem. While it is great to have a roof over my head, this particular roof is only six doors away from Betty's house. A perfect perch to watch Paul Scragg walk my heartthrob home every day. The Gartleys had decided, unbeknowns to me, that they would adopt me and make me sibling number four. In the light of after years, I now know that Dr. Logsdon, Betty's father, set it up. The Gartleys had been empty nesters for ten years. Alas, they had forgotten how demanding it is to have an energetic teenager under their roof. The arrangement only lasted for a month. The Gartleys were wonderful people who showed me much love and affection. It was a grand experience to live with them even if it didn't last. My pillar to post existence was a little rough, but I had made it. I graduated from grade twelve with flying colours.

Landing a job at the Coke-A-Cola plant, I could now earn enough money to return to the Sadlers' and board with them for the next two years. Needless to say, I was grateful not to see Paul Scragg walking Betty Logsdon home.

Chapter 12
The Coke Plant

Jack Daylor was the straw boss to whom I was assigned. Coca Cola was just as popular a drink in 1949 as it is now, and summer consumption demanded extra employees. Yes, I had this job and on my first day I learned I could have all the Coke I could drink. I finished eleven. My employer knew very well what would eventually happen. In no time I couldn't even look at a Coke. We tried everything to change the taste, even mixing it with milk. No luck. We could be trusted to handle the stuff and leave it alone.

Well do I remember that first day! I couldn't imagine such profanity, even in the days when I wasn't a Christian. By lunch time, Jack Daylor says to me, "What's the matter with you Woods? Are you strange or something?

"I don't think I understand what you are talking about," I reply.

"You damn well do, you idiot," says Jack.

"Sorry, but I don't get it. What's wrong?" I protest.

"Woods, you've been here for five hours, and you haven't sworn once. Whatsa matter with you – you crazy or something?" I smile and now I do get it.

"I guess you think, if a guy doesn't swear, he's strange."

"You bet I do," says Jack. "It ain't normal!"

"I guess I'll just have to be different then, because I don't swear." (If Grandma could only see me now!)

"Why not? Woods, Are you some kind of a pansy?"

"Sorry to offend you, Jack, but I don't swear because I am a Christian."

"Now that's all we need around here," says Jack. "A Christian who doesn't swear. Well, I'm a Christian who does swear, so what do you think about that?

"Well, Jack, maybe you are a Christian and maybe you're not, but I know I'm a Christian and I don't swear."

"Where on earth did you learn something as stupid as that?" says Jack.

"I learned that in the Baptist church I attend."

"Hey guys, get a load of this. We got ourselves a John the Baptist in our midst."

"Guilty," I proclaim as the men all laugh.

"That settles it. Guys, listen to me. As of this moment, I christen thee, Bruce, as "John the Baptist." If anybody here calls Bruce by any other name than John, he's fired."

The word of our straw boss prevails. From now on I'm "John the Baptist." or for short, just plain John. My new name sticks and I become the butt of every religious joke the guys can tell. I laugh just as heartily at their jokes about me as they do. I have since forgotten them all (just as well). When at last September rolls around, I quit, to go back to school.

Jack says to me in front of the guys, "You know John, we're going to miss you around here because with you gone, we don't have anybody left to razz." Then he adds this extra compliment. "I hate to admit it, John, but you're not a half-bad ass to have around, and you will be missed."

"Thanks for the compliment, Jack," I reply.

One interesting incident that arose from my summer at the Coke plant was that I got to know the janitor Werner Meyer (pronounced with a "v"). Vern was a quiet, middle-aged man who asked me if I minded the way the guys teased me about my religion. When I told him I viewed this as a subtle way of witnessing to my faith, he was surprised and promptly asked me to come to his house for Sunday dinner as he had something to share with me. The following Sunday, after church, I came to his house and met his wife. She was a rather plump Canadian girl who Vern explained to me was his second wife. His first wife had died in Hitler's holocaust against Jews. Vern then amazed me with pictures of his life before 1938. Vern had been a successful Jewish businessman in flooring, with his head office in Vienna. Vern was in commercial flooring doing major work for large retail outlets, servicing factories and warehouses all over Europe. I shall never forget one photo which showed him boarding a two-engine passenger plane that looked like it could accommodate twenty passengers. There was Vern with a mustache, looking quite dapper dressed in a business suit and carrying his briefcase (so different from his janitor's togs). The photo revealed a man who had an authority about him, showing him to be a confident businessman of the pre-war world.

When Hitler's "Anschluss" absorbed Austria, Vern's world collapsed. The Nazis confiscated his business and eventually put Vern and his wife into a concentration camp. Vern never heard from his wife again. One incident he related to me was the occasion when he was made to stand at attention in his underwear on a winter day for eight hours. Vern was tough; he survived to live and immigrate to Canada where he met and married Angela, his second wife. I marveled at Vern, who did not seem to be bitter but had accepted his lot as fate. At that point, Vern surprised me by saying he was searching for God. To this end, he had attended Central Baptist Church and was impressed by the closing hymn. I was intrigued by all this and wondered how it could be that the hymn impressed him, but not the sermon. Dr. Franklin Logsdon was well known to be an effective preacher that I personally admired, so I was a little disappointed that it was the hymn that he remembered. When I asked him about it, he sang the verse of a now almost forgotten hymn that was current in those days.

Almost persuaded now to believe.
Almost persuaded Christ to receive
Go Spirit, go thy way
Some more convenient day, on Thee I'll call.

We spent the afternoon discussing the gospel, and I tried to explain to him that Jews are no different from Gentiles, and that we both come to salvation through Christ's atonement on the cross. I'm afraid I was unable to convince him. After all what did a seventeen-year-old teenager have to say to a survivor of the Holocaust. In the end, he did most of the talking, and I just listened to his remarkable story of courage, perseverance, and survival. I prayed for him often after that memorable Sunday, but have long since lost track of Werner Meyer.

I fared better with Eric Ward. We met on the street in front of my boarding house. I sensed in him (a guy older than me, at twenty-four) that he seemed to have no direction. I took him to Central Baptist Church. I had versed him in advance of what to expect and how to invite Jesus into his heart. He made his commitment that very Sunday and afterwards said to me,

"Bruce you are a soul winner."

Right then and there I learned that if someone is to accept Christ, God has to prepare the heart. Our part is simply to tell the good news.

Chapter 13
Will the Real Terry Fox Please Stand Up?

Gospel! The word means "good news." I spent six of the best years of my life in Vancouver. It was there that I had the privilege of watching a unique sweep of the Spirit at work in that very special city. I refer to the Jesus people. Beginning in California, young people who were rebelling against the older generation referred to themselves as Beatniks. When I came to Ruth Morton Baptist Church in 1966, I was quickly informed they wanted to be called Hippies, not Beatniks. It is derivative from the word hipster which meant, "wake up, world; we are the now generation." They gathered at Wreck Beach in the west end of Vancouver by the thousands. Living without rules, and some would say without morals, they were a force that garnered attention just as 1967 ushered in Canada's Centennial Year.

They were soon to learn that you cannot live the life of a libertine without creating a vacuum of meaning. That's when hundreds of them turned to the gospel and the Jesus movement was born. I'll never forget the Sunday afternoon in the spring of 1970 when a group of about thirty singing young people passed by our window. They were led by a man with a guitar who seemed to be their leader. Soon, they were at the edge of the Frazer River (our house overlooked the river). Testimonies were short. About half of them were new converts. The leader waded into the river followed by those who were to be baptized. They didn't stay long. In springtime, the Frazer River is swift from the melted snows of the mountains. One by one they were baptized in that chilly river while everyone sang and hugged those who were making their way back to the river's edge.

Watching them from our window, I turned to my wife Joan and longingly said, "God is at work among those young people and we're not a part of it."

In actual fact, that seemed to be a season of evangelization because many youth of every walk of life were flocking to the churches, to give a fresh and welcome boost to aging congregations. Ruth Morton Baptist Church certainly enjoyed a thriving youth group, and I had the privilege of being their pastor.

One of the youth group was Rika Noda, a girl of Japanese descent. Alisa. her older sister, and our daughter Debbie were friends. The Noda family were Buddhists; but because they lived three doors away from us, the girls came with us in the family car to church every Sunday. Six of us plus Rika and Alisa (those were the days before seat belt laws). Well do I remember the laughter from the back seat as five kids there battled it out for a comfortable spot.

Rika's father was a hardworking, self-employed fisherman who plied the waters of the straits of Georgia and beyond for salmon. In 1942, Misaho Noda, like so many other Japanese immigrants, was informed that he was an alien. His boat was confiscated and sold, and Misaho was placed in an internment camp in Ontario. Many years later, after an official government apology, he was compensated with a check for $26,000. Of course, considering inflation, the money was a fraction of his original loss.

After the war's end, Misaho started from scratch to rebuild his business. Akiko, his wife, had spent the war years in Japan. In 1955, Misaho and Akiko were married and soon had two daughters, Alisa and Rika; and that's where we came into the picture. Rika became a Christian at the age of nine, following the example of her sister Alisa, and never looked back. In this respect, Rika mirrored my own commitment to Christ, and although she never entered a full-time ministry with salary, there never was any doubt that Rika was in full-time ministry.

By 1979, she had graduated from UBC with a degree in Physical Education and was working with Tim Frick, who was organizing volleyball games for wheel chair athletes. That's how Rika met Terry Fox. Soon, they were dating and in love. Betty Fox, who jealously guarded her favourite son, did not approve. I don't think Betty was capable of approving of any girl who could steal affection from her cherished son who she imagined was hers by exclusive right.

Rika Noda 1984, 22 years old
Photo courtesy Hamilton Spectator Archives

Terry Fox ran an unbelievable 3,338 miles from
St John's New Foundland to Thunder Bay, Ontario
when his cancer finally disabled him. Unable to
finish his Marathon of Hope, he nonetheless raised
millions for his cancer foundation.

Neither Terry's mother nor Terry Fox had any idea of the calling that God can have on one's life. It was said of Jesus, "knowing – that he was come from God and went to God" (See John 13:3), Terry was destined to follow those same steps. Terry Fox, unlike his three siblings who were gentle and gracious, was an angry young man with a fiery temper, like his mom. Is it possible that you can love too much? Rika had her hands full loving the tempermental Terry but threw herself into the task of taming the feisty stallion who was corralled by a virulent form of cancer. Her solution was to read books to Terry. At the time, Tolkien's books were all the rage, so she chose, the Hobbit, and read to him by the hour till it was finished. Terry, the red-blooded athlete who had no time for books, was charmed.

In typical Terry Fox fashion, he now became a Tolkien fan and read "The Lord of the Rings'. In fact, Terry even read "the Simlmarillion", in which Tolkien explains how he conceived of the series that has become such a worldwide phenomenon. Tolkien's books may be fantasy, but to the thinking mind, they raise the philosophical issues of life. The eternal questions are the same from generation to generation, and, when it gets right down to it, there are not that many of them. Tolkien used fantasy to explore these questions. With a little guidance from Rika, Terry Fox now took up the Bible, and with the same passion he had for Tolkien, he plunged into a quest to find answers to those life-probing questions. He concluded his quest by praying to Jesus and asking Him to be his Lord and Saviour. Terry was now ready to go to church. Rika brought him to Ruth Morton Baptist Church, creating quite a stir in the bargain. Terry's short life didn't afford much time to attend church. He would not become a church attending Christian, yet if he had identified with any church, it would have been the church that immortalized Vancouver's first settler whose legacy of love is still seen in that famous stain glass window. (see the back cover) I percieve similar lines of love in the famous Terry Fox.

I have made the statement that Vancouver's first settler and Terry Fox were from the same church separated by only seventy years. In actual fact, neither John Morton or Terry Fox were members of Ruth Morton Bapist Church. For John Morton he made the financial arrangements before his death. For Terry, he had no church. Rica was his church, his pastor, his counsellor, and mentor – however the few times Terry went to church, it was Ruth Morton Baptist.

Doug Alward, also a Christian, was Terry's closest buddy. As often as they shared friendship, they also clashed. It was impossible to have a friendship with Terry Fox any other way; but the thing that intrigues me is that it was with Rika that Terry always committed his heart.

"He always confided in me first," says Rika. "In fact, Terry told me things that he would never tell anyone else, including his domineering mother."

Terry's passionate vision to run the Marathon of Hope was first shared with Rika, whom Terry now asked to be his wife. After Terry died, Rika came east to spend a week with us and poured out her heart. It was during this very special week that we learned more about Terry Fox than the general public ever heard. I notified my friend Charles Wilkinson, who was a reporter working for the Hamilton Spectator. His findings made a full page in the Hamilton Spectator, Saturday, October 6, 1984. Quoting Rika he wrote,

"It seemed he didn't understand what a strong relationship could be, even though at times marriage was a very good possibility in the future. But I wasn't totally at peace with it because of his attitude towards different things. He was a very, very stubborn man; I thought, Can you live with this stubborn person? I was a little stubborn, too."

Rika agreed that Terry Fox had to be stubborn to make his great run halfway across Canada, raising $23 million for cancer research before that dreaded disease killed him in June 1981 at the age of twenty-two. As Rika said, "He sure wasn't a quitter."

In the end, much to Terry's disappointment, Rika decided against joining the cross country marathon. It certainly was not for lack of desire, but to protect her Christian testimony, she demurred at the last minute. Doug Alward would have to be companion for both of them. Without Rika's moderating presence, Terry fell into his old habits of anger and profanity. It is a pity that the script written by Ed Hume for The Terry Fox Story falls silent when it comes to Terry's essential Christian faith. Robert Cooper, who produced the (movie-for-theatre film) reaped the faint praise the movie deserved by ignoring these facts.

If only people would dig a little deeper and tell the whole story. Every great work of literature or film so often has a suffering redeemer figure that dies for a noble cause. Terry certainly fits the thesis. The example of the suffering redeemer is at the heart of life, whether Christ the Redeemer is acknowledged as that prime redeemer or not. If indeed, He is the creator of the world, why wouldn't this invaluable life principle be part and parcel of the creation that bears his workmanship in so many remarkable ways? The story told in the (made-for-theatre film, but now seen mostly on TV) is the poorer for its lack of candor at this crucial point. 'The Terry Fox saga makes for exciting Canadiana, unfortunately the film and the facts are blurred. The movie when it was finally released is a classic example of selective story telling. Who would remember Rika after seeing that movie, yet Rika was the most compelling and influential person in his life.

What a revelation that summer when we found out the real Terry Fox story. Unknown to his mother, as long as Terry was master of his own destiny, he continually phoned Rika for encouragement on his cross country run. When it became apparent he could not finish the race, it was to Rika that he turned. Wilkinson, quoting Rika, writes, "Terry revealed the news to me when he discovered his cancer had broken out in his lungs. 'I've developed cancer in my lung.' he said."
Rika's heart was breaking with him.
"And I could hear that he was crying. He was trying to be strong, but I could hear his voice was breaking, said Rica, and he started to cry."
"Of course, I had to be strong, too. I said, 'Well, when are you coming home? I'll meet you here, and don't worry." He came back. I think it was at that point he started to realize he wasn't invincible and could not control his destiny. I think he realized with this second bout of cancer that he was vulnerable. He didn't like to admit it. Nobody does. His helplessness now came home to him his helplessness, and how God is in control."

Thus, Terry died in true suffering redeemer fashion. The research his foundation established would ultimately discover a treatment for his kind of cancer so that others who suffer from the same strain of this disease can live. Had this know-how been available in Terry's day, he would have lived at least another twenty years. But the question nags us: without the martyrdom of Terry, would that foundation have been what it became?

Had Terry survived, as he related to Rika, he would have been ready to witness to the world about his Christian faith.

Again quoting Wilkinson, who is quoting Rika: "At his funeral, the head nurse took me aside. She knew how I was feeling, and I found out that she was a Christian as well. She said, I just want you to know that Terry was very much at peace when he died, and he said, 'I'm ready to go now. I'm ready."

"That made it worth it all, when I heard that, because I didn't want him to die in a panic, in a total 'lostness.'" Rika also added this statement:

"I think Terry learned a lot from his run."

Did his contact with Christianity and his Bible help a lot in that regard? Wilkenson queries.

"Oh, definitely! He phoned me once and said, 'If I get back – and he wasn't sure that he could make it back, he had told me before he left – I'm going to tell everyone it was God who helped me all the way to come across, because I could not have done it without him.'"

Miss Noda paused. "I learned a lot from Terry, about discipline and giving 100 per cent. He really put me to shame a lot of times. He lived as if there was no tomorrow – ."

The last two months of Terry Fox's confinement was complicated by his mother who was blinded to Terry's need for love of friends by her own devotion to her now famous son. She forbade all visitors except family, an order that she failed to tell her children. After the funeral, Terry's brother Daryl expressed his disappointment to Rika and Doug Alward that for the last two months of Terry's life, they didn't come to see his brother at his most trying hour. It was at this time that Daryl first discovered the frigid wall that Betty imposed around her son. A subsequent conversation between Rika and Betty explains all. Rika, attempting to console Betty Fox at her loss, said,

"At long last Terry is with the Lord to whom he belongs."

"No! That's not true! My son belongs only to me!" was her feisty reply.

Rika went on to marry and is an active member of the Ruth Morton Memorial Baptist Church. She is the mother of three children and is married to

The Terry Fox foundation has done so much for cancer research. It is under the able direction of Daryl Fox, a man with impeccable credentials. Daryl took his brother's loss with deep sorrow and many questions. Compensation for this kind of sorrow comes hard. Daryl became a biking phenomenon. He acquired a passion for cycling and mastered his craft. At the time he was one of Canada's best.

A footnote to his accomplishments is in order. Daryl acquired a top-of-the-line bicycle for $7000. His pride and joy caught the eye of a drug addict who was looking for a quick fix. His stolen bicycle showed up for sale a few months later in a second-hand bicycle shop. Price, sixty dollars. A Christian pastor from Port Coquitlam spotted the bike and recognized an unprecedented bargain, and bought it. He was soon troubled with an uneasy conscience. He concluded, "This must be a bicycle that has been stolen."

He phoned the police and described the bicycle to the officer, who shortly informed the pastor that the bicycle resembled one they were looking for belonging to Daryl Fox. The next day Daryl Fox got his bicycle back.

Chapter 14
From Rags to Riches

The second chapter of Ephesians in the New Testament tells us that when we become Christians, God has a plan for our lives. I was always excited about what God had in store for me and could never have foreseen what an amazing enterprise it was going to be. Often I thought I had missed God's best and wondered what life might have been like, if only I hadn't made so many blunders. I am convinced God allows those blunders to teach us humility; then, He takes over and makes things new. I never stop making blunders. It's just that now I don't worry about it anymore. I now know better than in my youth when I imagined I knew it all.

I was from a family of salesmen on my father's side, and although I had very little to do with that side of my family, I guess I inherited their genes. Like Rika Noda, I was at ease witnessing. One day, when I witnessed to Don Wonnacot, he told me I was a religious fanatic. To my surprise, I learned years later he had become a United Church minister. I don't remember how many guys I witnessed to in high school. I was an active member in the Inter-School Christian Fellowship (ISCF). We met every Thursday over lunch break. I guess somebody else noticed as well, because one day in a high school assembly, the drama club decided to do a spoof on our weekly meeting. It was a little skit making light of things that make up high school life. Our Christian Club came in for a little mockery in a song they made up:

"Come in for your religion, if you really want something more,
You might even go to heaven, but you have to know the score.
So come on in, and park your gum, with Rastus at the door."

Since I was the official greeter for our club, I guess I was Rastus. I laughed just as much as the kids. Ridicule never bothered me although not everybody shared my point of view. Some of the best Christian kids never darkened the door of our meetings, although to their credit in later life, they came through as solid Christian leaders, openly declaring their faith. It takes guts to live openly as a Christian in high school. Peer pressure keeps many Christian kids quiet. I think it comes easier when one has experienced a conversion in one's teens.

With school out and the summer coming on, Barry Moore organized one of his famous church baseball games at Springbank Park. It was memorable for me, not only because we had fun, but also because Bill Foster invited me (after the game) to see his study. Bill Foster was at the University of Western Ontario, and is one of the smartest men I've ever met. I was intrigued by his personal library and the learning it represented. Bill showed me a study in the prophetic announcements of Scripture concerning the coming of Messiah. I was mesmerized to think these remarkable prophecies beginning four thousand years ago could, with pinpoint accuracy, depict the coming of Christ and the manner of his death and resurrection. From that moment on, I decided that I would study the Bible for myself, giving an hour per day for personal Bible study.

With this new resolve, I determined that after a full day's work at the Coke plant, I would go to my desk and take the Bible verse by verse with the goal of covering the entire Bible, however long it might take. Why should I wait for Seminary to learn the Bible? I was determined to know it now. The task was not onerous. I loved every minute of it.

That summer I discovered a pamphlet written by Dr. Walter Wilson entitled, Whose body is yours? The essence of the pamphlet was that each sincere Christian ought to consciously kneel in prayer, at some moment in his life, and surrender his body to the Holy Spirit of God, asking Him to completely occupy every part of life. I remember kneeling by my bed and praying that prayer. It was a good prayer and I would shortly be put to the test.

I was in grade thirteen when I encountered my first lethal temptation with a girl. You already know I lived with the Sadlers. Soon after the school year had begun, four new boarders (all girls) booked into the rooming house. Ron Sadler invited two of the girls to go for a car ride, and I went along as well. I quickly learned the back seat of an automobile can be a dangerous place, where things can get out of hand. Mercifully, the Spirit of God has his ways, and I managed to escape unscathed. At times I have remembered that fateful evening, and thank God that I don't have to recall a bad experience.

Five months later, the same girl that shared the back seat of Ron's car with me offered to share her bed – an offer I declined. (I was of the conviction that the scarlet sin of immorality disqualified me for the ministry. I had to think that over again when one of my ministerial friends succombed to this lethal temptation. It was at that time that I decided that forgiveness reigns. He repented of his sin and moved to the United States and started over again.) This particular temptation would arise again in my pastoral ministry. I remember one woman who asked for counselling who revealed to me that her husband denied her sex.

"If I can't get my sex from my husband, then I'll get it somewhere else." She said. I'm not sure what that meant for me, but it was no temptation to a happily married man in the ministry. I guess I understand sex and don't understand it either. It is one of the unfathomed God given mysteries that is both awesome and beyond explaning all at the same time.

The following spring, when the four girls at Sadlers' finally graduated. I told Art Sadler what I had kept secret. He was shocked at the disclosure and commended me for my Christian stance, and later told his wife, Margaret. I could have informed them sooner, but what good would that do. I reasoned that kind of information would affect their attitude towards the promiscuous girl. I didn't want to poison the conversation around the common table we shared at mealtime. Sex is a wonderful gift from God; however in a fallen world, the age-old temptation is still the most appealing of forbidden fruit. Happy is the one who has the wisdom to wait till the right person comes along.

Grade thirteen brought me into the toughest academic school year I had ever faced. University, which was tough enough, was nothing like grade thirteen. To begin with, even though I only needed eight subjects to pass, I took nine. I soon found myself doing homework at midnight and sometimes later. To complicate matters, I had now decided to tithe my time based on fifteen hours of my waking/working day and give ninety minutes a day to Bible study and prayer. In addition to all this, I had to work after school and all day Saturday, just to pay my board. I was either on the job, working with Young Canada (a department store catering to children), or at my desk. Besides all this, I attended two services every Sunday and never missed Young

People's and mid-week prayer meeting. I knew this was sleep deprivation, but I counted on a miracle to keep me going.

That's when God taught me that common sense comes before miracles. Halfway through January 1950, I came down with Mononucleosis and slept for thirty-six hours. For two weeks I could barely lift my head. My zeal cost me my job working at Young Canada and nearly cost me my year at school. Although I returned to school two weeks later, it was all I could do to drag myself around till Easter, when at last I recouped my strength. I passed grade thirteen, but now the critical question loomed large. Would my marks be high enough to qualify for a bursary of $200, which I hoped would give me a flying start at the University of Western Ontario? I could only wait and pray that somehow I would make the grade.

I did get a miracle, but it came in an unexpected form. My guidance counselor was Mr. Lloyd Jackson. When my turn came up for my vocational interview, Mr. Jackson gave me a favourable report when he learned I was on my own and was working my way through high school. He commended me for my effort and decided to help. I failed to notice at the time that he was musing on something that concerned me. He said, "You'll be hearing from me again." I supposed that was the end of it. Unknown to me, Mr. Jackson was an influential member of the Lion's Club. It was their custom to give a $50.00 bursary to one student in each of the London high schools under the moniker "Good Citizenship Award." Usually, it went to whoever was president of the student council. With Mr. Jackson working on my behalf, it went to me. The manner of disclosure came as follows: T.S. McTavish (Tish for short) our principal was reading out the awards at the last assembly of the year. We were all in high spirits anticipating the summer holidays. Suddenly, as the awards were being read out, I heard my name associated with the prize money. I was so shocked that I had to confirm with my classmate if I was hearing things. Harold Hommer assured me that I had heard right.

When I finally discovered the good news was really true, I was given the privilege of attending the Lion's Club monthly dinner to express my gratitude. Jack Reese, a businessman who lived on Ridout Street, was there and took notice. I was always going from one financial crisis to the next, and I needed summer employment, so you can understand my enthusiasm when Jack, sales manager of the Fuller Brush Company, offered me a job. I was filled with enthusiasm and soon discovered my talent in sales. It was 1950 and I made $55.00 a week. Big money for an eighteen-year-old in 1950! Suddenly, I had come into wealth. The simple things of life, like shoes, and clothing, were open to me, not to speak of the luxury of going skating at the London Roller Rink. I had it made. This opportunity came my way in June. I hadn't worked since January. My savings had lasted till early May but after that I couldn't pay my board. Graciously, Mrs. Sadler continued to keep me on the proviso that I would catch up with paying my board from summer employment.

Sales runs in our family. My great grandpa Thomas [left] was a real estate salesman. My grandfather Arthur with Clarissa his wife [standing left] was a salesman. With the rest of the family looking on they are admiring my great grandfather's 1920 McLaughlin touring car. [made in Oshawa]

Well do I remember my first sales meeting with all the guys who sold Fuller Brushes. Jack Reese gave us a pep talk on enthusiasm. He has a convincing line: "I am certain that Fuller Brushes is the housewife's salvation from the drudgery of housework." However, after an hour, Jack is suffering from "the oversell". There comes a point when, having made your case, it is better to quit while you are ahead. I am grateful for the sales job. I have the salesman's gift to make it pay. However, I am unconvinced that the Fuller Brushe Company is salvation to overworked housewives.

For six weeks I made double payments to Mrs. Sadler, to repay my debt of board money. With that little matter now settled, I became a little more generous. I voluntarily raised my weekly board from $12.00 to $15.00 to a grateful Mrs. Sadler. Like a lot of us, she never seemed to have quite enough money to pay the bills. I've never met a woman who worked as hard as Margaret Sadler.

The summer of 1950 was great fun. It was made better by six mature school teachers ages twenty-five to forty who had come to summer school and were boarding with Mrs. Sadler. They joked about their kids and the experiences of teaching school. We were often in hysterics around the evening meal as they related their tales of teaching kids. I remember Susan Chambers who was a chunky girl, homely with short, thick, straight black hair. She was clever and witty. One day, halfway through our meal she stood up and entertained us with a song complete with actions she would use in kindergarten. The song positively doubled us over with laughter.

> "I'm a little teapot short and stout.
> Here's my handle, here's my spout.
> When I get all steamed up, hear me shout.
> Tip me over and pour me out."

I laughed so hard I could hardly finish my dinner. These schoolteachers were full of fun. I'll never forget Mrs. Sadler's menu that day, which happened to be beef stew, because no sooner had Susan finished her song when she said, "This meal is so delicious I think I'll have a second helping. Pass me the galosh."

"Gou-lash!' chimed in Mary Soper feigning disapproval, while we laughed even harder.

I don't know when I enjoyed the conversations at Mrs. Sadler's boarding house like the summer of 1950.

I am now a bona fide Fuller Brush man. I knock on doors and sell people my wares. I have forgotten most of my unusual encounters but two linger in my memory. The first was a young lady who welcomed me in with such enthusiasm that I wondered if I was going to make the biggest sale of my career. After I was seated on the couch, she came and sat beside me so close I could feel her body. (Uninterested in what was in my case,) she had other things on her mind. Pretending, I played the part of the naive Fuller Brush salesman. At long last, she finally agreed to buy a hairbrush. Dutifully, I wrote up the order and wondered why I was feeling so uncomfortable. Despite her pleadings to serve me a coffee, I beat a hasty exit on the excuse that I needed to make more sales to reach my quota. A week later when I delivered the hairbrush, I found myself again sitting on the couch which to me seemed unusual, since all I wanted was the $3.25 payment. It became all too obvious that the real reason for the sale was not because she was interested in hairbrushes. When at last I got through the exit door with my money, I sighed with relief. Next time I meet a girl my age that friendly, I shall pretend I am the Gas Man reading meters.

The other incident was sobering to say the least. The lady at the door of this house on Emmerson Street gasped when she saw me. Nonplussed, I stumbled over my opening routine, but still the woman was obviously in shock. Finally she said, "Please, you'll have to forgive me, but you look so much like my son-in-law who was killed in the war, I just couldn't help myself."

What to say in a situation like this? Although the war had been over for five years, obviously I had innocently opened a tragic sorrow. Then she spoke again. "My daughter came home from shopping last week and said to me, 'Mom, I saw a young man downtown who looked so much like Ralph, I nearly reached out and grabbed him.'" She explained to me Ralph was a Canadian pilot who was killed in action. Apparently, I resembled Ralph. Needless to say, I felt it inappropriate to attempt to sell brushes after that. Not to this household! I excused myself and continued on further down the street.

At church we are challenged to be generous. I soon get an opportunity from unexpected quarters. My sales manager, Jack Reese, has a god. It is money. When somebody from my territory phoned the office for an order, it was supposed to be referred to me. Considering that it took a lot of effort to produce $125 of sales per week, a phone order was a bonus. Jack would always refer the little orders to his salesmen. If it was a ten-dollar order, he would fill the order himself and pocket the profit. Sooner or later his salesmen would find out, but short of quitting, there was little we could do about it. I was surprised when Jack announced that he was leaving his very well-paid job to set up a store selling appliances. I figured that Jack was counting on making a bundle in his new venture, and he did. Later Jack phoned me and asked if I would buy his leftover surplus brushes. He didn't offer me a bargain. I could have bought the same stuff at company prices. He asked me to do it as a favour. Since it was of no consequence where I got my supplies, I agreed. Mind you, I still had to sell them, but I knew that would not be a problem.

I was on the horns of a dilemma. This guy Jack Reese, who has money to burn and has cheated me with his small-time raids on my territory, now wants me to take goods for which he has no further use and clean up his personal inventory. Two weeks before, we had had a conversation in which we talked about church givings. He had attempted to impress me by declaring that he gave $100.00 to his church every year. I countered by telling him that I gave $250.00, which was only my tithe. Jack's response was, "For a man of your small means, that's too much money."

So what's my dilemma? Over time, I figure Jack has cheated me out of $50.00 in profits on lost phone call business. Now he wants a favour that will net him over $100.00 that will cost me nothing but once again line Jack's pocket. I weigh the issues. I have told Jack that money is helpful, but I have a higher goal in life; I want to be a minister. It cost me nothing to be generous to this skinflint and take his merchandise for resale. I decide that as a witness to things that really matter, I would do it. A fellow salesman found out about it, and chided me for being magnanimous to a guy who didn't deserve it. Nonetheless, I felt I made the right decision.

With a year's experience behind me, it was now 1951 and I was looking forward to summer when I could work forty hours a week and overtime if I wished. I was set to make myself a lot of money. Out of the blue, I received the opportunity to be a summer pastor at a fraction of the wages I would be earning. The decision was a nonstarter. I gladly quit my sales job, and took a Kitchener mission church sponsored by Benton Street Baptist Church. It would only be for four months, but the challenge of it was for me a dream come true. I was nineteen and in the ministry, even if it was just for the summer. But let's leapfrog two years ahead.

Chapter 15
The Arthur Baptist Church

I was twenty-one years old with a year of Bible school under my belt. I had completed two years at Waterloo College (affiliated at that time with London's Western University), but I was a graduate of nothing. The only diploma I possessed was from high school. But I had a pastor, Hugh Horner of First Baptist Church, Waterloo, who believed in me. The Baptist church in Arthur had a speaker who cancelled on short notice. They needed a preacher for Sunday, September 6, 1953. Hugh Horner put us together and I was booked to preach in Arthur. The following day, York Road Baptist Church in Guelph called me with a similar dilemma. I deferred in their case to another date, September 27. It's either a feast or a famine. I preached in Guelph the last Sunday of August and in Arthur the following week. The Labour Day weekend was warm and beautiful, but to my disappointment, Joan, my wife, had come down with a sinus attack. I had to embark on this adventure alone.

On that Labour Day Sunday, a congregation of eighty-five greeted me and surprised me with their appreciation. They had spent a year looking for a pastor. After the service, right then and there, the deacons had a huddle and decided to ask me if I would consider a call to be their minister. Pleasantly surprised, I agreed, provided they were okay with my continuation of studies for my B.A. at Waterloo College. That afternoon, the deacons phoned every member and adherent who ever darkened the door of their church to attend the evening service. When I was finished preaching, Elmer Beer, the chairman, called for a vote of approval. Whoever said, "country folk are slow"? The vote was unanimous. I returned that night the most unproven yet astonished preacher-in-the making to be found.

The parsonage of Arthur Baptist Church and the church 1953

When I announced this sudden turn of events to my wife Joan, she replied, "While you were away, I thought to myself, what if they called Bruce to be their pastor. So maybe the Lord was preparing me in advance."

For my Anglican friends, who cannot imagine how a church congregation and an un-ordained pastor can get together, let me say, Baptists are like that. Two years later I was ordained and a month after that I graduated with my B.A. from Western University. While my case was unusual, there is a flexibility in our circles that accommodates guys like me. To illustrate, consider my watchmaker friend, Eric Penny. Eric was a member of our congregation and a wonderful speaker. His trade in 1953 was a necessity, everybody wore a mechanial watch. Since the advent of electronics; modernity has wiped out the watch repair business.

The Presbyterian Church had a two-point charge in Singhampton and Feversham that was dying. Unable to get a minister, these tiny congregations asked Eric to speak, and suddenly Eric had a Sunday job. Eric was naturally gifted and sensed a call to the ministry. The churches flourished and started to grow. Finally, they asked Eric to be their full-time pastor, but the Presbyterian Church had no flexibility for ordaining a full-time layman. When the Baptist church in Meaford became available, they asked Eric to be their pastor. Sorrowfully, the two Presbyterian churches said goodbye to their beloved Eric. However, the good news was that now that they had become two healthy country churches and they were able to call an ordained graduate from Knox College.

September is harvest time and in 1953 the combine had replaced the old-fashioned thrashing machine that I remembered from childhood.

Likewise, tractors were replacing horses. Howard White, the local blacksmith, had foreseen the decline in shoeing horses and was now the town blacksmith and welder. The local grocery store owners were bemoaning the large A & P store that had just been built in Fergus, only twelve miles away. Even worse, there was a rumour afoot about closing the small country schoolhouses, which abounded, and building one central school in Arthur and busing the kids in. It had already happened for the high school. The logic was irresistible. Also affected by modernity, the rural churches with their tiny congregations of twenty or less vowed they'd never close their doors. It wasn't that their loyalty was misplaced; it's just that the kids kept moving to the city. The advent of the large farm with labour-eliminating machinery had arrived, and rural populations were moving to the cities. Alas, the day of the small country church with its rich heritage of friendships and support was in decline.

In Arthur everybody had a vegetable garden, so we planted one, too, and grew potatoes so large that we had to cut them in half, cooking one half for one day and the second half for the next. If only the fall fair had been in October, we would have won first prize for sure. It was beginner's luck. We tried to replicate those potatoes the following year, but they were as pedestrian as all the rest. For a novice like me, those potatoes were the talk of the town.

Mrs. Prentice lived right beside us and for entertainment watched the neighbours through her 'bernoculars'. Mabel Prentice had the distinction of being the best informed lady in the village. Alas, television has swept away that kind of entertainment. Nobody walks the sidewalks anymore; the persons who made this spectator sport possible are also indoors watching television. The Mainlands lived on the other side of our house and kept us posted on country ways. Not that their ways were that different. We could pretty well figure things out for ourselves. It was the metaphors that took getting used to. At the time, for sake of gas economy, I drove a British-made Ford which had right and left signaling arms. Turn left and out flew a flag-like contraption that indicated my intentions. It was the latest in technology and made the farmers think that the Brits were certainly on top of their game. When Elmer Beer lifted the hood of my car, he marveled at the motor. "So small, you could put it in a bucket." I learned quite a few metaphors when I was in Arthur from the locals. Such sayings as "mad as a wet hen" took on more meaning when I actually saw one. "If you want to succeed, you'll have to scratch for it" or, she was "tight as bark on a tree," or, "all wind and no water". These were new sayings to learn. I could rattle off a few more but the point is made. English is a metaphor-rich language with many of its roots in our rural past.

One never realizes till you live it how fresh the country air can smell. In June it was the fresh-cut hay. In September it was the apple trees. In between it was the manure piles, which remind me of a companion story. Bob and Marion Norris were new at farming and had friends at our church by the name of Charles and Grace Mortley. One day Grace suggested that I ought to pay a visit to the Norris farm and invite them to church. For some reason I had our-three-year old son Mark to care for and took him along for the visit. Making our way to the farmouse required some dexterity, because it had recently rained. I made the mistake of going through the barnyard, and wound up picking my way through an old, rickety fence. The problem was that the path I chose took us through some soggy manure and you can guess the rest. After our shoes were cleaned, Marion invited me for a cup of tea. That's when my son Mark decided that he had to go to the bathroom. This embarrassed Marion, because they had no indoor plumbing. I was compelled to take Mark to the backhouse where an ancient "two-holer" was still the only plumbing on the Norris farm. Ten minutes after we returned to the kitchen, young Mark said he had to go to the bathroom again.

"I just took you to the bathroom," I said

"I have to go to the bathroom," Mark insisted.

To Marion's further embarrassment, I returned with my young son to the backhouse. Before that visit concluded, at Mark's insistence we made four trips to the backhouse. I had long forgotten the episode, but Marion did not. Fifty years later when we could laugh about it, Marion concluded that my young son was so fascinated with that "two-holer" that he just had to go back and see it again.

Every Sunday was a treat, because we always had an invitation to go somewhere for dinner.

"The Pastor and Mrs. Woods are coming," was the rally cry, and the inviting host and hostess always made sure that the meal was a feast of either roast chicken, pork, or beef. Each of the farmer's wives had their specialty. For Mrs. Clark, it was her homemade bread. For Olive Beer, it was her butterscotch pie. How I laughed when the leftover pie was devoured by her two teenage sons. Out came the ruler, and before witnesses, the measured pie was meted out with such care that the division of pie was precise. How those hard-working farmers' wives could go to church, prepare a feast, and show up for Sunday evening service at 7:30 PM. is testimony to the flabbiness of today's generation that sleeps in on a Sunday. If they go to church at all, they do it through a television program. How impoverished! No wonder in old age people are so lonely. How truly rich are those church people who gather for special occasions with everybody chipping in to make social event a success. Associations that are enriched by a lifetime of interaction reap a rich harvest when the aging process makes the going tough. Fifty years later Charles and Grace Mortley are still our close friends. We follow one another's kids, their marriages, their adventures in life, as though they were cousins to our own children. After years apart, we can still sit down at their table and never lack for conversation, thoroughly enjoying ourselves. During my three years at Arthur Baptist Church, Charley was my prayer partner and Grace our church organist. She only needed to hear a tune once and she could play it by ear.

It was at Arthur that I discovered that I cry at parades. It's not that I don't like them; it's just that for some deep subterranean reason, parades make me cry. I found this out three weeks after we moved into the parsonage located on Tucker Street. It was time for the annual fall fair, a big event for farmers who made up the bulk of my congregation. In association with the fair, the Boy Scouts and their Cub Scout companions were marching. They came right past our house and we joined the neighbourhood to cheer with the locals who all came out to watch. That's when I discovered this incurable weakness.

"What's wrong with you?" said my inquiring wife.

"Don't ask me," I stammered. "I can't help myself."

I have been a social liability to my wife ever since. Any time we ever watch a parade, I have to have Kleenex on the ready. I can't help myself. I cry at parades.

I met so many wonderful people in Arthur that if I were to speak of them all it would make another book. Nonetheless, let me introduce you to three. The first is Fred O'donnell, who owned the local Chevrolet dealership and Texaco Garage. Fred had been in the Canadian Army and been in France, Belgium, and Holland. Too young to go to war myself, I had nonetheless been fascinated by that war and followed it through to its conclusion. Fred and I had been talking after I had some repair work done on my car. Somehow our conversation turned to the war years so fresh in both our memories. Fred told me this incredible story.

"A few months before the war's end, we were stationed near the Holland-Germany border. We were busy on operations when suddenly we heard German aircraft overhead and dove for cover, something we weren't used to doing since we hadn't seen much from the Nazi air force after we won the Battle of the Bulge. That's when we witnessed an aerial dogfight between three RAF Spitfires and eight Messerschmitt 109s." said Fred "I tell you Bruce no air show you could ever imagine matched what these eyes witnessed that day. The Germans had taken our planes by surprise and outnumbered them. We expected the worst, but the Spitfires took evasive action and soon had turned the tables. You cannot imagine the sound and the dramatic diving, guns blazing. We watched as one by one the German planes went down. Finally, after five German planes were destroyed, the other three Messerschmidts fled the scene. It was the most spectacular event I ever witnessed in that entire war," said Fred.

Naturally, I drew my own conclusions from the story as you might also do. Years later through my reading of the War Annals of the second great World War, I learned that the Germans, due to gasoline shortages, were sending young men up to fight in their newest aircraft (every bit the equal of ours) with only fifty hours of airtime training. Our pilots were not allowed to enter combat with less than 800. I mentioned all of the above to a seasoned pilot many years later. His response was revealing.

"With so little training as that, those German pilots didn't have a chance."

Reflecting back fifty years later, I realize that today's generation are so different from mine. We lived and breathed that war every day for six years. We even trembled that we might lose. It affected us in a way that modern young people simply cannot understand. With the steady diet of violence available through media, today's generation is entertained by the things we feared might actually happen to us. It makes decent people who read the Bible long for the time when "And he (God) shall judge among the nations, and shall rebuke many peoples; and they shall beat their swords into plowshares, and their spears into pruning hooks; nation shall not lift up sword against nation, neither shall they learn war anymore." (Isaiah 2:4)

The second man is Dr. John Scott Hogg, who attended our church. When our first son was born, he came breech. Joan had a terrible time of it, but Dr. Stanley skillfully saved the day. When our second child was born, Joan wanted Dr. Stanley. John Hogg would have served us free of charge. John was a likeable man and loved by the townsfolk. Fearing complications my wife wanted Dr. Stanley. (Doctors can establish an undeserved reputation for doing miracles) When Deborah was born, Dr Stanley was delayed and didn't arrive in time. The nurses at Kitchener-Waterloo hospital delivered our second child. Dr. Stanley's fee for $50.00 was never paid. I didn't think he earned it, especially when Dr. Hogg would have done it for free. Seven years later, a bill collector came to our door. Dr. Stanley was demanding payment. Scrimping our budget, we paid. What a blessing today's Canadians enjoy with Medicare.

The third man was Lloyd Dixon. Lloyd was socially disadvantaged and lived on a farm with his mother. He was an able farmhand for his brother but was otherwise a quiet recluse. Lloyd never missed a service but at heart was a convinced Pentecostal. Lloyd was always trying to show me why I should be a Pentecostal. One day Lloyd dreamed that he would be a prophetic evangelist. During the Sunday service, Lloyd sat at the back instead of his usual seat beside his mother. Unobserved, at 11:30 AM, he slipped out and walked the two blocks to the Catholic Church. Boldly, he marched to the front of the startled parishoners and interrupted the Mass with a prophetic utterance that all Roman Catholics needed to be saved. Quickly, two strong armed ushers removed him and delivered Lloyd back to the

Baptist church to a very embarrassed Mrs. Dixon. The good-natured priest forgave him for his foolhardy venture. Needless to say, there was a good deal of fodder for Catholic sheep over Sunday dinner. Perhaps it was just as well the mission failed. How could we have handled 400 new members at our little Baptist church?

In 1955, I completed my B.A., and in the bargain met an old classmate from grade eight (Romeo School, Stratford). Jim Miller was the smartest kid in our class and was now teaching school in Sarnia. Later he taught high school and eventually taught at Western University. He was as surprised as I was when we met at summer school. I told him that Jesus Christ had changed my life. Now the former quick-to-cuss classmate he knew was a Baptist minister. I met him again 53 years later when he said to me,

"I shall never forget that meeting, Bruce. I honestly have to say that you blew me away with your Jesus style. I didn't know what you were talking about. Of course, today I know exactly what you were talking about." Jim Miller, after twenty-five years, retired from teaching school and today is still an active Anglican minister.

I cannot close this chapter without reference to our church annivesary which was always held on the first Sunday in May. In rural Arthur there were three events not to be missed: the first was a wedding, the second was a funeral, and the third was a church anniversary. Our church was no exception and on this occasion was typical of all. I will choose Sunday, May 2, 1954, because that was my first experience. Our special speaker was Rev. Leander Roblin; by this time, we had reconnected after our separation which I describe in a future chapter. The morning service was always held at 11 AM.; and was followed by a feast to remember. A roast beef dinner lay waiting prepared by the ladies of the church. Looking back I marvel at the energy of those farmer's wives. They had cooked the beef at several locations at home and brought their meat hot to the church, keeping it warm in pots wrapped with towels. Delicious roast beef gravy was also brought and kept warm in a large crock. The potatoes were boiled downstairs on the basement stove while the service took place in the auditorium. Vegetables were of the canned variety and warmed up after the service. Salads were easy to keep and the pies took care of themselves. Every variety of pie you can imagine was available for such a special occasion; apple, pumpkin, lemon, Olive Beer's famous butterscotch pie and of course, plenty of chocolate cakes. Such a feast was remenicent of the old fashioned threshings of yesteryears when harvest was also a gathering of local farmers.

The tables had been made by Howard White out of eight feet long plywood mounted with cast iron sockets. The men's duty was to screw in the pipe legs and set them up because they were heavy. Modernity had made a large paper spool of newsprint paper available for tablecloths. Chairs were borrowed from Goulding's funeral home; now we were ready for the seating of a hundred hungry parishioners. What a celebration. Appropriate giving of thanks was always done by the pastor. I assure you this twenty-two year old pastor, mature beyond his years, offered the giving of thanks which was followed by a chorus of hearty amens. Mary Hines (not her real name) who lived by the church always attended every anniversary service of every church in Arthur. Not bad for a non churchgoer. Elmer Beer lost count on how many pieces of pie she ate after she consumed ten.

The afternoon service was at three and was packed with visitors. Our usual attendance of 100 swelled to 200. At four o'clock we broke for a light supper at home. Chores were done by our farmers because remember, those cows had to be milked (this is the day before milking machines). At seven-thirty (the posted time for evening service) we were all back in church for the grand finale. In truth we always started late, more like a quarter to eight. The special music was always provided by the Fergus Baptist Church. Sermon number three was duely digested and at last the benediction. Church anniversaries, the highlight of the year, went away with the coming of television. Such occasions, (which brought the congregation together with so many visitors), have ceased. Times have changed and I'm not sure if we are better off.

Education has a way of making you feel you need more. After three years pastoring and preaching at the Arthur Baptist Church, I resigned because I was longing for a formal theological training. In September of 1956, I moved to Dallas with my wife, Joan, and our two children, Mark and Debbie. Four years later, I graduated from the Dallas Theological Seminary with my Master of Theology degree.

Twenty-seven years later, my now grown-up and theologically-trained son, Mark, accepted a call to the Arthur Baptist Church. He enjoyed seven fruitful years of ministry in the same Arthur Baptist Church building, preaching from the same pulpit as his dad.

In 2006, the Arthur Baptist Church closed, but two new ones started up. One numbers twenty and the other numbers six. In my day the Arthur Baptist Church had a congregation of eighty-five, with an evening service that numbered fifty-five. The new Pentecostal Church in Arthur numbers 125. There is a new evangelical church six miles away in Alma, that just seemed to come out of nowhere; they number 175. The Grand Valley Baptist Church twelve miles away didn't exist in my day although they tell me it is very small. It seems to me, we are forever building new aquariums for Christian fish to swim in because for some reason or other, we find reasons to disagree. The malaise is not confined to Baptists. The Presbyterian and United Churches in Arthur are a third of what they were in my day. However, it is good to see that other churches pick up the pieces and thrive.

Chapter 16
We Thought It Was the End of the World

September 25, 1950, was a warm fall day and even though it was Sunday, I had determined that I would hitchhike to Stratford to see Grandma. She was unaware of my decision to enroll at London Bible College, and I wanted to tell her all about it. As ever, hitchhiking was easy, and I soon had a ride. On my way to Stratford, the sky turned pink and the sun turned to a purple ball. I arrived around noon and for a little nostalgia walked past our old home at 156 Brunswick Street.

Now the sky had turned cloudy and lowering. I was sure it wouold rain. I had never seen anything like this before, and I knew this was no usual sky. As I made my way to 475 Albert Street, the day kept getting darker and darker and the streetlights came on. Even the Starlings were confused and were flying into the branches overhead to nest for the evening. By the time I reached Aunt Elsie and Uncle Gordon's house, I was getting uneasy. It was only 1:30 in the afternoon. It was night and starting to get cold. To add to this mystery, an eclipse of the moon had been reported in all the papers, and we knew that it was to happen that very Sunday night. A bizarre co-incidence indeed! Is this the end of the world that I had heard Dr. Dunkin mention in his sermons? I was beginning to feel uneasy that I had missed church. The atmosphere was surreal. I had already talked to several strangers and the conversation was always the same:

"Do you know anything about this weather? I asked.

"Don't ask me; I've never seen anything like it. Maybe somebody has launched the atomic bomb, and this is the aftermath. I'm frankly afraid," said the stranger.

"Never saw anything like this before." said another.

"Maybe, it's an eclipse of the sun."

"A blackout at noon? What is happening to us?"

And so the talk went, up and down the street. People had gathered in small groups and were holding animated conversations everywhere. Another lady was more philosophical about it. Having just taken a taxi to get home, she said she wasn't scared, "If the good Lord wants to take me, I'm ready to go."

By 2:30 PM, the clouds began to lift, and finally the sun broke through. We all sighed in relief, and conversations now turned to the cause. In the end, it turned out the source of this bizarre weather was a forest fire in Alberta. The smoke clouds driven by upper air currents leap-frogged over the Prairies and descended on Ontario and some of the northern states.

The next day made for interesting reading in the newspapers. A major league baseball game in Cleveland normally would have been cancelled. The newly installed floodlights enabled them to play the entire game under the lights. Seems like everybody had a story which they told over and over again. (See *The Stratford Beacon Herald*, September 25, 1950.)

"Cows demanded to be milked ahead of schedule. Chickens headed for their roosts. One terrified young woman wept to think that the world she knew was over and her husband was away. She had hoped that he would return in time so that they could die together."
"What a day to schedule a wedding," said one disappointed bride.

By suppertime, things had returned to normal, and I had explained to Grandma that in four years I would be in the ministry and pastor of my own church. Aunt Elsie said,
"That would make you twenty-two. Sure is young to be a minister."

I suspected by the tone in Elsie's voice that she thought that would be too young. As I have explained in the previous chapter, due to some very enthusiastic farmers, I had entered the ministry a year earlier than that. As I reflect upon it all sixty years later, knowing what I know, I wonder: would I go to a church to hear a twenty-one year old man preach?
I'm not sure.

Chapter 17
A Triangle of Women

The three women who figured so largely in my life were Grandma Gillatly, my wife Joan, and my mother. Grandma Gillatly was not a complex person. She had no agendas except to live a Christian life without pretense; what you saw was what you got. Grandma taught me logic. When she confronted me with something I didn't like, and I asked her why, her reply was always, "because I said so." The only time she ever laid a guilt trip on me was for my cussing. For this, I am eternally grateful; it taught me that I was accountable, in this life and in the life to come. Her clear-headed assessment was my pillar, especially as my mother slowly lost her grip on reality.

My wife Joan My grandmother Rachael My mother Ethel

As my mother became increasingly paranoid, my grandmother had every right to protest my mother's unreasonable accusations. She didn't need to defend herself before me or others. She had her Presbyterian faith that sustained her and the radio preachers that comforted her in her trials. She especially enjoyed Dr. H.H. Barber of Calvary Church, Winnipeg. I can still hear his sonorous voice as even I would listen to his radio sermons. To the end Grandma and I were soul mates. When at the close of her life the thought of dying troubled her, I was her refuge. In my growing-up years I needed her; in her last days she needed the encouragement of her now preacher grandson.

To this end, my wife and I invited her to come and stay with us for a few days. What a joy to drive the ninety minutes from Arthur to Stratford to pick her up and take her home with us. The drive took us through Mackton and Millbank and is almost a straight line to Stratford.

It was a pleasant drive through rural Ontario and prosperous farms.

Our son Mark was three; our daughter was nine months old. How she enjoyed their antics. I remember taking her to the church and showing her the place where Sunday by Sunday I preached. I wish she could have heard me preach one of my sermons before she died. Alas, she was too weak to sit through a service and had to content herself with my wife's stories about my sermons. After two days, Grandma was anxious to return to the security of her final earthly home, made pleasant by Aunt Elsie's kind and helpful care. I wish I could say the same about her son. Gordon could be cruel. He spared neither my Grandma, nor his wife. He never went any further than words. I suppose he imagined that he was a good son and a providing husband. He just had to be ignored for his ungracious remarks. No wonder he wept so bitterly at Grandma's funeral. After all the things he said to her, he needed to.

If only men realized how hurtful their abusive language can be, they would save themselves a lot of grief. My grandmother was an honourable woman; it was a privilege just to be present at her funeral. Fifty-four years later, I'm beginning to contemplate my own.

The most influential person in any man's life is his wife. I count myself fortunate to have had a good one. By any man's estimate, she was the most beautiful girl in Waterloo. I would not have dared to date her had I met her there. Gerald Thiele said of my wife Joan, "She was the prettiest girl in my grade eight class, definitely 'out of my league.'"

I met and wooed her at London Bible School where the competition was not so tough. I remember the first time I saw her. She was wearing a yellow short-sleeved sweater with a brown silk scarf at her neck that matched her skirt and her dark brown flashing eyes. Gorgeous eyes!

Her skin colour was naturally golden, making me wonder if she didn't have some Latin blood to match her temper. Her posture was erect and she walked like an aristocrat, her head always tilted up. She had high cheekbones and ruby lips that formed a heart-shaped smile. I was fascinated to watch the movement of her mouth when she talked. In short, she had style. After we were courting, she told me an interesting story. She was going to an office party at the Bell Telephone Company in Kitchener. Her mother had made her a long black velvet ballerina style dress with a large green bow at the neck. Her date had brought her a pink corsage that clashed with the bow, so she wore it on her wrist. The wife of one of the bosses was a buyer for Simpson's Department Store. Later that evening, she walked across the dance floor and said, "I've been watching you all night, you look absolutely stunning in that outfit. You are the best-dressed girl at this party."

Two leaders in one household can sometimes have its challenges. After fifty-seven years of marriage, four children, and ten grandchildren we both know that, in spite of the differences we have had and will have, God has put us together and we love each other deeply. At the tender age of eighty, she is just as gorgeous as she was in youth. Not a line on her face anywhere. Wherever she goes she is always taken for fifteen years younger than she really is. It's standard fare for humour around our house: our kids tell her her birth certificate is incorrect. I do have to add that I am taken for younger than my years as well.

Now to get back to our topic, I cannot say I am a self-made man. Joan made me what I became, and I dare not think of what my ministry would have been without her. For starters, every sermon I ever preached for three years in Arthur was first preached to my wife in the kitchen of our house after the dishes were done on Saturday night – first the morning service sermon and second the message for Sunday evening. She was merciless. Every lapse of logic, every irrelevant idea, every corny joke, every tediously involved and complicated thought pattern was scrutinized. No fledging reporter answerable to a red-pencil-wielding editor faced a challenge stiffer than mine.

Often her own ideas would supplant my mine, as I gave way to a superior way of stating my case. I sometimes wondered if I was preaching Joan's sermon or mine. She was the best homiletics teacher I ever had. Nothing I learned at Dallas Theological Seminary ever matched the kitchen lectures of my wife in Arthur. I could have skipped the four years I spent at Dallas Theological Seminary, preached in as many churches as would have me, and no one would have been the wiser. Joan has kept her word when she stated, "I may not always agree with you, but I will always support you."

For character and personality, I am what my mother made me. I was eleven years old before I noticed her irrational behaviour. By then, the mould had been set. Her lavish outpouring of love on her son was her compensation for mistreatment by men. I can understand (although disapprove of) why she lashed out at grandma for her naivety. Her misplaced trust in men who betrayed her may point to some flaw in her make-up, but that came at birth and had nothing to do with her upbringing by her mother (my Grandma). Her gratuitous blame came when it was too late to remedy her situation. Sadly, Grandma paid the price. As I write, I think of three men who are guilty, two of which, if discovered and charged, would have gone to prison. The third could have pulled her through except my father romanced another woman and abandoned my mother when I was born. Mother's fragile defenses could not stand up to the tribulations she experienced. Yet, look at the record.

In 1934, in the heart of the Depression, my mother set up a beauty parlour in Grandma's house. It succeeded. She became the breadwinner and provider for three people. When I wanted to make a punt to navigate the mighty Avon River in Stratford, she indulged me. She did it again when I wanted to enter the Soap Box derby, where I won second prize ($15.00). That same entrepreneurial spirit that she had is lived in me.

Fear of failure or the idea that the project is too big to tackle hold so many people back from opening the door of favour when it comes. In 1983, when opportunity knocked at my door, probably in spite of my congregation, rather than because of them, I led Stanley Avenue Baptist Church into Hamilton Baptist Non-Profit Homes. We built 166 townhouses with government money for low-income families that are presently owned and operated by our congregation. So Mom, where did that come from? I learned it from you.

Mother was artistic. She painted landscapes with oils that grace our home to this day. I can still hear her play Beethoven's Moonlight Sonata which celebrates romantic love – the love she longed for and never had. She died thinking her life had been a failure. I shall disabuse her of that notion when I meet her someday in heaven. Her tenderness and compassion had its lessons. I like to think that I reflect them and pass the love along.

These then are the three women who have molded my life – a triangle (a trinity?) that has made my character.

Chapter 18
My Big Opportunity

When I graduated from seminary, I knew I was ready for a challenge. Instead of the big church I expected to pastor, I accepted a call to a struggling little congregation of forty-four members that met in the Georgetown Oddfellows Hall. In the six and a half years I ministered there, we purchased a wonderful property on Maple Avenue right across from the new post office and built a beautiful church.

My ministry at Maple Avenue Baptist Church was marked by some very memorable events. First, let me mention the good things that happened to me. I drew the plans for the church and oversaw every detail in its construction. It was colonial in design with a traditional white steeple and became the talk of the town. On opening day, we sponsored a kids meeting with Frank Wellington "the Musical Storyman" and had 500 kids spellbound on each day of the Easter week vacation. Second, it grew from forty-four members to 130 in six years. Third, I was elected vice-president of our denomination at age thirty-three, the youngest man ever to hold that office. Fourth, when Canada's Centennial came along, I proposed a new head office for our denomination. Hal McBain, our elder statesman, was opposed; he had other ideas. The all-powerful executive council, in my experience, rarely considered anything without his support. It was a tough sell, but on a vote of six to three, I was able to steer the project through the executive council. We would buy land and build – before the astronomical rise in real estate values. The financial return of this decision was liberating for our denomination, to say the least. I was not alone in all this, and it took the expertise of other godly men to bring it all to pass. Fifth, I was elected to the Baptist French Board. Meeting the French pastors and becoming acquainted with the churches was a great experience. Those wonderful French pastors opened up for me that "Other Solitude" which takes us back to the very foundations of our country. However, liberating as all that was, life is still personal and memories that have depth always involves our association with people. Those kind of things are the "memorable." All else are merely the good things. For the memorable, I begin in no particular order, but I will list a few.

*Maple Avenue Baptist
Church Georgetown 1961*

Interior: the auditorium

— Peter Jones, Georgetown

FIVE HUNDRED FASCINATED

DURING EASTER WEEK the attendance at the Maple Ave. Baptist Church Bible School reached a high of 550 children. They were entertained by the Musical Story Man with illuminated flannelgraph and puppets.

In my previous book, I described the struggles my mother had with mental illness. Naturally, her struggles were also mine. One day, out of the blue, mother announced to me that she was going to marry Sid Jones of London. Sid was a retired CNR pensioner; their marriage was a mutual blessing. It also released my responsibility for her wellbeing. I was overjoyed at the news. They attended the Pentecostal church. When I urged them to consider a Baptist Church, mother replied, "Why should I do that? The Pentecostal congregation is such a happy people, I like it better." I acquiesced; at least mom was going to church.

114

The second memory is my association with "Crippled Civilians". That was what the Toronto organization called themselves before they changed the name to Goodwill Industries. To support myself and our little family when I attended Dallas Seminary, I had worked in Public Relations on behalf of Goodwill Industries. When I dropped in to see G.E. Smith, the CEO of Crippled Civilians, he immediately queried me about how to generate more materials to keep the 325 C.C. employees more fully occupied. It was easy to see the problems, because we had already faced them in Dallas. I take no credit for solutions that I had learned from others who had gone before me. Nonetheless, I had the expertise that the Toronto organization desperately needed. The mainstay of Goodwill Industries has always been used clothing. Short of materials, the items the employees of C.C. were processing were scarcely better than rags.

Smith hired me for one day per week to solve the problem. After clearing it with my church, I began organizing the Boy Scouts for clothing drives. The results were wonderful. The availability of used clothing was obvious (so different from today). But how to get at it. Toronto households were stuffed with clothing that was passe, but still hanging in Toronto closets. The Boy Scout drives for clothing in 1962 reaped a bonanza for C.C. (now Goodwill Industries). Within six months, we had turned things around. When we moved to Vancouver in 1966, Crippled Civilians had enough material to keep the employees going for six months without a single donation of used clothing. What a difference three years had made. Eighteen months into my Vancouver pastorate, the board was so impressed with the results of my efforts that when Smith retired, I was invited to become the executive director of C.C. It was an attractive offer because the one thing I hadn't counted on was how homesick for the east I would become. Vancouver is great in the summer, but oh, those dreary gray rainy days in the winter. A quick ticket back to familiar home territory was appealing. However, in the end I declined. God had called me to the preaching ministry. To the preaching ministry, I would stay committed.

The third memorable event was Uncle Norman's funeral. I loved my Uncle Norman. I also respected him. He was so much fun. I remember the second Christmas after my conversion, telling him that he may not realize it, but the two dollars he gave me, turned into a hundred dollars in four months. Half serious, but in his typical light-hearted manner, he asked, "How so? I've got a few more two dollar bills. Tell me your secret, sounds like a great way to make money?"

I proceeded to explain what you have already read in chapter three. However, when I came to the God part, he didn't want to listen. Politely, I changed the subject.

For so many who have grown up in a church setting, the faith of parents passes on a goodly heritage. Norman was an elder in his Avondale United Church. However, involvement in a church is no guarantee of experience. The words of Jesus are still true: "You must be born again."

Norman could not identify with my conversion experience. In 1962, Norman was stricken with cancer and became my special prayer concern. Eventually, he died of Hodgkins Disease, a form of cancer. Determined to pay him a visit while he was still alive, I was shocked to see how he had failed.

Visiting someone like an uncle strips away confidence. I still feel like his nephew, which I am. I wanted so much to tell him about the love of God and His purpose for our life. I had no liberty but tried. I did talk about heaven where there was no more fear because Norman had been sharing how "scared" he was. For someone like me in the ministry, it was not a satisfying experience. That was the last time I saw my Uncle Norman alive. He died January 3, 1963. The funeral took place three days later. It proved to be a memorable event.

When I looked at the program, I was surprised to see that Gordon Stephenson, a Baptist layman, was to deliver the message. Rev. Lowenberger took the rest of the service. Gordon Stephenson was Norman's barber. Gordon had frequently talked to Norman about the gift of eternal life. With cancer on his mind, Norman listened. When Norman was hospitalized, Gordon visited him regularly, and somewhere along the line led Norman in the sinner's prayer for salvation. Gordon spoke freely of Norman's new life in Christ, and I shall never forget the introduction of his sermon:

"Some people here will say that Norman Gillatly is dead, but I say Norman Gillatly is more alive this moment than he ever was on earth."

Instantly, I could put all the pieces together, and the tears rolled down my cheeks. All the things I wanted to tell my Uncle Norman but couldn't seem to say were said by his barber. It was one of the most memorable funerals I have ever attended.

By way of contrast, I now refer to the fourth memory. My father died of cancer when he was fifty-seven. Norman was only fifty. My father never went to church and steadfastly declared that he was an agnostic. I witnessed to him as best I could, and was bolder in that witness than when I was with Uncle Norman. I made no headway with my hard-shelled father. Slowly, as his health declined, we both knew that death was imminent. Life has both triumphs and tragedies. Few of us can escape disappointment. In Dad's case, everything seemed to go wrong in his prime. My father finished life by a double blunder that ruined him financially; then to compound the tragedy, he discovered he had cancer.

First, the partner he engaged in the aluminium window business cleaned him out. Second, was the terrible bargain he made when he bought the Westwinds Marina on Lake Simcoe. It was grossly overpriced. A seasoned real estate man could have told him so, but my father didn't need any advice. He found out too late that he had been taken. What little he had salvaged from the sale of his house was lost. He had good reason to be bitter. He had taken his life savings and thrown it away. Now he was dying with cancer and was blaming God for everything that went wrong in his life. How human. He never looked inward to find personal blame. Again, how human. At his bedside, I wanted to have prayer with him and remind him that God loved him. My lot was not made any easier by the presence of my Uncle Ross, another agnostic. I reasoned with my father that if Jesus could turn to the thief on the cross and say,
"This day you shall be with me in Paradise," then the same offer was good for him. To my utter astonishment my father accepted my comfort. I at last felt the unseen barriers between us vanish.

Ross, ever the skeptic, said,
"He was delirious; he won't remember a thing you said."
I had more confidence than that. Well do I remember the drive home that summer evening. The times I spoke to Dad about the good

news of the gospel had made their mark. Dad had denied it, but he did think about it. He did see his need. It was brief but it was swift. That's just how the Lord would have planned it. As I drove home to Georgetown the sun was setting in the rural landscape of Ontario. The sight was glorious. The exhilaration I felt that memorable day was even more glorious. I would meet my father again one day in heaven.

A few weeks later the funeral took place at the chapel inside U. of T. (University of Toronto). Dad said it was for medical research that he donated his body. Perhaps, but I cannot help but wonder if it wasn't a way to help Phyllis out financially. His disastrous investment in the Marina had wiped out their finances. In his deathbed repentance, he had hinted as much. Dad was not a good man, but he was not a bad man either. Does it matter? We are all sinners who need God. How I would have loved to take his funeral, but Phyllis made sure I only received an invitation. The officiating clergyman was handpicked because he believed in nothing. Unfortunately, there are too many Tom Harper types around offering a nebulous future despite their high-soaring philosophical ideas. Feel-good funerals without substance let the mourner down the following day. Dad's funeral was the most morbid affair I've ever attended.

Phyllis's daughter Pat surprised me by attending the funeral. She had so little respect for my father that, although he was the only father she knew, she had vowed not to attend. She always called him BL (Bruce Leigh). She was not without cause. My father was unfaithful to Phyllis and everybody knew it. Like a lot of wives, Phyllis just put up with it. Pat was not so forgiving. If my father had died an agnostic's death, I would not have been disillusioned, but I would have been disappointed. He had put two wives through an earthly purgatory and only took an interest in me at the end of his natural life. Does that matter? Not really. The apostle Paul put it so well, when he wrote, "Jesus Christ came into the world to save sinners, of whom I am chief."
If there's room in heaven for Paul, there's a space for Dad. What a reconciliation party in heaven awaits my arrival.

The fifth memorable event in those days took shape without my knowledge. I learned of it after the fact. I relive it now in memory. In 1964, my friend Jim Madge committed suicide. As my life was growing richer, Jim Madge's life was growing darker. Jimmy Madge lived four doors down the street and was smart – I would even say a genius. He taught me how to play chess, but I could never beat him at his game. We were often in one another's house. His parents were blind, so Jim had to help out a lot around the house with the chores that neither of his parents could perform. He certainly was a conscientious kid who was smart enough to learn how to read Braille. Jimmy would go to bed and smuggle a book under the covers, and when his parents imagined that Jim was sleeping, he was reading their books. Like so many brilliant kids, Jim was lonely, industrious, and always working. His problem was his maturity. When ordinary kids like me couldn't relate to his level of intelligence, we tended to avoid him, so Jim simply made his own way.

Cornel Wilde was a popular movie star in the forties. He starred in a movie with Merle Oberon, depicting the life of Chopin, the famous Polish composer and pianist. It was called a Song To Remember. I was so inspired by that movie that I decided to take piano lessons. That didn't last long. Jim Madge decided the same thing, but first he had to buy a piano. Incredibly, he not only bought and paid for that piano, but he learned to play it as well. But that's not the end of the story; he actually mastered Chopin's "Polinaise in A flat," an achievement reserved for a virtuoso. That's how talented Jim Madge was. Jim read voraciously, including the Bible, but claimed he was not a Christian. Jim eventually married and even had a child to bear his name; but unbeknown to friends, Jim's was a mind in disarray. Jim had dreamed of starting up his own restaurant. He wanted a partner. Out of the blue, he approached Harold Erb to lay out the project.

Jim had the experience; all his jobs had involved working in restaurants. Now he was ready to launch out on his own. Unfortunately for Jim, people skills were lacking, and Jim did not relate well. I suppose he thought that other people should understand him, when in fact they didn't. When the hoped-for partner (in this case, Harold Erb; it could have been anybody else) backed out of any suggestion of a two-owner restaurant, Jim decided in an instant what he would do. He drove to an isolated spot north of town; he closed the windows and sat in his car with the motor running. Jim made sure the carbon monoxide escaping from the tailpipe entered the car and, sadly,

Jim went to sleep forever. Imagine, that brilliant mind snuffed out in a tragic moment when Jim concluded that life was not worth living. Harold Erb said, "Why he chose me as a potential partner, I do not know. How was I to know his state of mind?" Of the guys I used to play with, that brought the number of suicides to three.

Which brings me to my point! I'm telling my readers about the life of a young man who went into the Baptist ministry. But here I am contemplating death. At the time of writing (I am now seventy-seven years old), I know my turn is not very far away. I have a very interesting story to tell and in a moment, I'll get back to the story; nonetheless, in a flashback, I see all the old faces. Some young when they died, others older, still a few like me, vigorous and reasonably healthy. Our number is dwindling. From time to time, I return to Stratford and walk those streets where once I played. As I pass the households I relive Thorton Wilder's celebrated Broadway drama of the thirties, Our Town. I suspect most people do that kind of thing when they're old, if they can. I relive the days when I was young. I name the kids who lived in those familiar houses and wonder why, if I knocked on the door that a stranger would answer instead of a familiar face, still young and ready to go out to play. It all seems like it was only yesterday.

The sixth significant memory is in reference to our Georgetown millionaire, Rex Heslop, who developed Toronto's Rexdale Plaza. When he moved his operation to Georgetown, he got into trouble. Like so many big time operators, when he thought he could make Georgetown into a significant city over the heads of the locals, he made enemies. His big city ways reaped the undying contempt of Mayor E.T. Hyde. I knew both these men and liked them. I had asked Mayor Hyde, if he would do the honours of the sod-breaking for our church, which he accepted. Wishing to do things with flair we broke sod with a bulldozer operated by the mayor. The photo appeared the next day in the Georgetown Herald.

Rex Heslop was a sharp businessman who, at times, could bend the rules to his liking. A stand off between the mayor and the businessman was a pyrrhic victory for E.T. Hyde, and Rex Heslop went to jail – for one month. The sentence was* really just a slap on the wrist. The court case had cost a lot of money. The only winners were the lawyers. I visited Rex in the Milton jail and learned a lot. Rex entertained me with many stories of how he had started from scratch and become wealthy. In regard to the court case, he told me, "The judge sentenced me to thirty days of hard labour. The sentence is a joke. The only hard labour that I have done around here is to sweep the floor.

When my visit came to an end, and I was leaving the jail. Rex Heslop said to me, "You know Bruce, I know every minister in Georgetown, but you are the only one that came to see me here in prison. I want you to know I appreciate it."

My seventh memorable experience started out badly but ended well and concerned our son Mark. Why are boys always getting into scrapes? Our second son, David, nearly bled to death when he was only thirteen months old due to a simple accident consisting of a slashed tongue that would not stop bleeding. I am so thankful for modern medicine. Today we moderns imagine the old timers didn't know how to practice medicine. The year 1959 half a century ago may seem ancient to some, but thanks to a skillful doctor we reaped bountifully through that doctor's medical knowhow. Thankfully, medicine in 1959 was far enough ahead to save David's life.

However traumatic the accident was to David, a more serious accident happened to our son Mark six years later. He was playing with the neighbour boy who thought it would be fun to swing a bullrush at Mark's head. He missed but caught Mark's eye. Mark was eight years old and his bloodshot eye revealed trouble ahead. A stint at Guelph General Hospital availed nothing; except for some peripheral vision, Mark lost the vision in his left eye. Four years later the same horrible accident occurred again. Mark was playing with his cousins. Our nephew Ken had received a pellet gun for Christmas; many kids want dangerous toys. Ken lowered his sights for something, the pellet ricocheted off the target, and it went straight into Mark's eye – the only good eye he had left.

The same horrible nightmare all over again! Mark lay in the back seat with his eye bandaged. The fear of blindness haunted us all. When we got him to Guelph Hospital, we took him to Dr. Cowan who was the specialist under whose able care Mark was treated earlier. Mark had only retained peripheral vision in his left eye which was still much appreciated. Dr. Cowan immediately transferred him to Sick Kids in Toronto. Not meant for our ears, but we found out later, that he had said to an associate, "That kid will be blind for sure; I just couldn't handle it. Someone else can give him the bad news."

The trauma of those days still makes me break out into a cold sweat. The next day when Joan and I came into the hospital to see our son, Mark started to cry. That made three of us crying. The vigil of those days was fraught with worry. The climax came when I phoned Dr. Cowan and asked him point blank, "Will our son be blind?"

"You've asked the hardest question an ophthalmologist could ever face. I'm afraid there is very little hope that your son will see again."

Never will I forget December 31, 1964. I went into the bedroom, collapsed to my knees, and sobbed, "Our son Mark is blind; he will never see again."

The next twenty minutes are a blur. Joan's mother was there. Our daughter Debbie was ten years old, old enough to understand. We were all weeping when God gave us our miracle. Dr. Aska from Sick Kids Hospital phoned us to give us his report. He was an understanding man to say the least.

"Dr. Aska, will our son be blind?" I asked, hoping for anything that would give a glimmer of hope. "I have already heard that he will be blind."

"Well," said Dr. Aska, "I wouldn't just give up like that. Your son's eye is stable, and we have him under twenty-four-hour care. So as long as there is some vision in that eye, we need not despair, at least not yet."

"You mean there is still hope?" I stammered

"Provided there is no more hemorrhaging, your son will see. How much vision he will have is a question that will have to wait. In the meantime, be encouraged."

Now the crying began all over again, only this time, it was tears of joy.

Our church had a New Year's Watchnight service scheduled for 9:30 P.M. I determined I would not let my troubles affect what is usually a joyful time. However, after the clock struck midnight and the New Year wasushered in, I shared the events that had taken place earlier that evening. Then I asked our Sunday School Superintendent, Bill Ganton, if he would close in prayer remembering our son. Bill was a compassionate man, and although I no longer remember his prayer, we all went home a little comforted. The next few days were crucial. Mark's eye recovered slowly, and there was no more hemoraging. Everyone rejoiced and cousin Ken's dad, Ross Amy, bought Mark a new bicycle, to show his gratitude to God that things had turned out well.

Georgetown Hearld, Mark delivers papers

Thirty years later, my son Mark was in the ministry and pastoring Humbervale Park Baptist Church in Toronto. It was there that he heard groundbreaking stories about restored vision coming out of western Canada. A trip to Alberta was arranged where the world famous Gimbel Eye Clinic was pioneering laser surgery for people like our Mark. In Calgary, a remarkable doctor by the name of Howard Gimbel successfully completed an operation on our son. Mark got full vision back again. In a memorable phone conversation he said to his wife, Shelley, "Was it ever great to watch a hockey game on television, and be able to see the puck!"

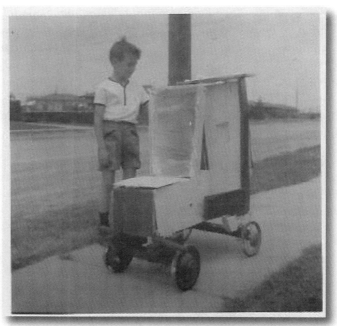

David age 8 was destined to be a builder of something
This photo made it to the Georgetown Herald, 1966

The final memory was the birth of our fourth child Sara. Our daughter Debbie was so excited when she knew the day of her arrival had come that she could hardly concentrate at school. Coming home that day she met our youngest son David who had beat her in the race to the parsonage. After Grandma Amy (she was babysitting while I was at the hospital) revealed the news to David, Debbie arrived breathless. Turning to his sister, he said, "Bad news Debbie."

Turning white, Debbie replied, "Did the baby die?"

"No," said David, "but it's a girl."

David's innocence was the focal point of laughter more than once in our household. One evening after dinner, when Bible reading was over, we asked David to conclude with prayer.

"Any prayer requests?" he said; to which his mother replied,

"You could pray for Daddy; he has to go to a deacon's meeting."

We proceeded to bow our heads while David prayed, "Dear Lord, please bless Daddy while he goes to the deacon's meeting and Lord, if it's your will, may one of the deacons be saved." Thus ended family devotions in gales of laughter.

Sara Joan Woods, our fourth child at 10 months

But now I'm getting so far ahead of my story, I really must return to where I left off. Remember? It is September 1950, and probably the most decisive events of my life are about to unfold.

Chapter 19
Kathy

When I lived in Stratford, I freely admit I liked girls. My only problem was falling in love; that was the hard part. Once I lost the stability that a solid home provides and lived in a boarding house, my love problem reversed itself. Now I fall in love at the slightest provocation with all kinds of girls. First, I think I love Margaret Dennett. Then, the next thing I know, it is Betty Logsdon. For at least two weeks, I thought it was Viola MacCorkadale. Jeanette Hardison came next at four weeks.

"Yep!" said Gerry Rowe. "You are the type that has to have a girl."

He should talk. He was madly in love with Ruth Horner and guess what, he married that girl. Meantime, I am happy at my sales job, and making good money with no one to spend it on.

I am anxiously awaiting my marks from Grade thirteen. In order to make it to university, I have to have my $200.00 bursary or I am in trouble. I must have an average of 66%. I am opening my high school report card full of anticipation. I cast my eyes to the all-important bottom line. Although I have passed my exams, my average is 64%. Those crucial days when I was so sick I could hardly lift my head, have exacted a price. University is beyond my financial reach. My mind is made up for the ministry, but I wanted to take the high road. University first, and then a top level seminary, with the goal of getting my doctorate. Interestingly enough, I traversed that road but God delayed the whole thing by one year. I never reached the doctoral level because I didn't have the smarts. Nonetheless, God had some special plans for me, because He knew I needed a wife. I found her in Bible School but first I got blindsided with Kathy. Meanwhile, Art Sadler says to me, "Don't be disappointed that you won't be going to university; set your sights a little lower and go to Bible school. They will accept you. If God's call is upon you, a ministry of His choosing will open up."

I accept Art's advice as the only alternative. I enroll at London Bible Institute. Little do I know that this decision is a watershed that will change the whole course of my life for the better. Next, I decide that as soon as I have enough money saved, I will buy a car.

I am vulnerable when the next shift of girls arrives at Sadlers' for Teacher's College. Kathy Harkness (not her real name) is pretty. I like her and the feeling is mutual. In no time, we are going for walks holding hands. On the other hand, at London Bible College, I notice that Joan Amy is a very attractive brunette, but Kathy is right there at Sadlers'. We eat our meals together and since neither of us have a heavy homework load, there is plenty of time for courting. Right from the start we are seeing too much of each other.

Our relationship goes smoothly except for the subject of church. For Kathy, church is something she can easily do without. For me, church is my life. Problems soon surface when I explain to her that she needs to be "born again." Since we are both in love, we decide to avoid the subject of religion altogether. It is a hopeless arrangement. How does a man whose life's calling is the ministry marry a girl who has never experienced a personal faith in Christ? Kathy had high moral standards but showed little interest in church. Emotionally involved, I determine I will have my calling and have my girl. Deep down inside of me I know it is an impossible arrangement, but how do you cool it when the only separation occurs on weekends. That happens when Kathy returns home to Watford. From Monday to Friday, there we are at the same table eating our meals together and living in the same space. It is almost like being married without the privileges thereof.

Teasing me a little, Kathy tells me about somebody at teacher's college that is showing interest in her. Next, the subject of other guys at teacher's college comes up. I reciprocate.

"I know; you see, there's this girl whose name is Joan Amy at Bible college." I describe Joan as a "Teutonic beauty."

"What do you mean by that?" says Kathy.

"A German aristocrat!" I reply.

"Humph!"

"You know what I mean; she probably is descended from some handsome Teutonic knight who married a princess."

"Well, then, maybe you should be dating her."

"Can't!"

"Why not?"

"Cause I'm in love with you."

Kathy smiles the smile of the victor, and we change the subject. She's on her first teaching assignment and will be staying in London for the weekend.

"Perfect!" I exclaim, "Now we can study the Bible together."

"Doesn't sound like a date to me," says Kathy.

"You'll like it; I've been thinking about it ever since we met. The Bible is the most interesting book in the whole world. Trust me, I know what I'm saying."

Kathy shrugs her shoulders and says, "Okay, I guess it won't hurt me to give it a try."

I can hardly wait for Sunday afternoon. I invite Kathy to church but she says, "Our Bible study will be church enough for me." I gladly compromise. I've had the most wonderful time with the New Testament book of Galatians. I eagerly sit down with Kathy to show her treasures she has never known. We bog down quickly. I have to explain every verse and Kathy is bored. After thirty minutes, she proposes an alternative: "It's such a nice day, let's go out for a walk." It is useless to protest. I give up the whole idea of converting Kathy, substituting a walk to the park for Kathy's salvation.

Monday morning, I'm sitting in class and glancing to my left where Joan Amy is busily writing notes from our lectures in Genesis. Terry Hulbert is a good teacher, and we are eager learners. Why couldn't Kathy be excited about learning the Bible like Joan Amy? I notice her flashing brown eyes and her happy smile. She is clearly a beautiful girl.

Ever since Barry Moore has given up leading the singing in our Monday Young People's meeting, I have been given the job. In those days, song leading is more about personality than music. (I was also convinced that this was so. In later years, I will have an altogether different point of view.) Meantime, I have found my niche. I am able to get the kids to sing up a storm. Rev. John Dunkin has taken note and invited me to lead the singing at our Sunday evening service, because our usual standby, Art McKenzie, is not available. My opportunity comes around in two weeks. I have the perfect plan. Kathy will be back at Sadlers' just in time to go to the Sunday evening service at (7:00 P.M.) to see me lead the singing. Pastor Dunkin will preach an evangelistic sermon, and Kathy will be saved. I tell Kathy about my big opportunity and ask her to my debut as a song leader in my church. She agrees to come, since it would be nice to see her boyfriend in action. I think, "It couldn't be any better than this." The fateful day arrives, and I am in the back room with Pastor Dunkin. We have prayer together, and walk into the auditorium where 200 people are waiting for the service to begin.

Kathy is seated near the front and is the only girl in the church wearing deep red lipstick. She stands out in marked contrast to the other girls in the church. Pastor Dunkin couldn't possibly miss her. I have not told him a thing about Kathy. He can figure that out for himself when he sees me sit beside her after the song service. Next comes the sermon. I am not disappointed. John Dunkin knows how to press home the point when he sees a prospect for salvation. The service comes to a conclusion, and as is the custom, pastor Dunkin gives an altar call for anyone in the service to come forward and be saved. Kathy is unmoved, and I am disappointed. As we leave the church, I introduce Kathy to Pastor Dunkin who politely shakes her hand. The next day is Monday, and once again I am to lead the singing for our Young People's meeting. John Dunkin is waiting for me, and asks me to come into his office after the meeting. I am apprehensive: I know what's coming.

"Who was that girl you brought to church last night?"
"Her name is Kathy. She is a boarder at the Sadlers'."
"Is she a Christian?" asks the pastor.
"Not exactly, but she's a very nice girl."
"I'm sure she is a very nice girl, Bruce, but not the one for you."
I know exactly where John Dunkin is coming from. I have heard enough sermons on the unequal yoke to know he would not approve of my dating anyone unless they were "our kind."

Next, John Dunkin gives me all the reasons why an immature Christian such as me should listen to my elders. I must give up this worldly girl and follow godly advice. He even suggests a few others but especially recommends a classmate of mine, Audrey Bell. I politely thank Rev. Dunkin for his concern. He doesn't interfere with my song leading in Young People's but I get no more invitations to lead singing on Sundays.

I have a question to ask Professor Hulbert about his lecture on Genesis. So does Joan Amy. Ladies first. Joan asks her question and gestures with her hands. I am captivated by her hands. I never noticed feminine hands before. I certainly never thought about Kathy's hands. Joan's hands are graceful and fascinating to watch. I am so captivated by her hands that Joan Amy notices and is embarrassed. When Dr. Hulbert turns to me, I have to think hard, "Now what was that question?" I am quickly satisfied with his answer, and on the way home to Sadler's, I visualize Joan Amy's hands. I watch the replay in my mind over and over again.

I have saved enough money to buy a car. I want a car so that Kathy and I can go for drives and get away from the boarding house. Dudley Collins tells me he has a 1931 Model A Ford in good shape for $125.00. The Lord's guidance for sure. I arrange with Gordon Duke to insure the car. It is an added expense I forgot to consider. Gordon gives me a little lecture on how he wouldn't insure just any teenager who comes into his office. Teenagers have too many accidents, and it is unprofitable to insure a teenager's car. He makes an exception for me, because he figures I am a conscientious Christian he knows personally, and therefore, he will take the risk. I assure him I will be a client that will do him proud. Meanwhile, I pay $25.00 down for the car with twelve payments of $10.00 per month. In one year, the car will be paid for. I am thrilled to have my first automobile. Henry Ford's creation is black. They all were. The styles changed so little in 1931 that I can look down on all those earlier models with disdain. There are plenty of older models around all painted black. The reliable Model A is still a hot product in 1950. I drop by the Gartleys to show them my prize. I really didn't impress them much. It didn't matter to me. What I really wanted was for Betty Logsdon to find out, and I knew the Gartleys would be sure to tell. Next, I pull out onto Dundas Street and promptly get into an accident.

In 1950, a driver's license was easy to get. As an inexperienced teen-age driver, what I don't know is that I am a menace on the road. I have discovered my shortcomings with a vengeance. Even though I am a conscientious Christian, my guardian angel is not that interested in giving me a helping hand. I am charged with "failure to stop at an intersection." I am grateful to have insurance but ashamed to face Gordon Duke. The car is still drivable, so I take it back to Dudley Collins and tell him the bad news. Dudley is upbeat and is sure it won't cost that much to fix. I am encouraged. The next day Dudley calls back and says the car is in fine shape, but unbeknown to him when he sold it to me, the car is burning oil and needs a ring job. One hundred and ten dollars later I have a car that has cost me double what I expected to pay. Not only am I broke, I've mortgaged my future. I have to take Kathy for one ride at least, so after it is fixed, we go for a spin down Wharncliffe Road for twenty minutes. That car ride has cost me four weeks wages. I'm beginning to wish I'd never bought this car. The dreaded phone call from Gordon Duke comes without delay. "What did I tell you about how carefully drivers must behave?"

I am ashamed and confess my guilt. I have a lot to learn in life, and my lessons seem to come the hard way. I decide I will sell the car. The price will be one hundred dollars and the new owner will take over the payments. I advertise my Ford in the London Free Press. I have no phone calls. Just as I am about to despair, I get a call from someone who wants to take a look at the car. It is a father and his teenage son. Apparently, there are other teenagers around as foolish as I am. They see the car and offer me $75.00, take over the payments. That would mean in one month of car ownership, I am out of pocket $125.00. At this time the salesman within me comes to life, and I extol the virtues of owning this valuable car. I tell them what I have lost and how they are passing up a bargain. We dicker, but I am resolute. I don't back down. They leave and I am left wishing I had accepted their offer. At this point my indifferent guardian angel decides to give me a break and five minutes later, they are back. They have decided to accept my terms. We close the deal, and I am relieved to be rid of a burden that is making my life miserable. I celebrate the next day by going downtown and for $100.00, I buy a brand new blue gabardine three-piece suit.

The shine on my affections for Kathy is beginning to falter through no fault of hers. I am troubled by our differences of opinion over Christianity. On the surface, now that I am rid of the burden of owning a car, I'm supposed to feel better. In reality, I am unhappy a lot of the time, and I don't know why. Looking back I know why: Kathy was not interested in my other world, the one I am more interested in than the present world I inhabit.

Chapter 20

Stanley Avenue Baptist Church, Hamilton, Ontario

The years we spent in Vancouver were wonderful. God called us and we eventually came to appreciate that beautiful city enough to stay. At the same time we couldn't help being homesick for the east. Sara was the exception. She knew nothing else but our home on 8490 Elliot Street. She would make us chuckle as we returned to our Vancouver house after a summer vacation in the east. The older kids, already missing their cousins, would complain, while Sara was esctatic with joy at the familiar landmarks that for her meant "home at last." Therefore, we were not a little pleased, when we received a call to return to our eastern roots.

We arrived at Stanley Avenue Baptist Church Hamilton in 1972

David, our third child, could have made an easy transplant to the west, because there were many teens his age in our church family. He ultimately went into a career in aviation, then midstream converted to a business career in house building in Grand Rapids, Michigan. Debbie, our second child likewise had friends both east and west. She could have adjusted nicely anywhere. She ultimately became a nurse and pastor's wife. Mark, our eldest, who followed my calling and became a pastor, like us, had the best memories of Ontario, and like us, was pleased to return to Ontario where cousins and old pals made our return appealing to him.

Excitement! Yes, when we moved East, we had an accident with our U-Haul in Salmon Arm B.C. Pastor Elmer Fehr [left] to the rescue. He mobilized his men and within 24 hours we were loaded into another U-Haul and were on our way. Miraculously, no injuries [oh-Joan scratched her thumb]. When the insurance claims were settled, we not only had all our belongings, we made a profit of $700.

We moved to Ancaster in 1972, a fifteen-minute drive away from Stanley Avenue Baptist Church, Hamilton. This church was the location of a Baptist schism that happened in 1926. The issue was modernism. At stake were the essential doctrines of Christianity, such as the deity of Christ, his resurrection, and the reliability of the Bible. However, in 1926, the person and work of Christ was the key issue.

It was an odd disagreement because the issues raised were not in question by either side. At issue was McMaster Divinity College and its independence from the Baptist denomination. The college board of directors had slipped into the hands of intellectuals who believed that the new modernity trumped the Apostles' Creed and that Christianity needed a facelift. To facilitate this new theological shift, a professor of theology was hired to reform the Baptist faith. Professor Marshall was not without his converts in Divinity College. The fight was on. Eighty years later, two Baptist denominations scarcely distinguishable one from the other still share the Dominion of Canada between them. So much for church fights. However, in 1926, Baptist evangelicals felt the very foundations of their faith were at stake. For them it was a crucial battle.

Eventually, McMaster Divinity College rejected the liberal views that divided the denomination and is today a distinguished evangelical seminary. But in 1926, it looked as though it were going the other way: hence the great Baptist divide. The old liberalism that aspired to make Christ a mere human and the resurrection a myth has long since died a natural death. At least this is so in Baptist circles. Liberal Christianity does not believe in the necessity of evangelizing anybody, including their own second generation.

The mainline denominations which embraced the new liberalism and social gospel exclusive of evangelism paid a high price for the imagined "better way." Many of their members surreptitiously just slipped away. Tiring of social gospel sermons which sounded more like the editorial page of the Globe and Mail, they just moved over to Baptist churches that preached the Bible. The biggest winners, however, were the Pentecostals who today make up the larger churches of just about any Canadian city.

The protesting ministers assembled for a showdown. In 1926, approximately thirty Baptist churches abandoned the battleground, and assembled in Stanley Avenue Baptist Church to declare themselves independent. The core of the Canadian cities was relegated to the older and established Baptist denomination. The splinter churches took to the suburbs, and grew to 450 churches. As people moved from the city core to the suburbs the emerging Baptist Churches that had started out so small, outgrew the older Baptist denomination. (They called themselves Fellowship Baptists; the older denomination called themselves Convention Baptists). Stanley Avenue Baptist was a church in the core of the city, but despite its downtown location, it continued to be a strong growing church. I would spend the next sixteen years of my life as the pastor of this congregation.

There is nothing that pleases a pastor's heart more than to be a guiding hand to someone becoming a Christian. I now relate the conversion of two very special men. I'll call one Mr. Brains and the other Mr. Brawn. The first was Mr. Brains, Michael Haykin, a University of Toronto Marxist who was in his last year of philosophy. Mr. Brawn was Alexander Clark, a rebel who loved his Harley-Davidson.

Michael Haykin met Alison Lowe working in a pizza parlour. Alison was also a bright young woman who made a career for herself in the health sciences. Discussions led to friendship, and friendship led to Alison's inviting Michael to church, at least that's what I thought. Years later, I discovered it was Michael who out of curiosity wanted to explore our kind of Christianity. Perhaps it was a little of both. Michael's father had distinguished himself at McMaster University by writing textbooks on electrical engineering, thereby making himself a world-class reputation. (He was originally from Iraq. Would that have put him under suspicion in these paranoid days?)

Michael's mother, a dear saint of God, actually found her faith through her son, but that good news was still a year in coming. Nominally Roman Catholic, she had a form of religion but not the essence. Michael was curious and a seeker after truth. He also had a fear of dying. He thought he had found utopia in Karl Marx and for a time was a Communist sympathizer. An inveterate reader, he soon found himself devouring philosophy with a special interest in Martin Heidegger, who wrote, "A man cannot arrive at the truth, until he faces up to the contemplation of his own inevitable death."

Michael was facing the eternal questions. Through a combination of Alison's testimony, attending our church, and a careful reading of the Bible, Michael was engaging the ageless dilemma of dying and its solution. He was too bright not to see the implications of Scripture and, like C.S. Lewis, recognized that Jesus Christ was either a lunatic, a liar, or the Son of God.

One Sunday evening, Ellwyn Davies, a guest preacher from the UK, gave an alter call for absolute devotion to Jesus Christ. About thirty-five people responded, including Michael. Still the issue in Michael's mind was unresolved. Restless and holding out, Michael returned to U of T uncertain and still afraid. Midweek in February 1974, the holdout gave in. One sleepless night, after retiring to bed, Michael slipped to his knees, and prayed again. The overwhelming presence of God sealed his assurance. He returned to Hamilton that weekend rejoicing and shared his decision to follow Christ. Shortly after, I had the privilege of baptizing him and extending to him the right hand of fellowship in our church. Four weeks after his conversion, he wrote me from university.

Dear Pastor Woods,

Since I didn't get a chance to speak to you last Sunday and seeing how my time is taken up by school during the week etc., and that I had a couple of things on my mind that I wanted to talk to you about, I decided to write to you.

Of late, I have felt the desire to do some concrete work for the Lord. Not that thinking about the Lord and His Word is not concrete, for it surely is; or that reading the Bible is not concrete, for that surely is too, as it is rapidly advancing my spiritual growth, awareness and freedom. But, I feel that the Lord wants me to do something more. And though I know that one cannot come by the Kingdom of Heaven by good works alone, but by faith, it is because of this faith, I desire to do good works. As John said, "My little children, let us not love in word, neither in tongue, but in deed and in action." And on top of this dissatisfaction that I am not doing enough for the Lord, I find a dissatisfaction with some of my courses. The earthly "wisdom" of some of my professors seems so useless and meaningless, as Paul wrote to the Corinthians, "where is the wise? where is the scribe? Where is the disputer of this world? Hath not God made foolish the wisdom of this world? For after that, in the wisdom of God, the world by wisdom knew not God, it pleased God by the foolishness of preaching to save them that believe."

Wisdom without its necessary and important relation to God is foolishness. The present day scientist who tries to explain nature and man without God finds himself hard put to do so. The wisdom of this earth is untruth. The truth is surely the wisdom of God, that God gives Christians through their belief in Jesus Christ as their Saviour.

The true philosophy is at one with the true religion, that is, the Christian faith. For Paul is not denouncing wisdom as foolishness, but only that "wisdom" of the world as foolishness. (see Romans 2:13,14)

Dissatisfaction with some of my courses with the dissatisfaction that I should do more for the Lord, have made me write this (though I feel it is the Lord that commands me to write).

I felt I would like to teach a Sunday School class, that is, if you need someone; I have no idea of how good I would be or even if I am fitted for such a task, but I feel the Lord has called me to do something like this. The only drawback is that I feel I am very serious; I find it very hard to be light hearted. My mother says I take life too seriously; she's right. But I feel the Lord wants me to teach, and think, and spread the Word. I feel that by doing such I can lead a fuller Christian life. I know nothing about how you conduct Sunday School, or whether you even need someone, But I feel much better for having written and having taken this initial step.

Please God, I shall see you Sunday.

Yours in the Lord,
Michael A. Haykin

Do you see why I love the ministry?

Michael Haykin felt the call of God to enter the ministry. His would not be any ordinary ministry. With Michael's brains, his was the calling of a scholar-teacher, and I was given the opportunity to point him to seminary. I recommended Wycliffe College, a participating school in the Union of Theological Seminaries within the framework of the University of Toronto. He has thanked me many times for steering him into this prestigious Anglican seminary. I would later do the same for other bright minds who trusted me for direction in such a crucial decision.

Michael's passion for church history led him into a scholastic world where he has now written over twenty books and countless articles which have appeared in theological journals throughout the Christian world. At first he taught history at Toronto's Central Baptist Seminary. Gordon Brown, the founder of that college and recently retired, was astounded. Michael had trained in an Anglican college. Unheard of! Denominational barriers are not what they used to be. Brown caved in and Michael was accepted as a bonafide Baptist lecturer at Central Baptist Seminary. Later, he became principal of Toronto Baptist Seminary. Today, he is The Distinguished Professor of Church History at the world class Louisville Baptist Seminary. At fifty-four years of age, he is only beginning to make his contribution to academia. While he was still young in the faith, he wrote me a note observing how my sermon from Psalm 33:6 paralleled the early church father Athanasius (whom Michael had been reading). His comment read, "God's truth remains the same forever. "Wow, my fledgling was reading the church fathers, something I had never done.

Now having introduced you to Mr. Brains, I introduce you to Mr. Brawn. The family of God never ceases to amaze me: Michael, the scholar, and Ace (Alexander) Clark, former rogue and ex-biker, are friends.

In 1959 at age sixteen, Ace Clark, lying about his age, joined the army. He was a rebel without a cause. When he finally quit Westdale high school after completing grade ten, he did it in style. His style. Placing his Harley at the entrance of the School and with a little help from friends, he roared up the steps into the hallway of his alma mater and rode up and down in front of the offices of his astonished teachers and back out again onto the street. Ace was such a rebel in the army, he got busted and graduated to hospital, with a beating he never forgot that included some painful broken ribs. Seems like some senior cadets decided to teach the rebel a lesson. Out of the army as quickly as he got in, Ace translated his troubled past into anger, and joined the Wild Ones motorcycle club, rising quickly to the office of secretary. With his sights set on nothing less than being president of the club, Ace gained a reputation of tough guy, and his moll was Joy Pimental.

Who would have thought Joy Pimental was a preacher's kid? Her mother, Evelyn, was a member of our church and a saint, if I ever met one. She often prayed for her wayward daughter who, thanks to the associations with the Wild Ones, was raped and gave the citizens of Hamilton some pretty racy reading as The Hamilton Spectator covered the court case. Needless to say Evelyn, agonized over her daughter, covering her with her prayers. A few years later, wiser and discontent, Joy experienced the mighty miracle of salvation. The incredible, Joy (now married to Ace) became a Christian and faithfully attended Stanley Avenue Baptist church.

One day, quite by chance, I finally got to meet the notorious Ace who had dropped by the Pimental house just as I was paying Evelyn a visit. He was cordial enough for me to propose a coffee some evening at his apartment. Ace grudgingly volunteered an invitation which he was sure I would forget. However, I meant business and one evening phoned Ace and caught him at home. After I hung up the phone, Ace turned to Joy and said, "If that preacher starts talking to me about God, I'll throw him out."

I have learned that if I'm going to talk to someone about becoming a Christian, the subject must be broached in the first five minutes or somehow it just doesn't come up for discussion. Following this self imposed rule, I did exactly that and discovered that the grizzly bear was a teddy bear at heart. A half hour after my arrival, Ace was on his knees, fighting back the revealing tears, and praying the sinner's prayer of repentance. His was an overnight transformation.

It took Ace another eighteen months to give up his membership in the Wild Ones motorcycle club, but not before his astonished friends had discovered he was a changed man. His fight to quit smoking took three years, but there was no mistaking the transformation: Ace was now a Christian. In contrast to his changed life, twenty-seven of his fellow club members are now dead, some of them last-minute Christians, as Ace was able to share his faith with them.

At the conclusion of our 1977 Christmas Eve family service, with no advance warning, I asked Ace to close in prayer. I cannot remember the prayer exactly, but my memory is nonetheless pretty accurate. The prayer went like this:
"Thank you, Father, for taking the most precious gift you had, and wrapping it up in love, and placing it under my Christmas tree. I

opened that present and found it to be none other than Jesus Christ, my Saviour. Help me Lord – help all of us to serve You with our best, for as long as we live."

What a jolt! Is this Ace Clark, the high school dropout, or is this Hamilton's poet laureate? Some of us had to clear our throats. Others just wiped the tears away. Ace had a way with words. Who would have thought that this truck driver was a preacher in the making. It started slowly, with Ace a favourite for a men's breakfast on a Saturday morning. Following the many invitations that came his way and going from church to church, he told the story of his conversion over and over again. Young people heard him and became followers of Christ. Christian businessmen clamoured to have him address their luncheons. All of this was part of his growing maturity. God, in his grace, took mutiny and changed it to ministry. Ace Clark is now the pastor of the Joshua Centre, a Hamilton downtown church which he and his wife Joy started.

I had heard that the Christian Science Church at 616 Main Street East was for sale and shared that information with Ace. Frank Gallant, a Roman Catholic businessman, arranged the mortgage (the banks wouldn't). Ace had his building and the congregation grew. Joshua 6:16 is an interesting verse. Somebody decided to look at Joshua 6:16 (note the address, 616 Main Street). Insert a colon and you have 6:16, a standard way of looking up a Bible verse. Apply this to the book of Joshua and you get chapter 6, verse 16. So what does Joshua 6:16 say? Now hear this:

"Shout, for the Lord has given you the city."

The Joshua Centre is a beehive of activity. Ace Clark, with an eye to opportunity, picked up the business block across the street – a tax write-off for the seller, and for Ace an opportunity to have a location for his Food Bank. Ace calls it the dream centre, where they also operate a used clothing store full of things which are given away to the needy. His feeding program aids 400 kids in the local public schools because the Joshua Centre is located in a tough part of town. Many of these families subsist below the poverty line. In his spare time (I speak in jest), he is called upon as a motivational speaker for High School

Assemblies. In this ministry alone, he has addressed over 250,000 students who always give him a standing ovation at the end of every address. Ace has now turned sixty-five and shows no sign of slowing down. He needs to stay vital for awhile. He wants to start a ministry for women, who are trying to escape drug addiction.

Chris Tolos and Bill Snip [Billy Red Lions] This wrestling match was a fundraiser for charity. Bill was a Hamilton hometown favourite. You can imagine the stir he caused when he started to attend our church. Photo, courtesy of the Hamilton Spectator.

In 1986 Ace published a comic book of his testimony. This Particular frame is of great interest to me

With an eye to the young who don't read books, Ace developed a comic book that tells his life story. One hundred and twenty-five thousand of these have been distributed throughout Canada and in twenty-eight countries around the world. So there you have it. Starting back where I began this lengthy story, on a Sunday morning I would preach my sermons with a budding historian, a grade ten dropout, and just to make life an extra challenge, Dr. Ron Childs, vice president of McMaster University. There were others: By way of contrast, consider Dac-Sinh Chu and his wife Sing-ha. They were our Chinese boat people from Viet Nam. We adopted them and their five children, clothed them, and gave them a house to live in. This was our contribution to the refugee problem created by the Viet Nam war, and their story is a book all by itself. Mel Cuthbert, a missionary of distinction who served in Brazil and Portugal and wherever Portuguese is spoken. His oldest son, Terry, became president of our denomination. Dr. David Parris who took a teaching position in Arizona, not to speak of plumbers and Stelco workers. We never had more than an active 250 members, but it was a well-balanced congregation including young and old, with people from every kind of background. It was a wonderful sixteen years that introduced me to every possible strata of life.

Chapter 21
Globetrotters

Why do churches underpay their pastors? No wonder most pastors' wives work. Any church that called me got two pastors for the price of one. (Mind you, it gave my wife time not only to minister to others, but also to minister to me. Not only did we discuss spiritual issues, but Joan also became a gourmet cook. Rarely do we eat a restaurant meal the like of what she prepares at home). I always had the same problem everywhere I went. There never seemed to be enough money to pay the bills. In Georgetown, I supplemented my income by working an extra day at Crippled Civilians. Vancouver provided no opportunities like that, but they paid better. Once again in Hamilton, I was having the same problem. My solution was to take tours. I didn't work for a tour company; they didn't pay anything, although tour guides got their expenses. I needed to set up my own arrangements, so that not only did Joan and I get our way paid, but after the expenses were covered, I would also make a profit.

With my venture explained to Joan, reluctantly she agreed. Ever the optimist, I arranged for a tour with two buses and advertised in our Baptist magazine at a bargain basement price of $350.00. My first venture was in 1981. I would take ninety people to New England. My grandiose plan would have been quite profitable but backbreaking to say the least. I had no idea of what I was attempting. Others did, and as one lady put it, "I might have considered a one bus tour, but two buses? Ninety people? Woods must be out of his mind."

In order to break even, I needed twenty-five persons to sign up by August. I had thirteen. Joan was sure I had made a terrible mistake that was going to cost us a lot of money. Faced with cancellation, out of desperation I came up with a plan to save the September trip. I had discovered that I could rent a fifteen-passenger van from Budget Rent-A-Car. I would call each of the thirteen, explain my dilemma, and offer the trip with myself as driver. One seat left for Joan. If they agreed, we could save the venture. Not one of them turned me down.

On Tuesday, September 22, we started out in high spirits for New England. Albany was our first stop. The weather was fair and the trip proved to be an adventure for all. We explored Stockbridge, Salem, and Boston with a stint in Vermont. The grateful passengers presented us with a thank you gift of money. In all, we had a wonderful holiday. I made $350.00 with a free vacation; all our meals paid for and an idea for future trips.

Over the next twenty-five years, I took fourteen trips to the USA, for the most part with a passenger list of anywhere from six to ten persons. We centered on New England, Pennsylvania, Washington (always to Gettysburg first), Virginia, and New York. We did three trips to California and included Las Vegas, the Grand Canyon, and clourful Sedona with its unusual red rock formations. Overseas we did eight trips to, England, Scotland, or Ireland. We did three to the continent seeing France, Holland, Germany, Switzerland, Austria, Italy, and Hungary.

In Canada, we did three trips to Vancouver and Vancouver Island. A very special trip took us to Nova Scotia, Prince Edward Island, and Newfoundland. We celebrated with Newfoundland their 500th anniversary, complete with the arrival of John Cabot and the replica ship, the Matthew.

Were there some high spots in all of this? I suppose so, but when all is said and done, I still love London, England. Paris is more spectacular, but knowing British history and walking on the streets that were trod by my spiritual forebears, like Cromwell, Dickens, and Wilberforce do something for me that I can't describe. All-Souls Church also helps. One has to go through Picadilly Circus (an elegant roundabout) to get there.

I agree with Alexander Pope: "He who is tired of London is tired of life."

At Windsor Castle

On the M5 heading from London to York we spotted this poster

I sometimes try to figure out what all those trips would be worth, if we calculated their value in today's currency. I'm sure it would be close to $200,000. Mind you, I worked for it, and those who went with me (always at below-market prices) said so as well. Furthermore, we did all those trips in the strength of our years before the slow-me-downs of older years curtail activities. Thank you, Lord; You sure have given me a colourful and wonderful life.

Chapter 22
Heart Attack

I never felt so exhausted in all my life. I was okay when we went into the restaurant, but suddenly, half way through my steak, I could have laid down on the floor and gone to sleep. We were in the Waterloo Charcoal Steak House and had paid good money for a sumpuous meal – a rare treat for a minister who doesn't splurge on restaurants. Glad to be in the car and going home, Joan said, "If you're that tired, maybe I should drive the car home."

"No. It will pass. I'll drive the car."

"Whatever you say," Joan sighs.

The truth is I should have accepted her offer. I was too tired to drive, but I persevered in manly denial. It happened again at the swimming pool. (I like to exercise). It was only 9:00 AM. I had just plunged into the water, and had begun to swim my laps. Exhaustion! I made my way to the shallow end, and pulled myself out of the water. My wrists were tingling. It felt like air bubbles were coursing through my veins. I staggered to the showers, shampooed my hair, and made my way to the car. By the time I was home, I felt well enough to go to the church office.

Evening and bedtime. It's three o'clock in the morning. I'm awake with nausea like I've never felt before. I'm not sure if I'm going to vomit or suffer diarrhea. I opt for the latter and stagger my way to the toilet. I can scarcely keep my balance. I think, "If this is cancer, what a horrible way to die." Back in bed I'm perspiring, while the room is going around. Vertigo for sure. By this time, Joan is awake and saying, "What is wrong with you?"

"Don't touch me," I gasp. (Joan had reached out her hand to mine.) I have never been so ill before.

"I'm so sick, I can't even move."

"You can't be that sick, you'll get over it." Joan is alarmed but also in denial.

"It will probably pass. Maybe I've got the flu."

I knew this was not the flu, but I had no idea what was wrong with me. A gnawing pain was growing under my left arm pit. It began to intensify. For half an hour I lay in bed, but the pain in my arm just wouldn't go away.

"What's wrong with you?" Joan asked with concern.

"I've got a pain under my armpit, and it won't go away."

"That's the sign of a heart attack!" gasped Joan.

"I don't have any chest pain," I defended.

"You don't have to. This is serious. You're going to the hospital."

"It's 4:30 in the morning. We can't go to the hospital at this hour."

"Oh, yes, we can. You're getting dressed and I'm driving you to the hospital." Joan is wide awake now, and so am I. We are getting dressed and the atmosphere is tense.

Twenty minutes later we are approaching the Emergency entrance of the McMaster University Hospital, and I am unaware of how ashen I look.

"Joan, I can't go to the hospital today, I've got the Ticats football chapel service to take at 3 PM. We have to go home I'll get over this Joan. Let's go home."

"Don't be foolish; somebody else will have to do the chapels. Now that we're here, you are going through with this."

"I'm not that sick," I declare.

"We're here and we're going in" says Joan, "Keep walking."

The automatic doors open before us and I stagger in. For someone who isn't sick enough for the hospital, I'm a poor actor. The nurse on duty greets us and turns to an orderly,

"Get a stretcher – we've got a patient that needs care right away."

"Don't I have to register somewhere?" I meekly ask.

"Your wife will do all that." Meanwhile – I'm already on the stretcher) – "You need to see a doctor right away."

Unbeknown to me; that nurse on duty was thinking, "I've seen a hundred of them, this man has just had a heart attack."

Later we discovered that we did everything wrong. Joan should have called an ambulance. I never should have taken the time to get dressed. Joan should not have driven me sitting upright in the front seat to the hospital. First-timers don't know these things. We were lucky; or was someone up above watching over us?

"The first twenty-four hours are crucial," said the doctor as he was putting me on intravenous with blood thinners.

"Soon you will feel nauseated; it's all part of the process."

I was beginning to understand the implications. For the first time it occurred to me that all this was happening to prevent me from dying. I breathed a short prayer. Then Joan came in, and after she had prayed and kissed me goodbye, I was alone with my thoughts. Tipped off by my wife, two hours later Rev. Walter Moore arrived. He was a returned missionary who had spent half a lifetime in Indonesia, and was now a member of Stanley Avenue Baptist Church and my deacon. He visited briefly, prayed, and left. From this point on things are a blur. I only remember that after being so sick for twelve hours and exhausted, I wanted to sleep.

As I slowly doze off, I suddenly awake. "I'm going to sleep; what if I don't wake up?" For the first time I am afraid. Many times, as a minister of the gospel, I had stood by others to pray a word of comfort. I remembered Walter Abraham. He had had a heart attack. I prayed for him. The roles are now reversed. Now others are praying for me as the word spreads. The all effective grapevine is at work in our our congregation. Elsworth Robinson, another deacon, comes by. Meantime, Joan is making some hasty arrangements. Sara, our youngest (seventeen) was on a missions trip to Belgium. Joan wisely decided not to call her at this time. She was homesick and was having adjustment problems with Belgium. After phoning our other three children, Joan arranges for our son-in-law Henry Dekorte to take my football chapels. After he did the Hamilton Ticats, he finished off with the Winnipeg Blue Bombers. Their response is gratifying. I have a poster of the 1983 team complete with autographs that now hangs in my study. A real collector's item. Next, she postpones an interview with a young couple who are planning their wedding. This preacher is out of action for the time being. With only five hours sleep, Joan is exhausted. Nonetheless, she returns to pay me a visit. As she makes her way home that fateful afternoon, she prays as she drives home, "Oh Lord, if you will spare Bruce this time and bring him back to me, I promise you, I'll never argue with him again." A desperate vow that after my recovery she finds is impossible to keep.

As evening darkens, my next challenge is to go to sleep. Just as I am dozing off, I awaken with a start. Suppose – I don't wake up tomorrow. "Am I ready to meet my Maker?" It's now time to practice what I have preached for thirty-two years. I rehearse a number of

Scripture verses. "The Lord is my Shepherd," etc. Nothing seems to work. All I can see is the blackness of the empty abyss. It was then I began to sing to myself a wonderful old hymn:

"The Church's one foundation is Jesus Christ, her Lord.
She is his new creation, by water and the word;
From heav'n He came and sought her to be his holy bride;
With his own blood he bought her, and for her life He died."

I could visualize that wonderful foundation like a massive Gibralter rising from the abyss. I saw myself stepping onto the plateau of that solid rock. I felt secure. The sense of relief assured me. I sang on to the final verse:
"Yet she on earth hath union with God, the three in one,
And mystic sweet communion with those whose rest is won:
O happy ones and holy! Lord, give us grace that we,
Like them, the meek and lowly, on high may dwell with thee."

I was at peace. I fell asleep. When I awoke, it was morning and it was Sunday. I was allowed to get out of bed by myself to use the washroom. I concluded my heart attack was not as severe as we first thought. I was allowed, (my intravenous), to make it to the sun room, and looked at my watch. It was church time. I imagined myself in church and sang with my congregation. I knew the hymns they would sing. I had chosen them earlier that week, so in my mind, I sang right along with them. I read the Bible and quietly spoke the pastoral prayer. I knew my people would be praying for my recovery. I added my prayers to theirs.

Monday, Alex Florek, a truck driver I had led to Christ, came into the room to visit me. Others came in a steady stream.

"Who is that guy in that room that he has so many visitors?" was the query of more than one nurse.

"When you are tired and have had enough, just close your eyes and your visitors will get the message," said one savvy nurse. That was good advice. I resorted to that ploy more than once. Sure enough, my well-intended visitors would say, "He's tired, I think we'd better go." (By the way, I was.)

Six days in hospital, and the welcome news arrives that I could go home!

"Coronary!" What a loaded word. My doctor said, "On the grand scale of things, your coronary was not severe as some. Provided you have no more, after seven years it will be as though you never even had one." Good news indeed!

My recovery was swift. Five weeks later, I was back in church for a standing ovation. The following Sunday, I was preaching again. The only hitch was Sara who was still in the dark. She had completed her tour of duty in Belgium and united with her friend Sarah Childs in England. Her homesickness evaporated as the two took in the south country together. When at last she flew home, at the airport she was looking for two parents. When she only saw her mother, she immediately exclaimed, "Where's Dad?" Joan was able then to explain everything, adding that the danger was past, and that her father's recovery assured. Somehow, it didn't sink in until she was home and on her own turf. When she saw me relaxed, but lying in an outdoor lounge, a big tear trickled down her cheek as she hugged me. She was home and secure. Her father's recovery was assured. All was well with the world. Time to retreat thirty-two years.

Chapter 23
Bible School

Dixon Hall

A View of Our Campus

Mahood Hall, Hooper Memorial Chapel

I am now enrolled at London Bible School and loving every minute of it. My misgivings at being a lowly Bible school student soon gave way to the thrill of sharing with a class of sixty zealous would-be-missionaries and pastors. I would make friends here that would last me a lifetime. The opening sessions were set aside for testimonies of how we got there. I rejoiced to hear of sacrifice and dedication that many had made. Some of them were former members of the Canadian army, and were there on their service benefits. Roy Lawson, who quickly became the class comedian, distinguished himself by eventually rising to the head office and presidency of the Fellowship of Evangelical Baptist Churches of Canada. Melvin Cuthbert and Ivor Greenslade became missionary leaders in their respective fields of service in Brazil and Peru. The students of LBI were pace setters in many fields of service, but the student that really caught my eye was Joan Amy, who was clearly a beautiful girl inside and out. Chapel was always the high point of every day where we heard the best of many speakers. The singing of the students never ceased to amaze me; it was like being in the choir. Sometimes, the students would spontaneously, break into two- and three- part harmony. The praise and song of those dedicated students was unlike any I had ever heard before.

Mt Elgin Baptist Church [now renovated into a home] where I preached my first sermon at age nineteen.

There was plenty of book learning for the head, but the sterling devotion of the students is what I remember most. If I could be young again, I would repeat the same process, just to experience the zeal and the devotion that would stay with me a lifetime. It was like being on a spiritual retreat for a year.

Chapter 24
The Pentecostal Divide

In March 1949, I was seventeen and never missed a Wednesday night prayer meeting. It was mainly older people, and only the most zealous of the young people attended – three or four at the most. Providentially, someone had placed a tract in my hands entitled, "Whose Body is Yours?" I have already alluded to the reading of that tract and, kneeling down, gave my body to the Holy Spirit. I felt no ecstasy, just a quiet decision that I wanted to have the fulness of the Spirit in my life.

Shortly after this event, I heard that the Pentecostal church was relocating a few blocks from our Baptist church. I was not pleased. At the next prayer meeting, I prayed a fervent prayer that went something like this: "Lord, help us to canvass our neighbourhood one more time for the lost, less they be attracted to the Pentecostal church and be led away by an excess of fleshly emotionalism." I reaped a chorus of "Amens" from the Baptist stalwarts at the meeting but went away feeling disquieted, as though I had prayed a prayer that was not pleasing to God.

My next encounter with Pentecostalism came when I preached a sermon on the excesses of that denomination at my first posting, the Arthur Baptist Church. I did no research for the sermon. I attended no service where Pentecostals meet. I preached out of my prejudice without any background information. I assumed much and offended many. While most of my membership forgave me for provoking many friends, Ezra Small did not. He requested a meeting with me, and both Ezra and I brought our wives. The Small family was interrelated with many of our members and might well have been Pentecostals if the new church in town hadn't been Baptist. (Arthur Baptist only got started a few years before I arrived.)

I was in hot water and I knew it. Ezra had met his wife at the Pentecostal Bible School in Peterborough. He had graduated from that school, but decided he was called to be a farmer. He attended our church because the nearest Pentecostal church was twelve miles away. He wanted to be a part of our church where his friends and family attended. His sister Grace had tipped me off that, thanks to my sermon, he would be leaving the church. That would indeed be a loss. When we met, he tactfully and graciously gave me his testimony, which included his Pentecostal experience of speaking in tongues.

I had never witnessed anything emotional or out of place with Ezra. He was a hardworking farmer and a sincere Christian. After he spoke, I said,

"Ezra, I want to apologize to you for preaching that sermon. I know nothing about Pentecostals. I've never attended any of their meetings. The few Pentecostals that I've met have all been fine Christians. I'm ashamed that I talked about something I know nothing about. I would not blame you if you left the church, but I hope you won't. Furthermore, you will hear no more sermons like that one again, if you stay."

Ezra did forgive me and we both put the sorry episode away. I learned a lot that day about truthfulness and pride. Ezra was true to his word, and I was a little wiser. I also as a deliberate choice put away my prejudice about Pentecostals. I still was not curious about them, I just decided I would leave that subject on the shelf and reexamine it at a more convenient time.

In the spring of 1958, I was a student at Dallas Theological Seminary and used to turn on a Pentecostal radio program as I drove the seven miles to school. I liked the music and the sermons. Finally, one Sunday evening, Joan and I decided to visit the sponsoring church of that radio program. First, we were disappointed that the pastor wasn't preaching (I've long since forgotten his name.) A young visiting evangelist was speaking and turned on all the trappings so obnoxious to Baptist ears. We left the service that night, certain that we would never darken the door of another Pentecostal church as long as we lived. When you visit another denominational congregation, it is easy to pick out the faults. There are other faults that Baptists have gotten used to within their own churches. Pentecostal Christians visiting our services would easily pick them out. Amazing how we can be so aware of the foibles of others, and be so blind to our own.

In 1965, the Charismatic movement was sweeping through the churches, bringing new life and blowing away the cobwebs of tradition.

No wonder so many comfortable Christians were speaking against it. Joan and I attended one such meeting where a young United Church pastor was sharing his dramatic encounter with the Holy Spirit. It warmed our hearts to hear him speak. Joan and I talked about it all the way home. We didn't really understand the "speaking in tongues" part but were not offended by it. How could we be? The reverence and respect for God had refreshed our spirits in a new and powerful way.

In 1971, there was a stirring of the Spirit amongst Baptist churches in Vancouver that paralleled the now fledgling Charismatic movement. Both were thriving. Large, well-attended meetings were taking place, and people from every walk of life were attending. We were going to church almost every night. The character of the meetings quickly became interdenominational. The evangelists were identical twins, Ralph and Lou Sutera. They preached the filling of the Spirit without speaking in tongues, something the Charismatics found unusual. It was a unique movement of holiness that gripped the churches and in its wake blessed us powerfully. I personally felt a fresh renewal and mark those meetings as a turning point in my life. I would call it a "tenderizing of the heart", and a delightful renewal of the joy of the Lord.

When I accepted the call to Stanley Avenue Baptist Church, Hamilton, I was fresh from the Sutera meetings that had been such a personal blessing. Bypassing our denominational executive, I proposed a day of prayer to be held at our church and invited any Baptist pastors in the area to come. To my surprise, about seventy-five men showed up, including our general secretary, Jack Watt. Later, I discovered that Jack showed up to make sure that nothing charismatic happened and to squelch it if it did. Baptists were paranoid about Charismatics/Pentecostals in those days. Shortly afterwards, someone mailed me a tract entitled, "The Charismatic Movement is Dangerous. WATCH OUT FOR IT'." It was published by the Fundamental Evangelistic Association, Los Osos, California. Such was the zeal to suppress unwanted Holy Spirit ministries. I guess, somebody thought I was at risk and in danger of catching the virus.

In 1976, I again ran into Bernie Warren. He was the United Church minister who had so inspired us eleven years earlier when we were in Georgetown. Bernie had now established the Bezack Centre. It was here that I first encountered "singing in the spirit." This exquisite form of singing happens when the congregation (at least those in the congregation who can pray in tongues) sing in tongues instead. It was quiet. It was powerful. It stirred my soul – but what was it? I was at a loss to explain it. I only knew that I loved it and longed to participate but didn't know how. For those who are curious, let me explain it this way.

Have you ever taken in a concert performed by a symphony orchestra? If you have, you will know that at the beginning, the concert master will sound a note on his violin. All the other musicians take their cue from that one note and start to play chords. They are not attempting to play the concert; that comes later. Singing in the spirit is a lttle like that – a sort of glorious cacophony of sound that has no tune, yet is pleasing to the ear, reverent and worshipful. I have wondered if Gregorian chant, so uncommon in Protestant churches but well known in Catholic churches, isn't "singing in the spirit" codified, while the practice of spontaneous "singing in the spirit died away in the second century. Such spontaneous song was thus preserved and set to music. Today we would call it a chant. I never had any appreciation for chanting when I was young. I totally love it now. It is so inspiring to hear, especially if you are in a cathedral like St. Paul's, London, England. (I can't explain it, but through all this, I found myself with a new appreciation for the Anglican service complete with prayer book). Whenever I hear this kind of music, tucked away in the back of my mind is "singing in the spirit". Today in Pentecostal Churches, praying in tongues rarely occurs in the public meetings, if ever. In Charismatic churches, it is present in every service, but it for the most part is sung and usually never spoken. In my view, it is a wordless announcement, "the power of the Lord is present in this place."

The following year I was leading a tour group in the England/ Scotland borders area. We had come to what I believe is the loveliest of the many ruins to be explored in that area. Drysburgh Abbey has adjacent to the main building an old stable which after 700 years is still intact, complete with the roof. You only need to whisper and your voice will echo off the walls, reverberating back and forth. Instantly, I recognized an opportunity. Inviting the group to gather around (seven of us), I started singing the first stanza of the well known hymn, "Holy, Holy, Holy, Lord God Almighty." The seven of us sounded like a cathedral choir that would make the angels fold their wings. Two of our little group had dallied at the gardens. They hurried to the entrance, imagining that a sixty-voice choir had somehow eluded their notice. That was the closest a group of non-charismatics ever got to replicating the hallowed sound of "singing in the spirit."

Pentecostals proclaim that speaking in tongues gives you power. I never found that to be so. However, there is a mystery dimension in this "least of all gifts" that gives a sense of edification that defies definition and borders on the edge of the supernatural. So if this gift eludes you, my advice is "live supernaturally!" Our problem is not the lack of power; our problem is our unbelief.

I rarely pray in tongues with my Baptist friends who are so prejudiced against it. So why did I pursue the experience, when I knew it would make me a pariah amongst the people I loved? I suppose it was because I hoped it would give me extra power to serve the Lord better. I affirm the gift of tongues, however, I still had some growing to do by its use. I am learning, but had little to show outwardly. In time, I found myself thinking, "If this thing is so great, how do I prove it to myself?" I needed a faith project, if for nothing else to confirm my own heart that my Pentecostal experience was real. That's when I set up Hamilton Baptist Non-profit Homes to benefit low income families. That is a story all by itself; I choose not to tell it here. One would think that such a project would need no justification, but many of my members felt otherwise. Little by little the opposition faded. We ultimately built 166 townhouses with government-approved loans. For me, that ministry alone justifies my "experience."

In those days, St. Clair Robinson was a kindred spirit and mentor. He was a British Baptist pastor who ministered at the Elliot Heights Baptist Church. I must say, he was one of the finest preachers I've ever had the privilege to hear. He had a blistering wit and could make his congregation laugh. He could quote the English poets at will and had memorized many famous Shakespearean passages. You can imagine my surprise when I found out that he had started out with the British Pentecostals. I suppose he wearied of the fleshly excesses. Yet he never got over their godly devotion and pined for its loss in conservative Baptist circles. St. Clair Robinson (now in heaven) could have been the pastor of the largest church in America, if he hadn't been such an irascible fellow. Too much unresolved anger handicapped his ministry. (When he was young, he used to be a boxer.)

Just once, he surrepticiously slipped away to a charismatic meeting. He found plenty to criticize but said, "The preaching was excessive, but the singing in the spirit was real."

Perhaps it was my "experience" or maybe it was simply the fact that I stayed too long at Stanley Avenue Baptist Church, but attendance was slipping. Whenever a church succeeds, it is to the congregation's credit; whenever it seems to slide back, it's the pastor's fault. I'm not sure whether my people hoped I would seek a pastoral change, or if it were me who felt it was time to go. On January 14, 1989, I left the security of Stanley Avenue Baptist Church and started Hamilton Christian Fellowship. I regretted having to locate so close to my former church, but the Hamilton Football Hall of Fame had just the right-sized auditorium. We were within a mile away. Before I retired, that venture grew in size from 25 to 170. We bought St. George's Anglican Church, renovated it, and moved in. The congregation continues to worship there to this day. I cherish many things about that church, but above all, the reverent and beautiful "singing in the spirit."

-oOo-

In 1999, I co-chaired with Hamilton's mayor, Bob Morrow, the Millennial Christian Festival which celebrated the coming of the year 2000. We brought Dr. Robert Schuller of California's famed Crystal Cathedral to Copps Coliseum, with 7000 in attendance. It was a highlight experience embracing all the Hamilton denominations, both Protestant and Catholic, and raising $13,000 for the food bank in the bargain. At the time of this writing, I currently worship with a small house group following the Anglican prayer book.

-oOo-

For the thoughtful student of evangelism, I need to add one more postscript. My most fruitful ministry in terms of conversions occurred at Stanley Avenue Baptist Church. I thought when I broke loose from my Baptist traditions that evangelism would increase. It didn't. My congregation grew faster, but that was because people were welcoming the fresh winds of worship in the charismatic style. As I reflect on these issues, I conclude two things. The Holy Spirit is Sovereign in such matters; I think the term 'soul winner" is a misnomer. When the gentle winds of the Spirit blow, people are attracted to Christianity. For a while at Stanley Avenue Baptist Church, there was a delightful freedom and some wonderful people coming to faith in Christ, including international students. I think evangelism is like a dance with two partners. One partner leads, the other follows. The lead partner is the Holy Spirit. We are the followers.

Chapter 25
The Girl of God's choosing.

I am supposed to be paying attention to the lecture on Genesis, but I am glancing to the left at a girl who is beautiful. I had told this to my mother on my last visit to her new place. (Thank goodness, she had at long last taken a job looking after an elderly gentleman whose grown-up children wanted help to care for their aged father.) However, my mother couldn't understand how it could be that I loved Kathy but was telling her about Joan Amy. Others see our inconsistency so easily. The inevitable has not yet occurred to me.

Anna Bastin was Joan Amy's classmate and constant companion and had been telling Joan that it was just a matter of time. "Lover boy is looking this way again," she whispered.

This was happening so frequently, it had become a standing joke between Anna and Joan. I am observant; Joan is a classy dresser and I can't help but notice but I think about deeper things than that. I think, "If only Kathy were sitting here instead of Joan Amy." Then we'd have so much in common. After lectures, I dutifully take up my Fuller Brush case and proceed to Victor Street where I canvass door to door.

"I can't give her up, I love her – but I can't continue on with a girl with whom I have so little in common – she doesn't even want to be saved – how can I convince her – I wish I had never met her – I wish I had met Joan Amy first."

It seems I am forever finding myself between two influential women. These are the thoughts that keep running through my mind. Absent-mindedly, I go through the routine of selling my products. About 4:00 P.M., I am knocking at the door of Vera Smith. I had met her three months before on my previous rounds in September.

It was the first week of Bible school, and I had been so excited and full of joy that my enthusiasm spilled out spontaneously to Vera. Vera had remembered me from the days when I would visit Central Baptist for the evening service. Remembering me she wanted to know what I was doing. When she found out I was preparing for the ministry, she had shared my joy. It was like talking to an angel about the subject that meant everything to me. Now three months later, I am knocking at her door so preoccupied that when Vera answers the door, I hardly know her. I trot out my usual routine,

"Good afternoon Mrs. Smith, I'm Bruce Woods your Fuller Brush man and if you will invite me in to see my products, I will gladly give you a free gift, whether you buy anything or not."

"Why, Bruce Woods," she says, "it's so good to see you again, but whatever has happened to you? You look so sad?"

Stunned at her honesty, I am instantly felled like a tree in the forest. I drop my case, bury my face in my hands, and fall apart in a convulsion of tears. Charismatics would say Mrs. Smith had been given a "word of knowledge" and said it with authority.

"I think you'd better come in and sit down, Bruce. Trust me, you can tell me all about it."

 Welcome words to a footsore kid lost in his worries. I stumble into her living room and completely break down. For ten minutes, the fountains of the deep overwhelm me. Here in front of someone I hardly know, every time I try to speak, I weep some more. At last I gain my composure and am starting to talk. It all comes out. I hold nothing back. When I am through talking, God has already shown me what I must do. However, it is comforting to hear Vera say, "As a Christian gentleman you have no choice. You must obey the voice of God and sever your friendship with Kathy and tell her why. Then you will have God's peace." Again, in charismatic language that was a "word of wisdom."

There are many forms of bondage which rob us of our freedom. Infatuation with the opposite sex is one. Infatuation can masquerade as love, robbing us of our freedom. It is a wonderful ecstasy with the right person. With the wrong person it is a road to a no-man's land.

In a moment of time, I have been liberated. The joy I felt in Vera's living room that day set my soul free. It was a God moment that I'll never forget. When I say goodbye to Vera, I am soaring like a bird, happy in the joy of my spiritual freedom. My next challenge is to tell Kathy that our relationship must come to an end. This is going to be tough, because we both live under the same roof. God comes to my aid. That night after supper, I notice that Kathy has her tennis gear ready.

"Going somewhere?" I ask.

"Yep, going out to play tennis."

"That sounds like fun. Who are you going to play with?"

"One of the guys from Normal School."

To hear these words with all the implications is like a second breath from heaven. If our relationship is a bit shaky, maybe Kathy won't take things so hard. I dreaded hurting her feelings. I had been given an opportunity with strength that comes from God to honourably, and forthrightly, break things off. Instead, selfishly I now play the hypocrite and resort to subterfuge to avoid the responsibility of a hard decision.

I feign betrayal. I lie when I should have been truthful. I could have used that moment to set Kathy as free as I felt. I could have said that I approve, because I did approve. I could have told her all about my afternoon with Vera Smith. I had been given the best of opportunities, but my duplicity made something that could have been simple into a tangled complication. I imagined I had to make my breakup with Kathy her fault in order to make myself look good. It was a display of ugly ego and hardly Christian. Remember, we have to share the same dining table for another four months. God had given me the best of all possibilities in what is going to be an awkward situation. Immature and clumsy, I was to hurt my ongoing witness as a Christian gentleman before the girls at the boarding house who naturally sided with Kathy. Thanks be to God who, despite our human failings, puts up with us and turns things right. Eventually I figure it out and have my private penance. I correct my failings, even going on to the high calling of the ministry. The world would be a much happier place if we could only be honest, even if it means a loss of face.*

In 1954, when Joan and I were married and with our first baby, Providence arranged a momentary meeting with Kathy. My wife and I attended a Billy Graham crusade at Maple Leaf Gardens. Surprise! There was Kathy Harkness with a colleague. It was a brief but pleasant exchange.

I return to classes unburdened and become a much better student. The God who cares for us all cares for Kathy as well, but that's another story. I am now free to talk to Joan Amy. The Christmas party comes early in December. Since classes end on Thursday, December 20, I pursue every opportunity I can to talk to Joan.

I am not without competitors. Some of the other guys are thinking similar thoughts. First, there was the party at a nearby church hall, followed by a trip to the local arena. I make my move early and ask Joan if I can walk her home to the dorm after an in-house hockey game is finished. Boldly I take her hand and she doesn't object. We talk as I had never talked with Kathy, because we share all things in common. We are off to a good start. Our romance consists of talking whenever the chance comes up between classes. In the five remaining days of classes, we talk a lot.

One of the topics we discuss is family. While we wait for the bus to pick us up for church, I ask Joan about her family.

"You have mentioned quite a few siblings. You've got me curious. How many brothers and sisters do you have?" The bus arrives just as I ask the question.

"Wait till we are sitting down before I tell you," She says. I detect a chuckle in her voice.

"Okay, " I say and now that we are seated, I ask again.

"Brace yourself." Joan smiles.

"I am braced."

"Are you sure?"

"Very sure; c'mon and tell me." Silence and then Joan replies,

"There are eleven of us."

"Wow, that's wonderful."

What I really want to say is, "That means our kids will have ten aunts and uncles." Wisely, I keep my peace. Instead, I say, "I think large families are wonderful." At this early stage in our romance, I didn't think it prudent to hint that we would one day be married.

My escapade with my Model A Ford has cost me my little nest egg to the tune of $125.00. I'm not broke and sales are good, but for a while, I don't have any extra money. I still have an ego. I decide I want to impress Gord and Elsie with presents and spend Christmas with Grandma and them. I will borrow $50.00 from George McBride. I promise to repay him in January with $5.00 interest. George rightly figures that's a ten percent return for a one-month investment. He agrees. I buy presents for Mother, Grandma, Gordon, Elsie, and their two kids, Bobby and Cheryl.

After all Mother used to spoil me with gifts, so now I try my hand on my cousins. Mother and I have Christmas early. The Christmas I'm really looking forward to is in Stratford with the Gillatlys and my beloved Grandmother. After presents have been opened, Elsie asks me where I'm getting all the money. It is a satisfying question which I delight to answer, especially telling them about my successful sales career. However, I didn't tell them I had borrowed the "present" money. The Bible says it is more blessed to give than to receive. I'm afraid my Christmas generosity had more to do with showing off than generosity. I will eventually learn the difference. It's just that it takes a little more time to reach that level of maturity.

I had already made plans to visit my father on Christmas day in Toronto. Hitchhiking is still easy in 1950. By 11:30 A.M., I am in Waterloo where Joan Amy lives. If I can skillfully execute my machinations I can have Christmas with the girl of my dreams. I plan to phone Joan Amy and tell her I just happened to be in Waterloo on Christmas Day. Who knows what might happen?

Shivering with bated breath, I'm in a phone booth looking up her phone number. I am excited as I hear the tone signal and nervously rotate the dial to make the connection. I couldn't have called at a more inopportune time. A few days before when I had said goodbye to her at Bible school, Joan had informed me that she was one of eleven children. Those future aunts and uncles had just assembled around the Christmas tree for the opening of presents when I interrupted the festivities. Bad timing to be sure. I hear a masculine voice (obviously one of her brothers) say, "Some guy by the name of Bruce Woods wants to talk to you Joan." What I didn't hear was the muffled voice that said, "Make it quick; we want to open our presents." I had just successfully managed to make a nuisance of myself. Meanwhile, Joan, who was just as anxious as her siblings to get on with their Christmas, has to be polite with her admiring suitor.

I have played the wild card and lost. I suspected my aspirations were forlorn before they were launched, but what can I say. I tried.

Prolonging the phone call as much as I dare, with feet growing colder by the minute, I finally say a reluctant goodbye and wish my new love a merry Christmas. I now hitchhike to Toronto, arriving in time for the evening meal. Unannounced, I had taken a chance that first, I would find them home, and second, that they would accommodate me. I tell my father and Phyllis that I am in love with the most beautiful girl in all the world.

Joan Amy grew up in Waterloo with two sisters and eight brothers. They are a handsome family whose Christian faith has made them a shining example. They grew up poor but were indescribably rich in the things that really matter. The family produced two businessmen, two ministers, two ministers' wives, a plant manager, and a college professor. Three of Joan's brothers served overseas in the Canadian army during World War II. All eleven of the siblings professed faith in Christ and are a legacy of blessing. Who wouldn't want to marry into a family like that? Any visitor who dropped in at the Amys' was in for a good time. Conversation with the Amy family was always a time of enrichment and laughter.

On Thursday, December 28, Joan and I are back at London Bible Institute. We all have part-time jobs and we need the money. Friday night, Gerry Rowe wants to take Ruth Horner and go for a car ride. I'm invited to include Joan and we get the back seat. Any date is a good time as long as Joan is beside me. We both have this thing in common: we have had enough of dating for its own sake. We are looking for a life partner who shares our Christian calling. Joan was such a beautiful girl, she never lacked for a boyfriend. I had had my own disappointing experiences as well. I wanted desperately to kiss her, but I was running with new rules. Everything had to be strictly Christian and frankly a little unrealistic.

As we drove around the streets of London, I decided it would the "Christian" thing to politely ask her for a kiss. So how do I accomplish this? I ratchet up my courage and finally say to her,
"May I kiss you?" A little surprised, she replies,
"I suppose so."

I lean in her direction and kiss her on the cheek, and then I add a second little peck.

"I cheated and took two," I whisper.

Fortunately, it's too dark for me to see the look on her face. The evening ends with a fond farewell at the Bible college dormitory.

No sooner is Joan through the door than the girls in her dorm gather around Joan and ask how it went.

"Fine," says Joan.

"Did he kiss you?" asks Anna

"Yes," Joan nonchalantly replies.

"What did it feel like?" says Anna, "C'mon, tell us the news."

"Like kissing my brother," says Joan.

Suddenly, the girls are doubled over in laughter. Since explanations are required, Joan tells them about her unromantic adventure. More laughter!

"I think that's so sweet," says Agnes.

"These are the memories that someday you'll cherish," says another.

"Perhaps," says an uninterested Joan Amy.

Our first date was not memorable. But there will be more. My guardian angel gives me another chance.

On New Year's Day, Wheaton Bible College Chorale is singing at Central Baptist Church, and Joan and I go to the concert together. Later that evening, we are alone in the entrance of London Bible Institute. I have discarded my unrealistic rules about romance. Meantime, Dr. Terry Hulbert is stopping by to pick up some papers. Our nocturnal reverie is shattered by an intruder. The entrance was so dark, our professor hadn't seen us. We were caught kissing in the foyer. The unflappable Terry Hulbert was not lost for words.

"Care to rent my office for the evening?" Without skipping a beat, he turned away and closed the entry door.

"He knows how we feel," we chorus. "He was young once just like us."

A photographer friend snapped this picture on our way home from church [Bibles in hand]

From now on we do everything together. We are zealous about our romance and our faith. Saturday night at the corner of Dundas and Wellington, we do street evangelism. The guys take turns doing the preaching. It is a rough and tumble expenditure of our bravery and energy, especially on cold winter nights. We are savvy enough when people give us that half-cocked look to know what they are thinking. We have an audience for a few moments, but they rarely stop to listen. People who are bundled up to brave the January winds make for an unresponsive audience. Still, there are enough people who stand around to hear what we are preaching to encourage our zeal. Young and enthusiastic, we last for about an hour and then head to a restaurant for a hot chocolate.

Later that evening, we are at the restaurant. I understand that holding warm hands is romantic; however, I am holding Joan's cold feet. First the right foot and then the left. In current parlance we are "chilling out", literally, but somehow that metaphor is limited. It just doesn't quite seem to fit. In fact, what I imagine I am doing is attempting to warm her heart. The ladies warm us guys by way of the stomach, or so the saying goes. I am working for the heart by way of Joan's cold feet. (Hmmn?) We are savouring our hot chocolate and talking about our relationship. I am looking straight at Joan's face. I've never seen more beautiful eyes. They are an Amy trademark. Most brown eyes are average brown. Joan's eyes are flashing. They are almost black. I am captivated by her eyes. I am hopelessly in love with Joan, and she knows it. I say to her, "You are sure of me aren't you." Joan agrees.

I say, "I'm not as sure of you as you are sure of me."

Joan smiles and looks away. Next, I boldly say, "I may not be sure of you now, and I may not be sure of you tomorrow; but eventually, I am sure of you in the end. Someday you are going to be my wife."

I really want to talk about matrimony, and I use the concept in as many ways as I can, but I'm too timid to use the "m" word. The meaning of my words is plain, but I am too enraptured to see the constrained look on Joan's face. Later on that evening in the dorm, she tells Anna, "Bruce Woods managed to terrify me tonight; do you know what he said to me?"

I have no report of what came next, except to reveal to my reader that once again, I have caused all the girls a great occasion for laughter. My terrified girlfriend gets over it. Maybe I'm marriage material after all.

One day after morning lectures, Joan tells me the menu for lunch is macaroni.

"I can't face it!" she exclaims, "Maybe I'll just skip lunch." I cannot bear the thought of the girl of my dreams going without her lunch so I propose to take her to the Rexall Drug Store where they have a food bar. Habits are easily formed. Every time Macaroni is served at the dining hall, I take Joan out for a ham salad sandwich. My landlady, Mrs. Sadler, quips,

"Now aren't you in the money, taking your girl out for lunch when you could be eating here for free. You're wasting your board money." I tell Margaret, "It makes me feel good to spend money on my girl." The ever practical Margaret retorts,

"Your girl should eat Macaroni like everybody else and you should be saving your pocketbook."

The younger generation always knows best. However, these things can be habit forming. I've been buying Joan Amy her lunches ever since. It's Friday and lectures are over. I have dallied and so has Joan. We slip into a small room by ourselves. Drawing her into my arms (there's nobody looking) I kiss her. We are in love.

Easter break means a long week-end. I am excited. Joan has invited me to Waterloo to meet her family. She has gone ahead with her brother Bruce and his wife Eleanor. I will come later on the bus. Joan, who has a sense of humour, has been talking to her best friend, Dorothy, who is married to Roy Shaub. She has invited them to meet her new boyfriend who, as she describes, " – isn't much to look at but has a gentle heart."

Dorothy who has confidence in her best friend says, "If you like him, so will we."

The first brother I meet is Bill, who is a student at Waterloo College. Later, he quipped on meeting me, "True to form, Joan seems to know how to get a good looking guy. I thought you were a movie star posing as a Bible school student."

Now where was I? Oh, yes, Joan introduces me to her life-long friend Dorothy Shaub and her husband, Roy. After we exchange pleasantries, Dorothy says to Joan (out of my hearing), "Joan Amy, you should be ashamed of yourself telling me all the stuff you said about Bruce, and all his shortcomings. And I believed you! He's a catch."

Roy says to Dorothy, "Joan sure strung you a line about her new boyfriend, and you believed her."

The weekend was one of the happiest times in my life. It was a joy to meet Joan's friends, her parents, and their children.

Joan's mother, Lillian, was a happy woman whose fulfillment in life was her family. Having given birth to nine children, she had paid the inevitable price of being overweight. Nobody ever seemed to mind. Oliver Amy was a distinguished looking-gentleman whose deportment breathed the dignity of a wonderful Christian life. At one time, he had been a well-to-do businessman in Elmira. However, he had lost everything during the Great Depression but emerged without bitterness. His was the quiet confidence of a man who walked with God. He worked right up to the time of his death at the age of seventy-eight.

"Bruce and Joan have it bad for each other, you can tell," quips Anna. The whispering grapevine is alive and well. The advice comes from several classmates again and again: "Don't you guys lose your head and get married this summer."

The reason for this advice is simple. In those days, there was a rule. If you enroll in London Bible College but decide to get married, you cannot return to classes for a year (I wonder why? Or was someone imagining an embarrassing event). For this reason, there were a few hurry-up marriages for couples who wanted to go to Bible college for three years. There were at least four couples who had married sooner than they originally planned, simply because they had decided to attend Bible school in 1950. One such couple was Elmer and Margery Cassidy, who said to us, "I know we did it, but don't you guys try it. Your life at Bible college is more important." We assured them we intended to return for our second year, going steady, but still unmarried.

It is the weekend of spring graduation. The day is warm, and the fresh growth everywhere was lush and green. Joan and I have planned a day at Gibbon's Park. The lovely old mansion that served as our alma mater was adorned with blooming lilacs. A sweet aroma fills the air. Joan and I walk hand in hand to the bus stop, and transfer at Richmond Street.

Our destination is London's Gibbon's Park. We arrive at 2:00 P.M. and stroll down the winding paths that lead to the spring gardens with flowers blooming their very best. We are enraptured with all the eye can see, and we have each other. I never tire of telling Joan how much I love her, and she replies in kind. I have the classified ads from the London Free Press newspaper. I show Joan an ad that reads, "Furnished apartment, $20.00 a month."

"See, Joan, with your income and mine we could afford to live here after we got married." It's all the stuff of dreams, but when you are in love, nothing is impossible. Three hours pass in an instant, and with the graduation schedule, we know we have to be back for supper. There are some things that are better than scheduled meals. That was a day I would gladly have stretched for another three hours. Reluctantly, we catch the bus to Queen Street. For me, the parting for two hours while we go our separate ways to have our evening meals at our respective places is intolerable. I will see her again that very evening; Joan's brother Bruce has loaned us his car so we can take a country drive after supper and romance one another again. May 10, 1951, was a day in paradise that we have often rehearsed – it was the most romantic day of our courtship.

Chapter 26
Boliva Bound

The 11,000-foot Culpina Valley in the Bolivian Andes is "far from the madding crowd." Isolated from Bolivia's main commerce, it should be brown and desolate. It's not. It is green with lush vegetation that produces abundant crops of potatoes, corn, barley, and red peppers that make the inhabitants of the Culpina uplands prosperous by Bolivian standards. Isolated from the rest of the world, it is a safe environment in which to raise a family. However, it wasn't always so.

German immigration not only benefited Canada and the USA, it also had its effect in Latin America. Some unknown German families saw the potential of the Culpina Valley, and bought cheap land. Next, they built a dam and irrigation canals. The virgin soil of the Culpina Valley made them rich much to the envy of their Bolivian neighbours. Then came the 1952 revolution by Victor Paz Estensoro, and the wealthy landowners of Bolivia paid the price. The new rulers of Bolivia redistributed the land. The peasants got what they for many years had viewed as rightfully theirs. The Bolivian peasanats did not reap the bonanza they anticipated. The problem with the peasants was that their poverty, compounded with ignorance of productive farming methods. They were still poor. Without capital and with deficient of know-how, the newly acquired land did not produce the wealth they imagined. Slowly, the Culpina Valley stagnated and slipped into perennial drought.

Dean & Evelyn Burns with son Tim, Santa Cruz mission compound

In 1951, Dean Burns of Fergus married Torontonian Evelyn Wallace in Bolivia. They were missionaries from Canada to the uplands of Bolivia. At first, the nominal Roman Catholics of that area were suspicious of them. Later, they would learn to love them dearly, especially Adrian Miranda, who was one of Dean's earliest converts. I first met the Burnes during my time at the Arthur Baptist Church. It was there I had met two generations of Burnes, and would eventually become intimate friends with the third. Tim Burns represented the third generation, born in Bolivia with joint Bolivian-Canadian citizenship.

Dean and Evelyn had a remarkable ministry in Bolivia with many converts. Baptizing new converts by immersion was a challenge. The only time there was water in the river was in winter when the temperature was just above freezing. When Julianna, was baptized she had an advanced case of melanoma. Within a week, her badly disfigured face was normal, a miracle that took Dean and Evelyn by surprise. News spreads fast. Everybody in the village who was sick now wanted to be baptized. What an opportunity to explain the gospel! Clemintina, who suffered from migraine headaches, heard about it, too. She walked fifty kilometers to find the missionaries. When Dean explained that baptism did not necessarily mean healing, she still wanted to be baptized. Her migraines never returned. Cold water notwithstanding, Dean loved it when people requested baptism. Again and again he braved the chilly waters to accommodate new believers. I asked him one day how many requests he had, but by that time, Dean had lost count.

"Perhaps something over 800," he mused. "After that I stopped counting." For skeptics who worry about cold water concerns, Dean was 89 years old when he died.

When I was the pastor of Stanley Avenue Baptist, son Tim and Phil, his younger brother, became members. Once again, we encountered the Burnes who were on furlough to see their sons. In 1976, Tim Burns indicated a desire to return to Bolivia to work side by side with his father. At that time, I persuaded Stanley Avenue Baptist Church to take Tim Burns on as a fully supported missionary to the town of Culpina in the Bolivian uplands at $12,000 a year. Never did so little money do so much for a far off country. In 1978, our church sent me and my wife to Bolivia to see for ourselves the mission field and for me to be the inspirational speaker for the annual gathering of GMU (the Gospel Missionary Union) in Bolivia. High on the 'to-do" list was my desire to see the work Tim Burns was supervising in the Culpina Valley.

For Joan and me, this was high drama indeed. When we changed planes in Miami, the first thing I noticed was that the plane destined for Santa Cruz, Bolivia, was losing some of its paint. The seats were older, and we were left to our own conclusions. Obviously, we were on an older plane. To the credit of Aero Sur, they got us to our destination safely. To visit Latin America in 1978 was an adventure. I was intrigued to see progress despite poverty.

Dean and Evelyn Burns met us at Santa Cruz. There they were in charge of the Missionary House which was right beside the seminary where Dean taught fledgling pastors courses in Bible and theology. It would detract from my story to tell of that fascinating city with its street vendors and money changers who worked right on the sidewalks by the curb. Suffice it to say that one week later, Tim Burns and I met at Cochabamba.

Now when it comes to Cochabamba, the temptation to digress is irresistible. Cochabamba is a wonderfully preserved new world/old world city. Its starlit nights bring out the locals in droves. Missionary Sandra Colerino is our guide; she is of American-Italian stock. She takes us under her wing. We walk through the lanterned streets with overhead arches that speak of an exquisite Spanish architecture fit for a Hollywood movie. The main street is more like a continuation of courtyards that indent the street in an irregular fashion. The main street is an architectural marvel of colonnade and arches. Charming alcoves and recesses reflect the joy of living. No vehicles here. This is for pedestrians only and there are plenty of them. Simon Bolivar, the emancipator of Latin America from Spanish rule, would have been right at home.

I asked Sandra, a former cosmetics salesperson from New York, what brought her to "Coch" as the locals call it. Her reply was, "God took me out of a messed-up life and called me to minister to the wives of equally messed-up executive wives and businesswomen of Bolivia."

Her church was her living room. Wives of executives and their wealthy friends met there for Bible study. It took a stylish, attractive girl of similiar rank to command their attention. Sandra was that girl. Sandra had come by the grace of God to a whole new life of meaning. Not only did she know those who were "somebodies," but also she was also known by them. Sandra was pastor and counsellor to those women and they respected her. I vowed to return one day to Cochabamba to see it in depth. I never did.

Leaving Cochabamba behind, Tim Burns and I flew to the Cupina Valley in a Missionary Aviation (MAF) four-seater. I had left Joan in Santa Cruz, at the mission house. We landed on the Culpina uplands before the green "transformation" had taken place; the valley looked desolate. That's when the pilot said to me, "Tim Burns is no ordinary missionary. Growing up in Bolivia, he speaks Spanish like a native; he even catches the subtle humour. Most missionaries learn the language quite well; very few ever reach the level of understanding the nuances of Spanish humour."

We landed on the airstrip that serves the town of Culpina. It was a windswept field marked by a few stones and an air sock. Half the valley was beyond use and suffering from drought. Woe betide the pilot who didn't know the aircurrents in the high Andes Mountains. Fortunately, our pilot knew his aircraft, and we landed safely.

When I first laid eyes on Culpina with its winding streets and sunbaked mud-brick buildings, I marvelled that they could endure heat and cold. Tim assured me they could. My response to Culpina was, "Tim, if we could pick up this slice of real estate, drop it in the middle of Florida, surround it with a chain link fence, and charge an entrance fee, it would be a number one attraction. Let's see – admission would be $20.00 a person just to walk around the town. You and I would be millionaires."

Tim showed me the main street where I could meet a member of his church, Fransisco Herrera, who had a dry goods store no bigger than a room twelve feet square. Although it seemed small by our standards, it was as good a store as might be found in Culpina. The proof that the Herreras were rich was that he had just purchased a

Mercedes. Tim smiled as I responded,

"A Mercedes – he must be rich."

Tim smiled but held his peace. Meanwhile, I marvelled at the contrast between a new green truck unloading goods, while a lesser merchant was leading a train of donkeys laden down with products for delivery up the street. Made sense. Trucks can't go where the only roads are donkey trails.

Chuckling, Tim pointed to the green truck and said, "That's the Mercedes."

As I have already implied, you couldn't take a truck to the mountain passes where so much of Boliva's salt comes from. "The salt of the earth", is what Christians are called. It is interesting that the mountain people experienced a Christian revival in the early twentieth century and many of them became Christians. That was the work of the early missionaries. They made them rich in spiritual life, if not in material wealth. That would come later. Those bearers of salt had now become Christians. Before the advent of the missionaries, the mountain people were basically animists. Away from home six months a year, but in possession of the knowledge of Christ, they literally and spiritually became the "salt of the earth," evangelizing the entire mountain area and the many tiny valleys that dot the Andes landscape. They surely were the happiest people on earth. These salt people prepared the way for the ministry of the Burnes, who were able to build on their pre-evangelism efforts. (Recent mineral deposits found beneath the salt plateaus offer material wealth. I hope the riches of this world do not corrupt the "real wealth" of those mountain people who like me are between two worlds with the better one yet to come.)

The Culpina tablelands had a problem: their irrigation ditches constantly ran dry. When the great land transfer took place, the early German landowners did not impart their know-how to the new peasant owners. Perhaps they couldn't have done so even if they wanted too. The science of irrigation requires experience and maintenance. After a decade of neglect, much of the water was lost in the ditches before it ever reached the farms. Furthermore, the water management was in the hands of incompetent men who could be bribed. At a town meeting fraught with ugly accusations and denials, a resolution to the problem gave Tim a breakthrough. A local man stood up and said, "We need a water manager who will not accept a bribe, and the only man who can find us that kind of person is Tim Burns." What a tribute to the fledgling church in Culpina. Adrian Miranda, a faithful member of Tim's congregation, got the job.

The crisis spawned a vision. Tim decided on a plan of action. However, Bolivia's impoverished budget would never consider Tim's vision. Instead, he took it to Ottawa and presented his dream to CIDA (Canadian International Development Agency). Tim wanted to line the ditches in the Culpina tablelands with concrete. Canada gave Tim $24,000 for his project – a pittance in view of the need, but at least it was a start. Had that money been turned over to the national government, it would have disappeared in the bureaucracy. Tim bought the cement and trucked it into Culpina. When the town found out about Tim's project, they wanted Tim to run for government office, an honour that Tim declined. In the minds of Culpina residents, he already was the 'honorary mayor" anyhow; at least that's the way I saw it. Using volunteer help, and the CIDA dollars as far as they would go, the mammoth task of lining the ditches with cement proceeded under the watchful eye of Tim Burns. In spite of would-be thieves, the project continued with only one bag of cement stolen at night.

In addition to lining the ditches with cement, Tim oversaw the building of three dams to create water reservoirs. Finally, the Bolivian farmers themselves took notice of the increased productivity of the Culpina tablelands. They finished the job with volunteer help and in the end, with their own money. Tim Burns was the local hero who made it happen. With his able church member Adrian Miranda, who helped oversee the project, the mammoth job was done. Tim's words are insightful:

"The ditch system took off. I agreed with the farmers' union, as I had done with the dam projects, that I would only provide cement. They had to supply the labour and other sundries, such as sand, gravel, and rocks. They took a look at what I had, and then they multiplied it. Reflecting on this, I think I witnessed something like the 5000 people did (2000years ago), when Jesus multiplied the fish and loaves of bread. When I left the area, the ditches were still being constructed in an on-going maintenance program."

A Bolivian engineer estimated the value of material and labour to be in the range of $450,000. Of course, little by little the farmers themselves had to raise that kind of money, but they were also the beneficiaries. All of this was accomplished by Tim Burns' vision and guidance. Of course, CIDA funds helped to get it started, but what a fantastic return for so little investment.

Now you see why I began this chapter saying that our financial support for Tim Burns was the best investment Stanley Avenue Baptist Church ever made. As always, the gospel and social-economic improvement go hand in hand. The building of those dams and the lining of the irrigation ditches transformed Culpina and reclaimed the drought-stricken valley. Furthermore, Tim's concern for their temporal needs opened the door to evangelism that saw the church prosper and increase in numbers.

However, I have a sad footnote to add to this story. In 1990, Tim's wife Denita abruptly left for Alberta, Canada, with their two children, Rachael and Robby in 1990. Tim was at the height of his career. He was now stationed in Sucre, taking his place on the national board of his mission. The marital breakup was one of those things that could not be forseen. If there were signs of dissatisfaction within the marriage, Tim missed them completely. Avant Mission (the new name of the now multimission union) had their rules. If for any reason a marriage breakup occurs, the affected missionaries resign! It was a devastating blow that not only hurt Tim but also affected an understaffed mission as well. With all avenues of recourse erased, Tim returned to Canada. In order to be near his children, Tim moved to Alberta, where Denita had decided to reside. All attempts at reconciliation failed. The inevitable divorce left Tim a lonely and disillusioned man and shortchanged Avant Mission of badly needed personnel. Wiser heads have prevailed and today the rules have changed, but in 1990 there were no exceptions. Everybody loses.

In 1994, Tim married Alvina Tjostheim, who had experienced a similar fate. They are happily married and Tim is a successful salesman in the Alberta oilfields, marketing high-pressure valves and fittings to oil companies. That same initiative that worked so well in Bolivia worked again in Tim's favour in the oil industry. The flawlessly fluent

Spanish-speaking missionary does volunteer work for prospective missionaries who are learning Spanish in preparation for work in Latin America. Given the circumstances, I suppose it's the best of all possible worlds. Asked if he has plans to revisit Culpina, Tim replies, "Perhaps some day I will return, but I have no immediate plans for it."

I have this feeling that if Tim Burns ever returns to Culpina for a visit, he will receive a hero's welcome.

Chapter 27
Marriage

"I can't believe the good news," I tell Joan. "I've just come from an interview with Rev. Leander Roblin, pastor of Benton Street Baptist Church, Kitchener. He has asked me to be the summer pastor of Bethel Baptist Mission." We won't be separated this summer; I'll be in Kitchener and you will be in Waterloo. We will see each other every day." (Waterloo and Kitchener are twin cities).

It didn't take me long to reason that after my work was done at the mission, I could bike to Joan's house every evening. It's a recipe for a blossoming romance. Brimming with happiness, I tell Joan, "I am now quitting my job with the Fuller Brush Company and moving to Kitchener this very week."

Ecstatic with the developments, I ship my bicycle to Kitchener, and ride with Joan in her brother's car, leaving London behind.

Sunday, May 13, I preach my first sermon to the tiny congregation of some thirty-odd adherents who attend the Bethel Mission, and Joan Amy is in the audience.

Leona Steinbeck says to Joan Amy, "We were upset when they told us they were sending us a nineteen-year-old-kid. But can that kid ever preach."

Mrs. Roberts is the Sunday School superintendent with an eye to opportunity and promptly signs Joan up to teach the primary kids (aged five to seven). We are in the ministry together. The only caveat about this position is that I could have been making $85.00 a week, selling Fuller Brushes; but I am only getting $35.00 at the mission. This, however, was of no consequence to me; I couldn't be happier. To add to my joy, our little congregation likes my preaching. When they heard that they were to get a Bible School student who was nineteen years old, they had grumbled that Rev. Roblin must have made a mistake. They had hoped for a mature student who was married. After my first sermon, they decided that I would do just fine.

I now get to know Joan's siblings a little better – four brothers who are married and six more siblings who are single (two sisters and four brothers). Of the married brothers, Ross and his wife, Irene go out of their way to know their sister's new boyfriend. After church on the second Sunday of my arrival, we are invited to dinner. They live in Bridgeport, a suburb of Kitchener and they own a lovely brick house. The upstairs was rented to a young married couple who are grateful for lodging. (Housing is still scarce after the war, even though this is 1951). Ross and Irene have two children – three- year-old Ken and six-month-old David, who is just as cute as can be. Joan picks up David and loves him up. I watch with pleasure dreaming of the day when the baby she holds will be our own.

One Sunday evening, we attend Benton Street Baptist Church. After the service, we meet the young people. (Today, those same young people are now old folks who have me speak from time to time at their dinners for senior citizens). They are curious to see who the student pastor is that serves the mission on Stirling Avenue South. Pastor Roblin had had misgivings about a Sunday School mission that once boasted a Sunday School attendance of 150. (It was only a mile from the mother church).

It had started on a Sunday afternoon in the basement of the Cecil Roberts home. This was the beginning of the baby boom. To their credit, the Roberts had seized the opportunity. Obviously, the Roberts home couldn't handle the crowd of kids that flocked every Sunday to their basement. The compromise for a Sunday School was a small church that could be converted back to a house if the need for a Sunday School passed. Meantime, I am so convinced of my prowess as a preacher, I am sure that within a few weeks great crowds will pack our little auditorium to hear my divinely-inspired orations. After all, I was a Premillenial Pretribulational Dispensationalist who knew exactly where I stood on every issue.

One day, Joan introduced me to her aunt, a nurse at the Kitchener-Waterloo Hospital. Mistakenly, I took her for the aunt that Joan had described to me as her spiritual mentor and member of the Plymouth Brethren. They were a small layman-led denomination similar to Baptists in doctrine but very exclusive in their views. Aunt Bert, as I finally got to know her, would say to me, "It's not that you are wrong, Bruce, it's just that you are living up to the light that you have. When you finally get more light, you will become a member of the Brethren church."

So now I'm being introduced to Aunt Edna, but mistakenly I think its Joan's super-religious aunt and want to make a good impression, so I say,

"I'm so glad to meet you, I've heard so much about you. I also hear that you are a Premillenial Dispensationalist."

Poor Aunt Edna looked at me as though I were from Mars and gasped while Joan quickly intervened, "Oh, Bruce, you have the wrong person! I will introduce you to Aunt Bert some other day."

Aunt Bert Hosea, 1923, 22 years old

Romance will not be denied. Joan and I are talking marriage, even if that flouts the Bible school rules. With the optimism of youth, we are sure that if we marry, London Bible College will make an exception for our return to classes in September. We go shopping at People's Jewellers on King Street. We pick out an engagement ring for $200 for which we put fifty dollars down. We agree to payments of ten dollars a month, until it is paid for. Next we go to the Queen's Restaurant for lunch, where I place the ring her finger. It's official; Joan is now my fiancee. Excitedly, after lunch we cross the street to show it off to Pop Amy who works at Walker's Dry Goods store.

Joan says to me, "I'll bet Pop will say to me, did you buy the ring at Woolworth's?" To our amusement, Pop says, "I'm not surprised. I could see it coming. Did you buy the ring at Woolworth's?"

The twinkle in Pop's eyes and the smile on his face revealed he was only teasing us. Joan's reply was swift as she chuckled, "I told Bruce how you would respond and sure enough I was right."

However, when I broke the news to Rev. Leander Roblin, he expressed his disapproval. When I asked if I could stay on as pastor of Bethel come September, he replied, "Only if you postpone your marriage and go back to Bible School."

I would later learn to appreciate Leander Roblin as a friend, especially when he regaled me with the history of how our Independent Baptist denomination was formed. Meantime, my decision to marry would separate us. I was beginning to learn that the rules of London Bible Institute were ironclad. My confidence that LBI would allow me back wavered. While I was sorry to lose my appointment with the folks at Bethel, I was too much in love to change my plans. However, I did find a new opportunity to do preaching. Dr. Hugh Horner of First Baptist Church, Waterloo, invited me to teach the Young People's Sunday School class. I had an audience of forty young people every Sunday.

In the year 1951, the marriage law required anyone under the age of twenty-one to have at least one parent's written permission. My mother had by this time done a short stint in London Psychiatric Hospital, and was diagnosed as Schizophrenic. Unsure if her letter would be accepted, I opted for my father who wrote me a letter of permission that was accepted for a marriage licence. I pay my five dollars, and now the wedding can proceed.

When we understood that London Bible Institute was not going to bend the rules for us, we made alternate plans for our future. Joan got her old job back at the Bell Telephone Company, and I enrolled at Waterloo College, which at the time was an affiliate school with the University of Western Ontario. Our honeymoon nest would be two rooms at the Amys'. All this with five siblings still at home and three student boarders who also attended Waterloo College, plus Jack who worked in Waterloo and lived in the basement. By the sound of things, one would suppose the Amys lived in a multi-roomed castle. They didn't. With not a little sacrifice, there were two bedrooms surrendered for our little apartment. Two more with bunk beds for the students. One for Mom and Pop! Joan's sister Ruth slept on a cot off the living room, and four brothers had the attic. Jack got the basement.

When I look back, I am amazed at the sacrifices that the Amys made for their children and how hard they worked. But at the time, it all seemed quite normal. By today's standard, it would have raised a few eyebrows. The amazing thing is that it worked. Not only did everybody get along, but we also had fun. The Amys were so highly esteemed by relatives and friends, there was always company dropping in for a visit. Life for the senior Amys was so full that neither of them had to go anywhere for a holiday. They were content and fulfilled living at 117 Albert Street. Years later, I have often reflected on how rich they were, though, by today's standards, they would have been considered poor.

August 31 is the night before the wedding. I saw Joan on the 30th, but today I have been banned from my future in-laws', house. I am not to see the dress or my lover until she walks down the aisle of the church. I am alone all day, staying at Aunt Margaret's house. All the women are at the Amys', helping in the wedding preparations. Sandwiches must be made for sixty guests, who will be at the wedding but are not invited to the wedding dinner. Our budget only allows for seventy. Time hangs heavy while I am "patiently waiting" in a hurry. Finally, Margaret arrives in her stylish 1938 Chrysler. She has a note for me written by my lover.

The original note 58 years later

September 1, 1951. At 3:00 P.M. I am standing at the front of the Immanuel Evangelical United Brethern Church. Rev. George Barthel faces me, and Lorne Pflug is at the pipe organ, playing Mendelssohn's wedding march. Joan's brother Bill is my best man. There are 400 people at our wedding because all the people who attended Catherine Sweitzer's wedding an hour earlier know both these church girls. After all, you can't beat a wedding for people watching.

At just the precise moment, Rev. Barthel gives me the signal indicating that I am to turn and look up the aisle in order to get my first glimpse of my beautiful bride in her gorgeous wedding gown. The train of her dress touches the carpeted aisle. It had been hand made by Lillian, Joan's mother. It is still perfectly preserved and hanging in our closet. It's a good thing because Sara, our youngest daughter wore it eight times when she starred in amateur theatre in the stage production Our Town.

I think, "There she is: Joan Amy is shortly to be my wife!" Accompanied by her father ever looking the part of the Christian gentleman, Oliver escorts his daughter to the altar. When Rev. Barthel says, "Who gives this woman to this man?" he smiles, and Joan steps beside me to change her name to mine. Joan's sister Mary is her maid

190

of honour. Her youngest sister Ruth is also there, along with two nieces, Nancy and Lynne, who are junior bridesmaids.

Waiting outside the church was the bridal car appropriately decorated by Joan's brother Ross [1950 Studebaker]

I have an issue to resolve at our wedding. Mother is recently remarried to a farmer by the name of Jim Langford who truly loves her. It is a marriage of convenience. Mother married Jim for security. She does not want my father and Jim to meet. My father will attend the wedding with his second wife, Phyllis. Mother does not want comparisons made between her former husband and Jim. As a farmer, Jim knows that, compared with the slick super salesman, he comes off second best. She convinces him to drop her off at the church and to put in the time elsewhere. I marvel at Jim's accommodation and admire him for his grace while he is being shortchanged. He is invited to a sandwich lunch for supper with about sixty others we couldn't afford to feed at the official reception.

My father's wedding gift was a car which he rented and provided for our honeymoon. It is a British-built 1951 Prefect. I explain to Dad that the situation is too touchy to have him and Phyllis at the reception. Mother will be there. He seems to understand and complies, returning to Toronto immediately after the wedding. Joan and I plan to visit them when we return the rented car. In spite of these complications, there seems to be enough good will to go around. Jim Langford should have been insulted, but he forgives mother for her vanity, hanging around long enough to pick her up after the reception. Later that evening he takes her home to the farm.

That farm is to be the occasion of some very happy times for us, especially after Mark, our first child is born. Fifty-seven years later, my wife not only bears my name, but also she is still the most beautiful girl in all the world. She has that rare gift that would be the envy of every Hollywood starlet. She never seems to age. At age eighty, she deceivingly looks sixty-five years old.

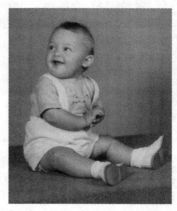

16 months after our marriage, our son Mark arrived
on December 18th. Fifty-six years later he is now
the pastor of Rowandale Baptist Church, Winnipeg, Manitoba

Chapter 28

The Honeymoon.

I used to wonder if it were right to love Joan more than I loved God. If that was an issue before marriage, it certainly wasn't afterwards. It doesn't take too long to realize that there is a significant difference. The New Testament uses two distinct words for love, one is for human love. The other is "agape" the word for divine love. When it comes to human love, a few arguments will take care of that issue quite nicely. Ollie, Joan's sister-in-law, had told us before we were married. "You will have more arguments that first year of marriage than you will for the rest of your married life." Armed with this information, which we promptly forgot, we plunged headlong into matrimony fully prepared for life.

Stratford, Sunday, September 2, 1951.

"Good morning, Mrs. Woods. This is the first day of our married life," I rapturously said. At least, I think I said something like that. I don't quite remember. That first day was memorable to say the least. Someone had spread confetti all through our suitcase, and the hotel room at the Stratford Windsor Hotel was a mess. Checkout time was 11.00 A.M. and we were hungry. We had just made it to our car in the parking lot when suddenly the hotel clerk was chasing us down. He was obviously all in a flap.

"Wait up," he cried, "I've made a terrible mistake. I've got to charge your seven dollars more than you paid."

"Why so?" I remarked, a little surprised and peeved.

"I gave you the Bridal Suite but only charged you the regular rate," He blurted.

Joan and I looked at each other as though we were being defrauded. We are both thinking the same thing: "Is this guy on the level or is he a charlatan? Or maybe he discovered all the confetti." We only have a hundred dollars for our honeymoon. By the time we leave the hotel, we are down to $93.00. We put this out of our minds. We go to Wong's Café and order a hot chicken sandwich. Next, we stroll through the Shakespearean Gardens and gaze at the Avon River. It is a beautiful day and the sun is shining. We want to get back to Waterloo for the rest of our luggage, because Aunt Marg has given us the use of her cottage at Sauble Beach (it used to belong to Pop Amy) for our honeymoon. We need to arrive before nightfall. I delay things a little with a visit to Aunt Elsie and Uncle Gord's place and introduce Joan to my Grandma. Our visit is brief, and soon we are back at the Amys' by 2:30 P.M. We are all hugs and smiles. As usual, the house is swarming with visitors. Everybody is greeting the newlyweds with fresh congratulations. Dorothy Shaub and her husband Roy are among the wellwishers. Suddenly, Joan gets a brainwave.

"Bruce, why don't we invite Dorothy and Roy to accompany us to the cottage? It will fun."

"Okay by me, just so long as you are there."

Dorothy and Roy are grinning. They are a little bit surprised at the invitation. Since it's the Labour Day weekend and there's nothing planned, they quickly agree and hurry home to pack. An hour later, two cars are heading north. The destination is Sauble Beach! We had an idyllic weekend at Sauble. The weather was warm, and the holiday crowd gave added excitement. We made some of our own excitement that has given us some laughs ever since. No sooner had we retired for the evening and turned out the lights than the bed collapsed. At first, we suspected shenanigans on the part of somebody to embarrass us. Later, when we related our "incident" to the amusement of friends and family, they all claimed innocence. The mystery of the collapsing bed is unresolved to this day.

Since Roy had to go to work on Tuesday, we said our goodbyes on Labour Day. Tuesday, we enjoyed a beautiful day taking in the scenery and just being together. However, on Wednesday the weather turned cold; furthermore, the beach was deserted. When the weather is bad and the beach is devoid of people, it is amazing how a place so favoured and beautiful can suddenly lose its appeal. By suppertime, we realized we were bored, so Joan suggested that we pack up and visit her Aunt and Uncle Ernst in Mildmay. Suddenly our honeymoon took on more zest when we knew that tomorrow we had a planned-for destination. We are already learning the richness of family. After a leisurely breakfast, we packed the car, locked the cottage, and said goodbye to a place that would include many happy days to come, so much so that our firstborn son, who is now more than fifty years old, speaks about the wonderful memories at Sauble.

The drive to Mildmay is pleasant. This is September and the fields are ripe for harvest. The trees are just beginning their annual colour festival. The corn is high. There is freshness in the air that speaks of fall. A very surprised aunt and uncle welcome these newlyweds, and served us an old fashioned supper of sausage and sauerkraut. By Friday, we were home at 117 Albert Street. Joan Amy, now Joan Woods, has a new achievement under her belt. During our honeymoon, I taught her how to drive a car complete with brake and clutch. Holding the car still on a hill, balancing clutch and gas, while waiting for a traffic light to change, is a real achievement. Joan passed with flying colours – that is, until she stalls the car two blocks from home. Panic is brief. She makes it right into the driveway with a little help from her tutor.

My wife Joan and me six weeks after we were married at a youth convention in Hamilton, Ontario, 1951

Thirty years later at a costume party at Stanley Avenue Baptist Church, Hamilton. Joan was Lydia, a seller of purple (see the book of Acts, New Testament)
I was C.J. Loney who was pastor of Stanley for 46 years from 1915 to 1961.
He was noted for his high collars and spats.

Chapter 29

An Old-Fashioned Sunday School Picnic

When I was a child, my mother took me to church (for a while), and it was then that I attended my first Sunday School picnic. I can no longer recall the events. I just remember how excited I was to go. A lifetime of ministry has its rewards. I now relate that nostalgic charmer with not a little regret at its passing – the old-fashioned Sunday School picnic. I choose only one of at least forty, I have attended. This one was special because it was the most memorable. It happened in 1970 when I was pastor of the Ruth Morton Baptist Church in Vancouver.

(Historical note: Ruth Morton was the wife of John Morton, Vancouver's first settler. Most are not aware that before Vancouver received its name, it was called Morton's Shack. Later as a love tribute to his wife, Morton gave the funds to build the Ruth Morton Memorial Baptist church. I call that place Canada's Taj Mahal.)

Our Sunday School superintendent Jay Perkins held up the jar of jelly beans before the children. "Whoever can guess how many jelly beans are in this jar wins the whole jar – provided you attend the the Sunday School picnic in June."

The kids are cheering. Every kid (over 200 of them) is sure he or shey can guess the correct number and come home with the prize. In today's affluent society, candy is no longer a bribe. I had already noticed the previous year that there was a decline in attendance at the annual Sunday School picnic and had my own challenge in the ready.

It was a Sunday morning in May and I had just read off the announcements, "Now for all you men who think the Sunday School picnic is just for kids, I have a challenge. When we come to the 100-yard dash, I have a dollar bill for every man in this church who thinks he can beat me in the race."

The congregation roared their approval and accepted the call to arms (well, in this case, feet). The talk of the church that day over Sunday dinner was how to bankrupt the pastor at the picnic.

When I first accepted the call to Ruth Morton Baptist, the aging campgrounds at Point Roberts was put up for sale by our denomination for a new facility on Vancouver Island called Camp Quanos. Our church purchased the old campgrounds for $15,000 and took over the twelve acres located on the American side of the forty-ninth parallel known as Point Roberts. Years ago by an oversight, that valuable land (accessible only through Canada) was ceded to the USA by sloppy Canadian ministers who were ignorant of west coast geography. Canada has tried many times to purchase what naturally fits into the greater Vancouver area but failed because of the valuable fishing rights that go with the peninsula. In 1970, crossing into the United States to Point Roberts was only a formality for Canadians, who make up ninety percent of the landowners. Our picnic was to be held on our own campgrounds in Point Roberts.

Saturday, June 27 was sunny and the best picnic ever was about to commence. Food preparation had been under the able supervision of Edith Patterson. My wife Joan was to make her famous egg salad sandwiches which included chopped up walnuts, onions, and a dash of sugar. All the staples of the annual picnic were arranged with ladies having made their salmon and ham sandwiches. Chocolate cake for dessert and home-baked cookies of every kind were packed in the picnic baskets that were now arriving by the carful. Car after car kept coming. Between the jellybean jar and the pastor's challenge for the 100-yard dash, the ruse had worked. In the end, over 300 parents and children were present. The festivities were on. The attendance was phenomenal.

Beatrice Blight was in charge of the little tykes, and mothers lined up for the toddlers' race at one end and the kindergaarden kids' at the other. Some of them didn't seem too prepped to run as they had to be persuaded by their mothers that this was a race to win. What this race is really designed to do is to demonstrate how sweet the toddlers look. Competition didn't really get under way until the older kids lined up. First came the six-year-olds, and so on up the ladder. Seven-year-olds complained that it wasn't fair to have to run against eight-year-olds when there just weren't enough of them to make a decent race. Not to complain; they would get their chance again in other races such as the three-legged race that tied two kids together (left leg to right with cloth bandages that didn't hurt when you tied the knot). Provided one could stay upright without falling on the ground, one could finish the race which in itself was quite an achievement. If that didn't net you a ribbon, then one could always compete in the sack race. Remember those old 100 pound capacity cotton bags for potatoes. We saved them up from year to year so that the kids could step into them and jump their way to the finish line. As the day wore on the children could proudly wear their awards. The blue ribbon was for first prize, the red for second, and for third prize, it was white. The last event before the adult races was the candy scramble. Individually wrapped kisses and carmels were pitched high into the air with each age group snatching them up as they landed on the ground. Proud parents brought out their movie cameras (provided they could afford them) and the action preserved for posterity.

The day wore on as the latecomers arrived. There was Clifford Gropp and his wife. They had responded to a Saturday blitz campaign when we dropped off flyers at every door in the neighbourhood. Cliff was now a Ruth Morton regular. (He was in trouble with the law when we contacted him, later I had stood up for him in court when the judge gave him a suspended sentence on the promise of good behaviour.) The best thing about church is how people from every walk of life fellowship together. Inner healing is a beautiful race in itself.

After the children's races were over the next phase began for the young people or adults who fancied themselves young enough to compete. The obstacle race is a case in point. Not exactly a triathelon but good enough for our crowd, it was our test for the strong. First it was the girls and then the guys. Lining up for the signal the competitors were required to crawl under a tarp. Next it was the run to the water pots all lined up which required a running jump to clear the last pail of water. Remember those potatoe sacks. That comes next. The final was crawling through the monkey bars with a final sprint to the finish line.

The last phase in the races was for the couples, married or courting or partners chosen that day for the fun. With everybody paired off the fun begins. First was the grapefruit race. In this event the girls lined up with half a grapefruit in their hands. With the signal given, they raced forty yards to their guy who proceeds to eat the grapefruit without touching it with their hands. The girls could turn their grapefruit any which way to hurry the process but the guys had to keep their hands behind their back. After the grapefruit was eaten, hand in hand they made it back to the starting line. First couple across the line wins the prize; a flashlight for the men and a doll for the girls. The needle and thread race came next. Usually the same couples paired for this race too. The guys race the fifty yards to their partner who is holding the needle. After threading the needle, they return to the finish line. For this race, good eyesight helps. In previous years, the biggest and most watched funnerama was the egg toss. This year "the beat the pastor race" has trumped everything. The event required married couples to line up ten feet apart and play a game of catch with an uncooked egg. After the first round, the couples take a step back and pitch the egg back and forth until one breaks (the yolk's on you). Lose your egg and you're out of the competition. Of course it gets better as each round is followed by one step back. The distance between couples is now stretched to the "breaking point" as one couple after another catches an egg that goes squish, and the crowd squeals with delight. Ed and Beatrice Blight were famous for winning this competition year after year. The egg toss really gets interesting when the couples are pitching their egg back and forth when they're forty feet apart. Usually by this time, by process of elimination there are only two or three couples still in the contest. Finally Ed and Beatrice Blight at fifty-five feet apart won the contest yet again for another year.

Saving the best till last, Ed Blight calls for the long-awaited men's 100 yard dash. I have twenty one-dollar bills in my pocket for a worst case scenario. My wife Joan is sure my challenge will cost us a week's groceries, but I am not worried. I have been training for three months and at age thirty-eight, I am fit. Ed Blight has a sense of humour. His call to action is prefaced by these words:"All the men who have taken the pastor's challenge, line up; the cardiac emergency unit is parked at the camp gate and we are ready."

The year previous, we had eleven men in this event; today we have thirty-three and three hundred spectators. The race of the century is about to begin.

"Get ready, get set, go!" Ed hawks and the race is on.

I have a slow start and most of the men are ahead of me. "This is going to cost me money," I think as we thunder down to the finish line. Most of the guys are my age and even if they are younger, they haven't figured on the need for training.

It was a great show because all the ladies were rooting for their pastor. At the seventy-five yard mark the lack of training showed as my competitors began to fade. A come-from-behind photo finish saw me in fourth place. The only guys that beat me were three teenage jocks, brothers John and David Duncan and Don Scott. I should have limited the race to married men. I would have come in first with a dazzling show of a come-from- behind win. Laughingly, I paid off the three teens who looked a little guilty taking their dollar from the pastor. Not too guilty. Nobody offered to give it back.

The Sunday School picnic-to-end-all-picnics finished off with supper at the tables set up in the dining hall. As the sun was setting, everybody agreed they had had a lot of fun. Of course, no Sunday School picnic is complete without a game of softball. We always choose up sides and I am the umpire. I have no intention of letting our people know that I can't play softball without striking out. Being an umpire has distinct advantages, and it gives me the authority to announce with gusto. "You're out at home plate!"

Many picnics have come and gone but this Sunday School picnic was the most talked about picnic for years. Alas, the tradition of an old- fashioned Sunday School picnic went out with the advent of the barbeque and the arrival of organized sport. In its heyday from Mark Twain's Tom Sawyer to the 1970's, it was the best social event of the year. About those jelly beans, I just can't quite remember who won that prize, but given the nature of the challenge, it must have been a boy – or was it a g—

Chapter 30
Dallas Theological Seminary

In 1955, Jim Langford died. What a shock, a heart seizure took him at fifty-five, leaving my mother with a small inheritance after the farm was sold. All this took time. Meanwhile, wanting to be near her son, my mother took employment caring for an elderly man from Elora. This arrangement gave her spending money, and a roof over her head while she waited for Jim's will to pass through probate. Jim had neglected to make out a will. With her husband now dead and bereft of the farm, Mother quickly succumbed to her depression. Mental illness defies the best of counselors. We were soon dealing with all the old demons. Every week, I could see her deterioration.

Two and a half years at Arthur were full of interesting events. One Sunday, out of the blue and unannounced, my father paid us a visit after the church service. His Cadillac, parked outside as we left the service, made the impression he desired on our rural congregation. Michael, my fourteen-year-old-half brother, was with him. As ever, my father asked about my mother and offered to take us for a car ride to Elora to see her. My wife, Joan, saw through that quickly and wouldn't hear of it. It would have stirred old wounds that I believe were at the root of Mother's illness. I have often wondered in later years if my father nursed a secret love for her. My Mother didn't need more frustration than she already had. Mental illness is not a stimulus for glamour even in a woman as beautiful as my Mother. She would have been horrified to have him see her. My father saw our consternation and let the matter drop. In the seven years of life he had left to live, we protected Mother from such an encounter. My father had to settle for carefully edited reports.

Later years: My dad and his Cadillac seven years after this photo was taken he died. taken he died.

My mom with her treasures, she had the better part.

Mother kept her little job until Jim Langford's estate was settled, then to my chagrin, she quit. Ever the generous one, her first endeavour was to hand us $3000 to buy a new car. We revelled in our new-found wealth for a week. That's when I had my epiphany. I announced it to my wife,

"I don't believe we should spend this money to buy a new car. I believe God wants me to use it for Seminary training. I want to go to Dallas Theological Seminary."

It didn't occur to me that my mother would be saddened by this; that came later. The joy of her generosity had unintended consequences. The transferred use of her monetary generosity would deprive her of my immediate presence, an ominous turn of events for a lonely widow with mental liabilities. Still, she reluctantly agreed.

Of more importance to me at the time was my wife's concurrence. That was assured; Joan instantly agreed. She wanted me to be the best in the ministry. To her, the sacrifice of a new car was worth it. We both subscribed to the idea that the road to success in the ministry lay through a first-rate seminary training. In our eyes, Dallas was it. I have since placed my confidence elsewhere but will speak of that later. My zeal for excellence in the ministry did not include my mother's need for the sole person left in her life. Years later, I would reconsider all that with a mixed review.

Dallas Theological Seminary 1960

*Pleasant Grove Bible Church, Dallas where
I spent a year as student pastor*

-oOo-

When we set out for Dallas in our used 1950 Dodge purchased in Detroit (cars were cheaper there), it was June 1956. Car radio blasting, we were full of anticipation of the adventure awaiting us. "Standing on the Corner Watching All the Girls Go By" was popular at the time. We heard it often along with other songs popular in the fifties. The idyllic weather of a Canadian summer was gradually exchanged for the oppressive heat of the south. We were a young couple with two children (Mark was three and a half, Debbie was eighteen months) on the trip of a lifetime. With enthusiasm, we plotted our course and pored over the map of the United States. Terre Haute, Indiana; Vandalia, Illinois; not the most exciting cities when you look at them up close.

East St. Louis appalled us but we pressed on. Little Rock seemed more progressive. At last we reached Texarkana and sacred soil. Well do I remember the Dallas city limits sign, "600.000 people cannot be wrong". We arrived midday at Dallas Theological Seminary; the temperature was 101 degrees Fahrenheit (36 degrees Celcius).

We picked up the keys of our school-owned apartment (there were plenty of vacancies until school started in September). I had not reckoned on how hot Dallas was in the summer. We had arrived and wondered if we had just made the biggest mistake of our lives. Strangers in an unfamiliar city, we had the name of our former pastor's brother. When we called Ken Horner, nothing would do but to meet for dinner at their house that very day. Once again we were to learn how valuable friendship can be for two lonely people.

It had only been five years since I had made good money selling Fuller Brushes door to door. I would repeat my Canadian success in Dallas.

What I didn't know at the time was that the advent of the automobile and the shopping plaza had revolutionized the way goods are bought and sold. In actual fact, you could say that Dallas's Casa Linda Shopping Center had been the prototype for all of North America. Casa Linda was the territory that had been given to me. I set out on a hot day (temperature 110 degrees Fahrenheit, or 45 degrees Celcius) with my sample case of products, rejoicing that at last I would be making some real money. When I returned home, sadly I had to report to Joan, that the day's earning was $2.15, and I was exhausted from the heat. Disillusioned, I went job hunting (green card in hand; they were so easy to get in those days). Later that week, I awoke one night to find Joan at the window quietly weeping.

"I'm homesick to see Mom and Pop." she cried. I had to admit, so was I.

When you feel a sense of call to the ministry, it gives you a determination to stick things out. We never entertained any ideas of quitting. Adjustments had to be made and that's the end of it. It helped to meet other married Canadian students who were toughing it out but were now in their second year. Rev. Norman Forge, who was an American but had served in my first home church in London, Ontario, also helped. He would have the Canadian students over to his house, serve us a supper in the church basement, and help us to meet fellow lonely hearts who were adjusting just like us. I eventually landed a job as a public relations assistant at Goodwill Industries. To this day I'm not sure which institution served me better, Goodwill Industries or Dallas Theological Seminary. The Goodwill movement introduced me to the working poor as well as the supporting rich.

However, perhaps I should explain how all this came about.

Chapter 31
Goodwill Industries

After I had worked for three weeks at dead end jobs, Joan was scouring the employment ads for me. The days were long for Joan who had two children to entertain. Like a lot of other seminary wives, she hung out with similarly bored and discontent women, while their husbands were away during the day at summer employment.

The children, blissfully unaware of their parents' discontent, played in plastic summer pools or traded dolls and tricycles. That's when Joan discovered an employment agency looking for college students for part- time work. I applied and they placed me with Goodwill Industries. The fee for the job was 40% of my earnings for the first three weeks, gratefully picked up by my Goodwill Industries boss.

At last I had a steady income making, $1.50 per hour at what proved to be a learning curve that paralleled the things I was learning at seminary. Had I put the knowledge acquired in promotion and public relations at Goodwill Industries to business, I could have had a lucrative professional career with Goodwill Industries or elsewhere. When the offer eventually came, it was no contest. Seven years later when I was in Vancouver, the offer came again from the Toronto organization with the same results. I had been called to the ministry; to the ministry I was completely devoted.

Just before school started, we moved into a subsidized housing complex in the west end of Dallas. It was in the middle of a rundown part of the city. There were six blocks of housing set aside for students who were pursueing their careers in a variety of professions. Eventually these students would become doctors, lawyers, accountants, and ministers. It was at last a solution to Joan's malaise because during the day, the wives, who were a gifted and intelligent bunch, had great discussions. Meanwhile, the children of all such revelled in the usual squabbles and conflicts at which preschool children excel. One such friend was Marilyn Salovich whose husband was training to be a neurosurgeon. One day Marilyn dropped in for a visit. Exasperated with her two year old, she blurted out, "Joan, how do you stay so calm with your kids when they misbehave?"

Her reply was classic Christianity.

"Why, when I don't know what to do, I just pray and ask God for wisdom, and God usually answers my prayer."

Startled, Marilyn simply changed the subject and the conversation ended when she crossed the back lawn to her townhouse some fifty feet away.

The following day, Marilyn came by the second time and said,

"Joan, I have not been able to stop thinking about what you said the other day about prayer and the children. Just what do you mean when you say you pray to God for wisdom." That was the beginning of a fruitful friendship that resulted in Marilyn's conversion and eventually that of her husband, Ed.

Unlike me, Ed was a great athlete and loved to play basketball. You can imagine my surprise when I learned that he was playing on our church team with Charles Ryrie, my theology professor, who was a recognized author and a favourite professor. We all attended First Baptist Church where Dr. W. A. Criswell was the pastor. Ed Salovich went on to become a leading physician in Minneapolis.

Another friend was Gloria. Her husband Bob Gromacki became my best friend at Dallas Seminary. We always sat together in lectures. In contrast to me with my mediocre marks, Bob graduated with 450 points out of a possible 450 points. In other words, he never suffered the humiliation of having a B in any course he took. Bob eventually became a professor at Cedarville College, Ohio. He was the author of over thirty textbooks that were widely used throughout the USA and the world. When I took a student pastorate for a year at the Pleasant Grove Bible church, Bob and his wife Gloria attended. He said he liked my preaching and predicted that I would win the Harry Ironside prize for preaching. I didn't. Fellow classmate Charles Sell won the prize, and to be truthful, I was jealous.

My boss Charlene McLain liked to use our family for promotional pictures for the Dallas newspapers. This one was to promote the sale of a surplus of donated shoes. The following photo was to promote the Boy Scouts' collection for Goodwill Industries

Goodwill Industries taught me style. I had the advantage of looking through the store and catching the good stuff after it had been processed.

I had only been there a month when I spotted the most gorgeous double-breasted navy blue suit I had ever seen. I needed a suit and it fit me perfectly. Shortly after my purchase that cost me all of $10.00, I was invited to speak on behalf of Goodwill Industries at the prestigious Park Cities Lion's Club. Naturally I wanted to look my best and wore the suit to class, then bolted quickly to the Lion's Club luncheon held at the Park Cities Country club. I was proud to be properly dressed for such an auspicious occasion. I even had a good car, because I drove the Goodwill Chevrolet station wagon and parked it beside the Cadillacs that lined the entrance.

That should have been the tip-off, but I was too naïve to know. I was warmly received by the greeter who promptly wrote out a visitor name tag. It was a cardboard pocket stuffer that should have fit my lapel pocket, except that my lapel pocket was covered by the very wide lapel that rendered his welcome service extremely difficult. That welcome pocket stuffer jammed sideways into my lapel pocket just kept falling out.

When I purchased my suit, all I had looked at was quality cloth. My problem was that it was ten years out of style. Sheepishly, I looked at every suit jacket in the room. All of them without an exception had narrow lapels. With my wide lapels that reached almost to my shoulders, given a good stiff wind, I could have glided to my next destination.

"My suit is old and out of style," I thought, "and everybody in this room knows I'm just a country bumpkin who has just had a humiliating epiphany." There I am party to a small group of businessmen, red-faced and trying to concentrate on a half-finished conversation by three polished gentleman who were discussing something about the track.

" – and five minutes after the payout, that horse dropped dead in its stall."
Suddenly those men were laughing and to be polite, I laughed too, even though I had no idea what the joke was. It took me till the next day to figure that one out. The ensuing chatter was all about business and fast women. I came to a speedy conclusion I was definitelyout of my element.

Rescued by the call to dinner, I sat down to the largest salad I had ever seen. "That thing is so big I'll never have room for my meal," I thought. The men seemed to know what to order, but the waitress could see that I was as green as the salad that was placed in front of me.
"Sir," said the kindly waitress, "what dressing would you like?"
I had no idea how to answer the question so to gain a little time, I said, "What kind do you have?"
"Catalina, Ranch, House, vinegar and oil, or Thousand Island."
Terrified that I might say the wrong thing, I replied,
"Thousand Island," hoping that I would like whatever that turned out to be. I composed myself, knowing that I had faked it; however, as things turned out, it was the right choice. It was a first time-experience and I liked it. Later that evening I told Joan all about the most delicious dressing I had ever tasted, and the salad that I thought was far too large for anyone to eat, and how I devoured every scrap. Next, I ordered the best steak I had ever eaten. When at last I was invited to speak, I finally gained my confidence. At last I was in my element and given the compliments I received, I knew I was on safe ground. Careful to remove that ridiculous name tag before I spoke, I prayed a prayer and things turned out well.

During my four years at Goodwill, as I completed my Master of Theology degree, I spoke at many service clubs where the members were run-of-the-mill ordinary types with whom I felt at home. Why my first club had to be the classiest joint in Dallas is beyond me, but it sure catapulted me into the world of fashion like I never could have imagined.

Charlene McClain was my boss and a seasoned newspaper woman who reminded me of my chain smoking stepmother, Phyllis. She taught me   how to write a newspaper article and the way to promote your big idea. She was a skeptic when it came to Christianity and never went to church. Hard as nails and demanding to work for, she knew her stuff. I learned the ropes by following her example. Gerald Clore was the CEO and pretty well delegated everything to a well-developed staff that was devoted to his leadership. When I graduated from Dallas Seminary, he invited me into his office. Imagine my surprise when he tried to convince me to stay on for a year as his understudy before moving on to a new opening in Washington. It was a lovely gesture on his part, but I never gave it a second thought. My calling was to the ministry.

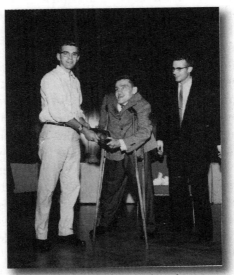

In 1959 one of our handicapped employees was chosen as "National Goodwill Employee of the Year"

Money was always a problem for a married student who had a wife and two children to support. I worked an average of twenty-six hours a week to provide. No wonder my marks were mediocre. I gave blood every six months because the hospital paid $20.00 a pint. I would have given it every three months if I could, but they had these rules. To complicate things further, our son David was born a year before I graduated. We conscientiously tried to pay our bills but eventually found ourselves three months in arrears for our rental accommodation. What a shock to receive an eviction notice. I can still hear the worried voice of my wife as she explained to her mother back in Canada that we might find ourselves on the street with three kids to feed.

"Mom, what are we going to do?" She exclaimed on the phone.
"Now don't you worry, Joan; maybe the family can help."
That's exactly what happened. Joan's eldest brother, Nelson, forwarded the necessary funds, three months rent to the penny, and at last we were caught up. When I finally graduated from seminary we had paid our tuition for four years and left for Canada with only $700 of debt that we paid off the following year.

My first church was Maple Avenue Baptist Church in Georgetown. We had members who met in the Oddfellows Hall when I came. One year later we had purchased land and built a brand new church. It was such a beautiful building that it was literally the talk of the town. We often thought of those eventful years at Dallas, however, we would relive them again on a very sad occasion. Three years later, I was in the car listening to the radio when a news bulletin interrupted the program. It was Friday, November 22, when the horrific news broke.

"President J. F. Kennedy has just been assassinated in Dallas." Talk about a flashback. I knew those streets like the back of my hand. I had often been in the radio station across the street from the Texas Book Depository Building, that Lee Harvey Oswald used when he killed President Kennedy. I knew the parade route and had walked those very sidewalks. Those momentous events registered with me as though I had actually been present for the whole thing. As the old hymn writer wrote,

"Life at best is very brief,
Like the falling of a leaf,
Like the binding of a sheaf:
    Be in time!
Fleeting days are telling fast
That the die will soon be cast,
And the fatal line be passed:
    Be in time!"

Chapter 32
Mother

When we left Canada for Dallas, I felt no guilt about using Mother's money for the furtherance of my education. I assumed the whole endeavour was from God; therefore the decision was God's will. As the Bible says, "Whosoever loveth mother or father more than me is not worthy of me." I clearly believed that attending Dallas Seminary was God's call upon our lives.

Fifty years later, I have a different viewpoint. My mother's nature was to sacrifice for others, especially if that meant the welfare of her son. Youth has yet to learn these lessons. If I could do it over again, I would have looked for a university like Western in London and taken an MA in communications or religion. Anything that would have enhanced my education. That way I could have kept an eye on Mother and pursued my dreams using another venue. Other seminary alternatives were available, I simply didn't want to consider any of them. I could have attended a Canadian seminary; in hindsight, the sharpening of the mind is the real issue. One can enlarge the knowledge of theology simply by the reading of books. Mother's mental deterioration was tragic, and the one person who should have been there was 1500 miles away in Dallas. I wrote her letters every week, but I should have been by her side when she needed help.

Thankfully, God intervened and in spite of my neglect spared her. After I graduated from Dallas and returned to Canada, I took a mother who was not much more than skin and bones to the London Psychiatric Hospital where she recuperated. She left the hospital to return to the only occupation she could handle, caring for a widower who wanted to hire a housekeeper. His name was Sid Jones and six months later they married. It was a gift from God who understands the zeal of his called ones. He is the One who compensates for our lack of insight due to immaturity and egotism.

My time at Dallas Seminary was not the rewarding experience that I imagined. I made the best of it, but in reality I was a fish out of water. Dallas, which demanded proficiency in Greek and Hebrew, was a great place for a man gifted in languages. My gifts lay elsewhere, but Dallas didn't offer the kind of courses I longed for. I found myself grinding at the mill where I was least proficient. My stint at Goodwill Industries was the compensating gift. I learned public relations and promotion which stood me in good stead in the ministry. It was God's wonderful way of coming to the rescue of a zealous disciple who was misplaced in a seminary where he didn't fit. Sometimes with the best of intentions, we pursue a less rewarding course of action. Isn't it wonderful how God can compensate us for an inadequate decision. Given the wisdom of hindsight, we would never make a mistake and wouldn't need any help from God. We are inefficient by design; that's how we learn humility. Learning to step aside and letting God do the work is how we really learn.

God rewarded my mother with a third marriage that gave her the best life one could have hoped for. Because Sid Jones was a retired CNR man, he had a lifetime pass to travel anywhere in Canada by rail. Sid and my mother were able to travel free to Vancouver when we ministered there. They often took trips to Toronto. Sid loved my mother and put up with her bouts of depression. I like to think that God rewarded her for sacrificing on behalf of her son. When Sid died, we arranged for mother to have a little apartment near our church in Hamilton. In the last three years of her life, I was able to be the son she deserved to have.

Chapter 33
That Unforgetable Day

It is September 11, 2001. There is not a man or woman alive that will forget where they were on the day that the Trade Center in New York City was destroyed by terrorists. Incidentally, that is my wife's birthday, and we were looking forward to an uneventful day concluding with a family party. To make the occasion special, we had travelled to Grand Rapids, Michigan, to visit our son David. Instead of celebrating the commonplace joys of life, like the whole world we were glued to the television and watched the awful events of that day in horror.

The following day when we returned to our home in Ancaster, crossing the bridge from Port Huron to Sarnia we witnessed the lineup of trucks on the Canadian side. The drivers were sitting together in groups, chatting. There was no need for explanations. Everyone knew what was happening at the border. As we sped our way home, the traffic lane on our left was stalled with the transports that a day earlier would have long been on their way to their respective destinations. Witnessing that growing lineup now twenty kilometers long gave us a foreboding malaise that lingered long in our spirits. President Bush had called for a day of mourning on Friday, September 14. I knew in my heart that our city of Hamilton must be a part of that memorial Day.

On Wednesday evening, a day later, I called Rev. Hannes of the Lutheran Church who was president of our Hamilton Downtown Ecumenical Ministerial. I said, "The two of us have got to make an executive decision, there isn't time for a ministerial meeting." Hannes agreed. With only two days for preparation, we planned a day of mourning on the spot. The full executive would find out after the fact. Immediately, I was on the phone informing all the radio and TV stations. Next came the newspapers. Thursday, Hannes and I were arranging all the participants for a Service of Mourning and Prayer.

Since I had initiated the whole thing, I determined that I would take no part in the service. Mine was the satisfaction that it had happened. I would have remained anonymous, but the Hamilton Spectator in their Saturday coverage blew my cover by calling me the "organizer." The service was uplifting and the various clergy did a remarkable job, especially Dr. James R. Dickey of St. Paul's Presbyterian, who gave the address. It was gratifying to stand back and see the whole day unfold.

The location of the service was the front steps of City Hall. I had informed the media without official permission. Next, I informed City Hall. Permission would have to come later. With this accomplished, I called the new mayor of Hamilton, Bob Wade. He was out of town on business. At last, I reached Deputy Mayor Tom Jackson, who came to our aid, and all the arrangements were finalized.

Hannes and I were involved in nonstop activity. The clock was ticking. Our ministerial executive gathered Friday morning of September 14, still unaware of our plans. Naturally, they were surprised. There was a moment's pause and then, Malcolm Curtis said, "Well, what are we waiting for?"
There was instant unanimity. When they heard the news, there could be no dissent. They understood. We quickly adjourned and headed for City Hall. The service began at noon.

As preparations were being made, it occurred to me that I should contact the Muslim community about our plans.   I knew they were grieving just as much as the rest of us. When Javed Mirja heard what we had decided, he immediately asked if his Imam, Ramzan Manek, could participate. At first, his request surprised me, but as I thought about it, I realized it was only right that they should have a part of what was, in the end, a civic gathering, albeit a Christian one.   Meantime, the word was spreading that the organizer of the event was me. That's when the Fire Chief phoned me and asked if they could participate. I said that it would be most fitting, since so many firemen had died in that tragedy.

The day for the service was warm and beautiful. With such short notice, I did wonder how many would be there. As things turned out, upwards of 200 people showed up. Later that night, the television coverage was gratifying. I had acted on an impulse. The impulse had proven to be good. Thanks to the liberal coverage by the media andthe city of Hamilton, everyone who shared a vital interest participated. A week later, Mayor Bob Wade phoned me and thanked me for taking the initiative. It was a fresh lesson to me that it's important to follow the leanings of our heart.

Chapter 34
Family

When you marry a spouse, you also gain a family. I was the richer for having married a girl who was one of eleven. My wife, Joan Amy, brought more to our marriage than I did. I was an only child. To tell the beautiful story of the Amy family, I must dip into the past. Oliver Amy was English but grew up in a German settlement halfway between Elmira and Elora, Ontario. He was fluent in both English and German. He married Lillie Marth who gave him two sons, Nelson and Reginald. Then tragedy struck when Lily died of an asthma attack at age thirty-eight.

A year later, the grieving widower married Lily Ann Seiling, a milliner from Mildmay, who gave him three sons and a daughter. Not a bad start for a second family now numbering six with five more to come. Oliver and Lily were prospering. Growing up in the retail business, Oliver learned and watched for an opportunity to start his own store. With a keen eye for business, he moved to Elmira in 1923 and went into partnership with George Drury, selling textiles and cloth of every kind. Drury and Amy developed into a general store located on the main street of Elmira. It prospered from the start.

After Oliver's first wife Lillie Marth died he married
Lily Ann Seiling on December 26, 1918

Tragedy struck again when George Drury died suddenly. After Dad Amy made an equitable settlement with his widow, Oliver was sole proprietor of the store. He carried a mortgage and a debt within reason for the assets. With six healthy children and a thriving business, Oliver and Lily Ann were rich indeed. The future looked good. In the fall of 1929, Oliver was stocking up, anticipating another profitable year. The Christmas rush was about to commence.

Unknown to the world, there was a dark cloud building over Canada and the United States that no one had forseen. November 1929 was the blackest business month of the century. The famous Dow Financial Stock Market on Wall Street, New York, went into free fall. No one could have foreseen the results, especially in Elmira. Like a falling house of cards, the chain reaction that reverberated around the world brought the economy of North America to a screeching halt. Millions were thrown out of work, including 200 workers at the Elmira Mill.

Merchandise on Oliver Amy's shelves lost half their value overnight. Buyers slowed to a trickle. By the summer of 1930, the wolves were circling the wounded. Forced into bankruptcy, Pop Amy (as he was affectionately called) went under. Oliver Amy had a family to feed. The car had to be sold. Next went the house. Miraculously, he was able to hang on to the family cottage at Sauble Beach. The banks saw no value in the place, and left it alone, saving many happy memories and underwriting the many happy memories still to be had. Apart from this little encouragement, the larder was empty.

RUPPEL BLOCK — Charles Ruppel built this outstanding "block" in 1892 on the northeast corner of Arthur and Mill Streets. (The beautiful brickwork is still visible on Mill Street). His furniture and undertaking business was in the north section; Jury and Amy's General Store in the middle, and A. Werner's Drug Store — also a Bell Telephone agent — on the corner. Later, Blair's Drug Store, Bolender's Shoe Store and C.D. Miller & Co. Insurance agents occupied the building.
(Photo courtesy of the Woolwich Historical Foundation Archives)

Oliver did the brave thing and took manual labour working on the Elmira highway alongside men who whispered amongst themselves, "How have the mighty fallen." If it had not been for a compassionate friend, the Amy's and their six children would have been on the street. They were given a house rent free for the winter of '31/32. With the help of friends, one more forlorn attempt to set up a general store was attempted. It was a gamble that failed. Under different circumstances, the venture might have succeeded, but this was 1932 in the depths of the depression. Oliver finally said goodbye to his beloved Elmira and moved to Waterloo, renting a house at 59 Menno Street. For a brief time, he was on relief. The once prosperous business man actually did his stint on the salvage truck which was a prerequisite for government assistance.

Then the enterprising Lillian came to the rescue. She had designed many quilt patterns for personal pleasure, and adorned her bedrooms with her craft. Why not sell prestamped patterns, door to door, ready for sewing. Quilting is still the passion of women who love to create things beautiful. It was the mainstay of the household, until emploment came at Albright's Sewing centre on King Street. The little business had by this time made a reputation for itself and continued after hours. Whenever a shortfall in the family budget came along, the quilts made up the difference. Oliver and Lillian (about this time Lily Ann decided her name was Lillian) Amy were no longer rich, in this world's goods. But, they were still wealthy in their loving and loyal family. For example, they had concern for the poor; those were the days when unemployed men came to the door begging for bread. Anyone who called at the Amys' always got a sandwich. The children remember seeing men sitting on the back porch and thanking their mother for her kindness.

In turn, the Fast family who lived next door, were watching out for the Amys. One day Mrs. Fast said to Lily, "Oh, Lillian, I made this stew for our family and I made too much for us to eat. I haven't the heart to throw it away. Could you use it?" Both women knew the real story, but neither would let on.

My wife recalled picnics when her mother would chop peanuts and mix it with home made mayonnaise. Those peanut sandwiches were always a hit, especially when Lillian and Oliver would walk to the park (via the railroad tracks) carrying a heavy jug of lemonade. After the kids swam in the river, the sandwiches would disappear one by one, carefully rationed according to age. Joan would say to me, "You could tell when times were tough in our family by the menu: creamed peas over toast."

The Amy kids didn't know they were poor. Oliver and Lillian were wise parents and accentuated the positive. In the eighth grade, Joan had one red dress which was washed when needed and ready to wear the next day. To this day she cannot look at a red dress without a visceral reaction.

When the Albright's store closed, a job opened up at Walker's, Kitchener where Oliver continued to work. One day, as he was growing older, his manager said, "Oliver, you are my most valuable employee. When a German-speaking customer comes in, we always send them to you." (After the war, Kitchener was full of immigrants from Germany who could not speak English). "Because you speak the language, our business prospers. If you find yourself getting tired, I want you to slip into the employees' room and rest." Oliver worked at Walker's for the rest of his life. Walker's gave Oliver ninety minutes for lunch so that he could take the bus home for lunch, rest and return to work. He was still working when he died at age seventy-eight.

Time for a roll call. Names are as follows.

1) Nelson, who established the Amy Coal Company, later renamed, Amy Fuels and Oil.
2) Reginald, who ultimately became sales manager for Schlichter Auto Parts.
3) Bruce, who was ordained into the Baptist ministry with a lifetime of service.
4) Ross, who established Amy Awning and Tarpaulin located in Bridgport.
5) Joan, who became my stay-at-home wife, taught Sunday School, ran a ladies' Bible study, headed up a girls' club and counselled so many troubled adults that we have lost count. She also raised our four children.
6) William, who earned his Doctorate at the Univerity of Toronto, became dean of Monmouth College, and wrote extensively.
7) Paul, who became plant manager of Warwick Stamp and Stencil.
8) Ruth, our beloved "spinster," who took care of all the grandchildren at one time or another (twenty-four of them) and distinquished herself caring for her mother, and volunteering at her church for just about everything.
9) Mary, who became a public school teacher and a minister's wife.
10) Donald who became second-in-command at Amy's Awning and Tarpaulin and everyone's favourite handyman.
11) Ronald, who entered the ministry but later transferred to Canada Manpower as a counsellor and teacher.

When World War II broke out, three sons of the Amy family volunteered. When Bruce came home proudly wearing his army uniform, Lillian excused herself, went into the side room, and wiped away her tears. (Her brother Clarence is buried in France. He was killed three months before the end of World War I.) Reginald, Bruce, and Ross came ashore on the third day of the Normandy landings in World War II and were in action with the First Canadian Army. Reginald cheated death twice. The first time was when, caught in crossfire, he hit the dirt with two ordinance companions. When the shooting was over, he was the only one alive.

"Why not me?" he sobbed over and over again. After being wounded in a V-2 rocket attack, he was repatriated to England and shipped home. Ross and Bruce were decommissioned six months later.

When at last Oliver, the Christian gentleman, closed his eyes in death, he had worked every day of his adult life. Five hundred people attended the funeral at Emmanuel United Church. I confess, before and after, I wept at his loss. The most moving funeral service I have ever attended concluded, when six of his eight sons acting as pallbearers carried his coffin to the waiting coach. What a comfort to know that as Christians, we will one day be reunited in the celebration of the ages.

After the funeral, I was party to a few of the sons who were rehearsing memories about their father.

They always called him "Pop." I'll never forget what Paul said that day, "Many times when I came home late, I had to go through "Mom and Pop's" bedroom to access my room in the attic. Sometimes, I interrupted "Pop" saying his prayers. He always said them on his knees beside his bed. I would tip toe my way past "Pop" on my way up to the attic. He would never look up, but I used to wonder if he wasn't praying for me."

All the brothers had had that same experience. Pop never preached at his kids. He just set the example. He never missed a Sunday attending Immanuel United Church unless he was sick.

His life was a quiet example of his Christian faith and commitment.

Chapter 35
The Boat People

Come with me while we leap ahead twenty three years. We are in Hamilton, Ontario and I have served two churches, one in the east and one in the west. I am in my third pastorate at Stanley Avenue Baptist Church. With the coming of the seventies, the war in Viet Name dominated the news. The peace settlement may have meant the cessation of war for some, but in the eighties, for others, it was the beginning of a conflict that would ultimately see Canada accept 80,000 Chinese immigrants. One such immigrant was Dac- Sinh Chu and Tea-Ha, his wife. During the war years, Dac-Sinh drove a truck for the Hanoi government. His only crime was ethnicly – he was Chinese. Like many others who had lived in Viet Nam for generations, he was forced to flee from his homeland. It cost him everything he owned to purchase passage for his family on a rickety boat that dumped them off at Hong Kong. The ensuing humanitarian crises gave rise to the moniker "boat people." Many of the boat people drowned in the attempt; others who survived were robbed by pirates. All of the two million boat people that were distributed around the world were stripped of everything they owned. Canada was moved with compassion for these people right down to ordinary citizens like the people that made up the membership of our church.

We had just purchased a small house behind the church. With the boat people news on the radio every day, it occurred to us, "Why not adopt an immigrant Chinese family and help them get established."] Our people responded with enthusiasm. Everything was in place. We had a house and we had people with accumulated household goods [that were] stored [up] in basements and closets just begging for a higher purpose. Canadian Immigration laws were tough, but had been set aside for the "boat people." In no time the paper work was done. My appeal to the congregation for furniture had met with a response resembling an avalanch. We had two kitchen tables and far too many chairs. We could have furnished two or three houses with the surplus. Everybody wanted to contribute and our congregation was full of anticipation for the family we might adopt.

Meantime Dac-Sinh and Tea-Ha Chu, Grandma Chu and five

children were on a plane heading for Edmonton. They were in for a shock. Having never seen a snowflake or experienced cold weather, they received their baptism in Edmonton with minus twenty degrees. [I suspect Canadian officials might have decided to deliberately do this to them so that Ontario March weather would seem like the tropics or some such thing, but of course, it is only a suspicion on my part.] Tuesday, March 18, 1980, Joan and I were at Pearson airport with two cars to meet the immigration people. We were not alone. The airport was filled with host families that were to meet their new adoptees. The melee was contagious and exciting. Efficiency! In no time we were introduced to the Chu family, all eight of them. Neither of us could communicate except with gestures. Body language can be eloquent. In no time the family was loaded in our cars and we were speeding our way home to Hamilton.

Be it ever so humble – our little house – home is where your heart is. Right beside the church on Stanley Avenue, we had our Chinese immigrant family. We had a brand new rice maker for them and a kitchen fully outfitted with dishes, pots, pans, and cutlery. I can't remember when a church had so much fun providing for a needy family. Sunday. March 23, 1980, was a day to remember as we introduced them to the congregation oozing with love for the new arrivals. The evidence was everywhere. As soon as the people had sized up the family, new clothes kept arriving as our members showered the Chus with shoes and sundries using every conceiveable excuse they could invent to show the family our love. Joan went every day to teach them rudimentry English and soon discovered that ESL classes have their place. I took Dac-Sinh to Stelco who hired him right away even though the language barrier still remained. Everybody wanted to help. After five Sundays, I knew that the place for the Chu family was the Chinese Alliance congregation which was only five blocks away. Now they could understand the service in their own language.

Naturally we were eager to show them the sights, so we took them to Niagara Falls and introduced them to hamburgers and french fries. Where? Where else but McDonalds. As soon as the Lilacs bloomed we showed them around the Royal Botanical gardens. In no time, they had us over for authentic Chinese cuisine, and frankly, I confess, they excelled themselves.

With no prompting from me, they immediately gave their five children English sounding names. We couldn't remember their real names no matter how hard we tried. When Stelco took a slump one year later, Dac-Sinh lost his job, but promptly found another job working nights with a flashlight searching for earthworms for a company that catered to anglers. In time the family bought a house located at 169 McNab Street. Today they have a brand new home in the suburbs. At the time of writing this book they have a stellar record of hard work and achievement.

Time for a roll call: today Alison, the oldest who graduated from McMaster with a degree in engineering married an electrical engineer who now works in Hong Kong. She is the mother of two children. David also took his degree in engineering and works at Almac, Dundas where Dac-Sinh is also employed. Lisa, like David is unmarried and is doing a career change studying architectural design. Amy is married, and is currently a medical management consultant, working in Shanghai, along with her husband who is a currency trader working for a Swiss bank in the same city. Janice who likewise took her degree in electrical engineering married a dentist who now practices in Edmonton, Alberta. The family loves to travel. They have been to Europe, South Africa, Bali, Singapore, and China. Alison and Amy stoutly affirm they are Canadians and are looking forward to returning to their native land.

I wish I could report that the family goes to church. As soon as they got established, they dropped out of the Chinese Alliance church, however as Canadians they have certainly become productive citizens. When I asked Dac-Sinh if he ever felt homesick for Viet Nam, he stoutly replied, "Never, I am a Canadian."

Chapter 36
An Innocent Abroad

David Green as a teenager

David Green was one of our young people who grew up at Stanley Avenue Baptist Church, but through Providential circumstances moved away to the United States. He enrolled in the U.S. navy with the promise of learning the electrician's trade. His yen to see the world would take him halfway around the world to the U.S. aircraft carrier Forrestal plying the waters of the Arabian Sea. This enormous vessel was a floating city of 4000 who serviced the jet planes it carries packing a frightening range of firepower. An amazing ship of technology, it was three and a half football fields long. The adventure of a lifetime soon lost its zest. David was homesick and wrote me this incredible letter which I now relate to you. It speaks of his memories of church life and how much he missed us. It is also a tribute to church going people anywhere on this planet and the value it brings to everyday life. I include it here without even touching so much as a comma.

David M. Green, 093624991
Attack Squadron 146,
P.P.O.
San Francisco, Calif. 96601

May 24, 1980

Dear Pastor Woods and Church Family:

Hello to all of you wonderful people up there! These greetings come from Gongo Station, somewhere in the Arabian Sea, about half way around the world. As hard as it may be to believe, I am doing fine, but I miss everyone of you.

How are things back home? I get a little insight on events and special happenings from letters I receive from some of the church family. The boat people finally arrived. Tim Robinson is back home. I imagine that you probably feel that things that happen to you all are unimportant but try to imagine what it's like being out here. I love to hear about what happens with and to my fellow members of the church family.

I get about one letter a week now so the mail service must be slow. I can't help but feel that sometimes the mail just doesn't get delivered. Recently I've received letters from the Clarke family, Tim Robinson and Kathy and Wayne Wilson. These help keep me in touch with what is going on up there.

Today is a sad day for many of us out here. One of our mates passed away in his sleep at about 5 o'clock this morning. They say it was a heart attack and he had been dead quite a while when they finally became aware that he was dead, as he didn't awaken when his buddy attempted to wake him.

That's a sad note to begin with but we've lost two others over the side in the last two weeks. One person jumped because he said that he had too many problems to cope with. We didn't find either of the bodies. There are a lot of sharks in these waters so it was assumed that these sailors were devoured by the sharks. Something like that is hard to prove.

Ace Clarke asked me what it felt like to see prophecy fulfilled right before my eyes. This area has a very important role to play in history. So much time is spent out here where you're on the go that not much time is left to contemplate what is happening. Life seems to be unaffected by our presence here. In fact, just about two hours ago we passed a tug towing an oil drilling platform. I feel honoured in a way to be allowed to see prophecy fulfilled but not yet having to be physically subject to its adverse effects. The only thing that we suffer is that we visit fewer liberty ports and that we are constantly at a subdued alert status.

When "General quarters" is called and we are asleep we have four minutes to waken, dress, don our flight deck uniforms and man our planes. We should be able to clear the deck in about 30 minutes. A plane flying at Mach II (twice the speed of sound, about 1500 miles per hour) would take about that much time to reach the ship after our defence systems spotted him. This month my squadron alone (12 planes) will log over one thousand flight hours.

I sometimes lay in my rack and wonder what it would be like to be at war. I pray every night that the Lord will see me safely home. I pray that he will protect and bless everyone of you at home and everyone I know everywhere. You really can't imagine what it is like out here.

David's soul mate during his Navy exile was Tim Robinson who in the exchange of letters had acknowledged homesickness when he was out west in Saskatchewan. For Tim it was Briarcrest College, hardly the kind of exile that David experienced, yet the mere mention of it was a comfort to David. Poor David. Even when the Forrestal tied up in port, his Christian convictions meant more confinement. David didn't want to go to the girlie shows his mates were hankering to see. Sometimes, he just stayed on ship to take advantage of a little peace and quiet. During David's stint on the Forrestal, the Iranian hostage crises broke. The Forrestal was immediately put on a war footing, that's why he prayed so fervently for peace.

The flight deck of an aircraft carrier is supposed to be the second most hazardous working environment in the world. The ship may seem big but imagine 75 airplanes, three or four hundred people, servicing equipment, three catapults launching, and about twenty of the airplanes turnging and moving all over the deck. About ten people so far have been sent to a land based hospital after being fairly badly injured on the flight deck. I can relate many stories but it's hard to relate them on paper. I know that you all must be praying for me because I can feel it and it is apparent by the protection the Lord has afforded me on the cruise so far. One time, two guys, one on each side, were both blown about twenty feet down the deck by an F. 14 as it turned its exhaust by us. I felt no real heat and just a mildly strong gust from the plane. The exhaust can blow you down even if you are eighty feet behind the jet. The temperature is about 1400 deg. F. when the exhaust comes out and you can hardly breathe because of the heat when you feel it at distances of 100 to 150 feet.

I have found that the easiest time to spend time with the Lord is after work but just before I go to sleep I even find that I never forget to have this chat with God, as I used to forget sometimes when I was home. I somehow feel closer to the Lord out here, may be just because I need Him more I hope that isn't the case but I hope that I am slowly but surely bending my will to let His will for my life have more control. Knowing that His way is best is easy to understand but to put it to work is harder to do. I'm glad that I have you all as friends and I ask you all to remember me in your prayers.

Tim Robinson has really helped me out a lot by being there to write to and by sharing experiences, feelings, and his love for Christ, with me. Of all the people back home, I can relate to him because he's experienced somewhat the same things as I have – loneliness, being where you know no one, being away from home and not being able to do anything about it, plus the fact that we are buddies, about the same age and have shared many good times.

When I think back on all the times I had at Stanley and with the church family, the good times outweigh the bad times by a great deal. I grew, learned lessons, met many fantastic people, dated many pretty and wonderful Christian girls and made friends that I will have as long as I live and will know so many people when I get to heaven.

I hope that everyone who hears these words, listens closely and remembers what I say. Make all of your moments at Stanley happy moments. Love everyone. Participate. Help out those less fortunate than you. Store all these special memories in your mind. All the things you do together will bring joy as you remember them, but if you miss out, what kind of memories will you have then? A little time spent helping someone out is more than repaid by the smile and thank you you receive when it's done, and the fond memory that person will carry of you for the rest of their lives.

I think of the things I missed by not participating and also the great times that I had with others, that those who didn't share, missed. We can never relive those events so why pass them up. – Retreats, Young Peoples at M.B.C., at Guelph, Church picnics, camp outs, roller skating, Good Friday service, Christmas, weddings. I could go on forever. Everyone who says that there's nothing to do at Church had better reassess themselves. I thought that I participated in enough but now that it's all out of my reach, I can see all the things I missed.

Thank you, Pastor, for the things you've organized, Jan Spring for the choir and special music, teachers for the message you put into so many people's minds, bus drivers and riders for you ministry, Deacons for your support in directing the church and everyone else for organizing, participating and making Stanley what it is.

Well, I must close. Thank you for all the memories, prayers and letters. I remember you all in prayer every night. Hello to everyone who doesn't know me and those who do. I'll write again sometime when I have more to say. I hope I didn't offend you or bore you, but I write exactly what I feel and don't hide or disguise my thoughts. Believe it or not, there are some good points in me, somewhere.

In His Love and as a member of His family,

David M. Green

P.S. Sorry about all the carrying on but I really feel that a lot of us miss out on so much just because we're shy, don't know about it, or just think that it's not for us.

Quite a letter! David survived his Navy service, married and had three children. Tragically he suffered another war in the battle of life, not of his choosing. After his Navy discharge with his electrian's trade completed, he was working on an industrial electrical service panel. It was assumed the power was off. Despite every precaution, from time to time, it is impossible to escape human error. The power was still on. Sixty thousand volts of electricity killed one man outright and left David with third degree burns, but still breathing. He was horribly disfigured and bears the face of an alien. His wife Sharon stayed by him through his terrible ordeal. Compensation was paid and they live reasonably well in Tennesse. They maintain their Christian testimony through all their trials and are a witness to the keeping power of the grace of God.

Chapter 37
For the Good of the Church

Pastoring Stanley Avenue Baptist was for me the best of times and the worst of times. If one is to measure a ministry by new converts, it was the best of times. In the sixteen years that I spent at this church, we baptized 176 new members. We established Hamilton Baptist Non-Profit homes, which grew to 166 townhouses owned and operated by our church. For eleven years, we were the driving force behind the downtown Christian Business Luncheon. Joan and I teamed up to provide a hot sandwich luncheon complete with salad, dessert, and coffee for downtown Christian business people (men and women) who would meet at Centenary United Church. We called it C.B.L.[Christian Business Luncheon] I brought a twenty- minute devotional and wound things up in time for downtowners to be back to work within an hour. In the eleven years we operated this, at one time or another a total in excess of 200 people dropped by, with an average attendance of around twenty-five.

Ground breaking ceremonies, September 1982, for Margret Mews, our other housing project to help low income Canadians. Left to right: Stan Hudecki, Member of Parliament, Paul Cosgrove, MPP [ministry of housing] and me.

Our weekly luncheon at such an historic church as Centenary United made me research their history. It was then I discovered that Centenary Church was the home of the Great Hamilton Methodist revival of 1859 and wrote about it (see Hamilton Public Library). When Billy Graham came to town, he picked up on that article, and the Hamilton Spectator published a synopsis.

Another facet of our ministry at Stanley was our Sunday School which ministered to hundreds of children, and I personally conducted children's rallies in four of our local public schools.

We helped establish the Hamilton Theological Society and for years met once a month with the local clergy. Again, Joan to the rescue: we always provided a hot lunch.

My most meaningful funeral was at Stanley. Albert Gadoury was a sixteen year old kid from our church who was killed crossing a railroad bridge on a fishing junket with his friend. Caught in the middle of the bridge with an oncoming train, John French, Gary Jones, and Albert made a dash for the other side. John made it to safety and Albert would have too but the seconds he took to push Gary to safety cost him his life. A member of the Westdale football team, the entire school mourned his loss. The Dodsworth and Brown funeral home was packed with 350 mourners with another 350 outside who could not get in. What a memory!

The ministry to international students was a cooperative affair with Philpott Memorial Church. Dr. Molly Abraham (originally from India) inspired our two churches to begin. Joan and Evelyn Fritz headed this ministry with the co-operation of others from each congregation, and enrolled over 100 multinationals each year of its existence. This ministry helped many homesick students to make the Canadian adjustment and meet new friends at their host families who would invite them for family dinners from time to time. When I think of all the ministries in the church that Joan spearheaded, in reality, the church got the services of two pastors for the price of one. My intent was to be the pastor of this church till I retired. I looked forward to being the grand old man. Instead, I was the centre of a controversy that finally resulted in a church split.

The early years of my ministry were idyllic. Both pastor and people were a healthy, happy lot. There were, of course a few who became disgrunted and leaf. When they did, a cloud of disapproval hung around for a while. The arrival of newcomers soon disippated that kind of damage. We often had visitors comment on how much they appreciated the church and sensed a warm and happy spirit. Years later I ran into a former member who said, "Stanley Avenue Baptist Church was the best church I ever attended."

So why did things come to an unpleasant end? Or should I say an apathetic end. Perhaps, I stayed too long. Towards the end of my ministry, the attendance had shrunk from 240 to 170. Who can say for sure why people leave a church, but we did have one liability. We were a downtown church and people had to drive the distance to get to us. Competition from local churches in the suburbs that are closer is tempting. Looking back, I sometimes wonder if the real reason for the loss of membership was my involvement with Pentecostal/Charismatic Christians. They were such a vibrant lot and full of zeal. We attracted this kind because they knew they were welcome with a pastor who identified with their Christian experience. My mainline Baptist people distrusted them. They would raise their hands in worship during the singing of hymns.

Because I approved, some of my members distrusted me. As a card carrying charismatic, the security of my mainliners, was more in my wife who was a decidedly traditional Christian. Our church was something like our marriage, a sort of mixture, with plenty of difference of opinion. One day an exasperated deacon said to me, "You watch and see the day will come when you'll change the sign out front to 'Stanley Avenue Pentecostal Church'."

I always felt that my traditionalists and my enthusiasts could live together in harmonious tension, but others disagreed and left our church, thereby precipitating a congregational crises. I encouraged my deacons to believe that once people knew that we could embrace both and live together in harmony, things would turn around and we would grow into an even stronger congregation.

The problem was that those who were discontented with the situation simply couldn't bend. At no time did the discontent ever amount to anything more than 15% of the people, but it was enough to divide our deacons' board who wearied of the phonecalls from the disaffected. Had I stayed on, we would have lost them. I could foresee that attendance would drop to 140 and then what. Finally, the deacons with my consent agreed that to salvage the church, I should resign. I wasn't adverse to this solution, since I believed that upwards of fifty of the people would follow me, if I started a new church. (They were so committed to my ministry that they would have left anyway.) I didn't have the conscience to precipitate this kind of move without cause (that would make me a church splitter); however, my deacons in all good conscience asked the very thing that would absolve me from such a charge. In the end, I was certain the church would suffer from this decision, but I wasn't interested in more controversy. The deacons (naively as things turned out) were convinced it was the only solution.

They meant well but didn't seem to understand how committed many of our members were to me personally. They were blind to the inevitable exodus they were about to precipitate. Christmas Sunday 1988 was my last service at Stanley Avenue. With a lump in my stomach, I turned in my keys. The stage was set for starting a new church, and try as I may, I did not avoid the moniker, "He's a church splitter. First, he divided the congregation. Next, he took his followers and started another church."

The solution now achieved was supposed to rescue the church. As things turned out the plan didn't work. With the news that Woods had resigned, all the dissatisfied members who had left were to return. They didn't. My very loyal supporters (about twenty-five members, not the fifty I had envisaged) wanted me to start a new church. With no other alternative in sight I gladly agreed. They would not have stayed under any circumstances. Another twenty-five members who appreciated my ministry, but did not feel comfortable in a Charismatic church (whatever that means) simply went elsewhere. I have to say that disappointed me, they were such a fine lot of people, but I certainly understood. The nucleus of Hamilton Christian Fellowship met in the auditorium of the Football Hall of Fame. News spread quickly. Within five weeks we were eighty-five strong. The first thing they did was to increase my salary by $10,000. Because of the discontent at Stanley, this vital issue was allowed to slide but was rectified when my replacement arrived. I managed to pay off all my debts by remortgaging the house. A congregation in controversy doesn't raise the pastor's salary to match the cost of living.

With all this going on, some of my detractors were demanding that I should repay the church an interest-free housing loan I received when we first came to Hamilton. You can therefore imagine my surprise and my delight to discover that my former deacons' board forgave the interest free $10,000 loan that had enabled me to purchase our house back in 1972. It was to be repaid whenever I moved on. In 1989, after all the losses they had suffered, they still forgave the loan as a severance package – a magnanimous gesture to be sure.

Oddly enough, the little minority that had lobbied for my departure left the church. Disillusioned with the results of what was supposed to revive Stanley, the malcontents couldn't face what they had envisaged would be a solution. They removed to other churches. The ninety faithful who stayed on had to make a painful choice. They could no longer support their missionaries. The missionary budget had to be axed. In fact, the givings had slumped so low that they needed a new source of income. Irony! The offices of Hamilton Baptist Non-Profit Homes that I had started against the will of the malcontents moved into the church. The rent helped to bridge the shortfall in givings. Had our deacons foreseen the outcome, they might have opted for a compromise and I'd have stayed on. It was a case in which everyone had good intentions, but misread the very congregation they sought to serve.

Meantime the new Hamilton Christian Fellowship became not the half-Pentecostal, half-Baptist church that I envisaged; rather, it became a fully Charismatic congregation. It grew to 170 until once again I found myself regarded as a liability standing in the way. I wanted the enthusiasm of the Charismatics, but I also wanted it curtailed. The zealots of the supernatural workings of the Holy Spirit – holy laughter, tongues-praying in the public service – did not appreciate my restraining hand. At Stanley I was too radical; at HCF I was too conservative (as the very zealous imagined). Solution! I resigned. Today the congregation numbers around seventy. It has become a Messianic church with a great interest in Israel. Amazingly, I am on good terms with both churches. In both cases they carry on, but I can't help but wonder what might have been if we could have found middle ground to accommodate tradition and enthusiasm. Perhaps others wiser than I will figure that one out.

Once again I had wrestled with the issue of being between two worlds. A good church needs to be better than a very human governance. It needs to have the eye of faith to the supernatural, to the world to which we are destined to become. Accomplishing such is a challenge that I only partially succeeded in and also partly failed. That said, God has worked on my behalf to bring about my circumstances for personal good.

I have become a playwright, an actor, an author, and entrepreneur to distribute and sell my books. I might have missed those experiences had I not gone through the struggles of being an unemployed pastor. The church I left continues as does the new church I started; may they both grow and succeed.

Our new congregation met at the Canadian Football Hall of Fame, one year old.

A further word about squabbling churches. Do married couples have arguments? Do they even divorce? Do families harbour grudges and wind up not speaking to their siblings? Do best friends part company over life's burning issues? The Church is made up of very human people who bring their issues with them. Sometimes these issues appear in strange and sublimated ways within the walls of the

Church. Look at the record. For all the church troubles that come and go, the Church is nonetheless a wonderful community of caring people. It's a good place to belong. It is the best example of the family village I know. Everybody gets a crack at raising your kids. Not a bad thing when as parents you are at your wits' end over discipline problems. I can't think of a better place to find a life partner. No finer institution than the Church will sustain you in old age when you are lonely. For all its shortcomings, the Church is the best example of a loving community on the face of the earth.

Chapter 38
Drama and a Career in Acting

I had often preached that if Christianity is going to impact this post-Christian generation, perhaps it might come through the arts. I would urge our young people to consider those fields of endeavour, such as the performing arts or writing, as a ministry. Little did I dream that, in my retirement years, I would enter both those worlds at simultaneously. My initial vision was one-man drama. Once, when we were touring Vermont, I had witnessed Julie Harris perform the Amherst Belle. It was a one-person drama depicting the life of Vermont Poetess, Emily Dickenson. What an amazing accomplishment. It was a two-hour drama that kept us spellbound. I had often wondered about how that might be applied to the stories in the Bible. Plenty of drama there!

Almost like a revelation, the unfolding idea came in a flash one sleepless night before Easter 1997. In time, I would perform my David and Bathsheba drama, plus others, over two hundred times in five states and in Canada. The drama format differs from preaching. Every line builds on what has gone before. One has to have it down cold or the drama falls flat. Eventually, one learns such things as the dramatic pause. Being able to carry a tune and dance a little also helps.

One day, John Huber of the Wilmot Centre Missionary Church phoned me and said, "We would like to have you do your drama for our annual Seniors Rally for September 2008." I was pleased to accept the invitation to do James, a Skeptic Believes. Of all my plays, this one is my favourite. Not only is it a crowd pleaser, but it addresses the key issue of our current generation, which I see as skepticism and unbelief. When you think about it, people were no different in the days of Jesus. (The gospels record the skepticism of the ancients when it came to the claims of Jesus.) Today's moderns are no different. Fueled by the likes of turncoat Tom Harpur, who is Toronto's most recent skeptic since Charles Templeton died, people are encouraged to dismiss biblical Christianity. Sure there are alternatives, but do they address the eternal issues the way Jesus does? The skeptic has chosen a hard road to travel. I call to your attention the record of the brothers of Jesus. The Bible plainly states, "for neither did his brothers believe on him."

So what made James, the brother of Jesus, change his mind and become the leader of the Jerusalem church? This is grist for a white-knuckle drama. When I perform it, I always receive a standing ovation. Of course as dramatist I depict what I imagine. First, Jesus announcing to his skeptical family that he is leaving the carpenter's shop for public ministry. With no formal education, what could they think? Next, the surprise popularity of his ministry attracting large crowds. The miracle stories would quickly make the rounds. What did James think about that? The fear that would inevitably come with the growing antagonism of the Pharisees. The despair after the crucifixion. Did James and his brothers consider moving elsewhere? For self-preservation, I think I would. The only information we have is that Jesus appeared to James after the resurrection. That would be the clincher. The intriguing thing about the Bible is that there is so much room for the imagination. What a fascinating read.

JAMES
A SKEPTIC BELIEVES

A Drama on the Life of James,
The Brother of Jesus
by Bruce A. Woods. A C.A.P.A. Production

ALSO FEATURING
The Music of our
Local Churches

FUNDRAISER
Proceeds go to the
New West Parry Sound
Health Centre Chapel

TUESDAY JUNE 1ST, 2004
7:30PM

Charles W. Stockey Centre for The Performing Arts

Box Office Tickets: **$19.00**

FOR MORE INFORMATION: (705) 746-5882

Dramatic presentation over and over again has sharpened my pen.
Without it, I don't think I could have written my first book Between
Two Women. It has helped me again to write this one; I hope you
like it.

Chapter 39
Preacher Woes

Preachers, teachers, writers, actors, and politicians all have something in common. They have learned a secret. It's fun to tell. They all have the insufferable gall to imagine that they can make the world a better place. And do you know what? They are right – provided they can do it in humility. There's the rub. This little annoyance of pride gets in the way because we all inherently know that of all our competitors, we are the best. Obviously, the most gifted have the right to be first and be recognized as such. Thus, when life treats us with an uneven hand, we suffer the inevitable jealousy. Passed by on the stage of public notice, we rage at the idiots who are too dull to perceive true genius when it is so patently obvious to us. Our petty jealousies get out of hand and wreck our personality. Pretty soon we are parading our talents and promoting ourselves ad nauseum until even our best friends are avoiding us. Churchillian, we are such misfits in this rough and tumble world that depression overtakes us.

Preachers, teachers, writers, actors, politicians. Really, when it gets right down to it, in order to be a successful minister you have to be a little of all five callings rolled into one. It's a tough call, to be sure. Small wonder that fifty percent of the pastors I know have dropped out of the race in favour of something else. Once more, they can never be quite satisfied, until they can go back into the ministry. There is no misfit like a failed preacher. They are always trying to get back into the ministry, although they rarely do. So what is it that makes us tick? We really are an odd lot. I can't think of any profession that brings the best and the worst out of a man. Give me a list of guys who are ministers and I will tell you that it will include men that I love and guys that I avoid like the plague. They are the most interesting of men and the most boring of men. Again, I ask the question, what makes us tick? Analysis of the problem is beyond me; I will simply tell you about my own case, and you can judge for yourselves.

When a man is called to the ministry, it is a high calling. I can't imagine any man responding to that call with less than the best of motive. Still, things can go wrong; of all the temptations known to man, pride is the most subtle. This is and was my greatest conflict.

For right or for wrong, most congregations revere their minister. I know I did. You can't imagine the thrill I experienced the night of September 6, 1953, with the knowledge that Arthur Baptist Church had actually called this twenty-one year old kid to be their pastor. Accepting that call placed me amongst the "elite," or so I supposed. I couldn't conceive, at that time, that ministers were really human (of course I knew better, but you know what I mean). I was sure that they were a breed "apart." I would be numbered amongst them. I took this seriously and prayed often that I would be worthy of the "high calling." One year later, when the annual convention gathered, I was a pastor of a bona fide Baptist church. I couldn't imagine a higher honour. When I and others were called to the front, and our names read off and we were publically acknowledged, I was ecstatic. One year later, at a pastors' conference in Muskoka Baptist Campgrounds, I carefully noted the names of all I met. I wanted to be able to call them by name. I felt I was walking on holy ground and talking to the gods. The last day of the conference, the gods were dethroned.

The last meeting of the pastor's conference was held in a rickety, screened-in chapel. It was early June. The weather was hot and humid. The old ramshackle building was scheduled for demolition. A new chapel would be built the following year. It was long overdue. The screens were so old that they were full of holes. Every mosquito within a half a mile had discovered the place. If the blood of the martyrs is the seed of the church, that night the blood of preachers was making saints out of every mosquito in Muskoka. You could tell they were religious creatures. First, they would sing over you, and then they would prey on you. I was sitting near the back, and suffering the indignity of these invasive creatures, just like everybody else. Why Noah didn't exclude the pair of mosquitos from the Ark is a mystery to me. When I get to heaven someday, I intend to ask him for an explanation. From the front row to the back, there was the inevitable clap of a hand against the neck or forehead as we battled it out for supremacy over the lowly mosquito.

In some cases, impatience ruled. A wary preacher seeing an unsuspecting mosquito would clap him to death in midair. The war against the mosquito was on and sitting from my vantage point, I found myself straining my ears to hear the visiting speaker above the clamour of the clapping. I declare that no rousing Pentecostal camp meeting had more excitement than this one. At other times the speaker's face would disappear for the multitude of arms and hands in the air. Soon to follow was the inevitable scratching of the itchy evidence and distractions thereof. No wonder I cannot remember the speaker's name or the sermon he preached. Gratefully, the final hymn was announced. Although I can't be sure, I think it might have been "All Creatures of our God and King lift up your voice and sing." As things turned out, I slowly discovered that in the end, we are only mortals.

We have all heard the phrase, "He worships the ground she walks on." Just let them marry and the mirage evaporates. In many ways, to enter the ministry is like the proverbial marriage that removes the scales from one's eyes. Guess what – pastors are human, just like everybody else. Being a minister opens the door to theatre. We can preach good sermons, but they had better be interesting. Jesus was the consummate story-teller. Tell it well, and we have entered the world of theatre. Men who pursue the ministry are also called to theatre. Furthermore, we get compliments. Sometimes it goes so far that we have trouble getting our head through the door. Here are a few I have received.

"You are a good preacher."
"That sermon really inspired me today." Said my deacon one day. Four years later he was so upset with me, he left for another church.
"Our church needs your ministry. Please don't accept a call to that other church."
"That sermon was so good you ought to write a book," said a missionary to me one day.
"You are as good a preacher as my boss," said Billy Graham's secretary. Her sister was a member of our church.

Pretty soon, we are sure to imagine that we are heading for the big time. That means a call to a large church. I remember well when I was a candidate for Campbell Baptist Church in Windsor, Ontario. They had turned down Bob Brackstone and Bob Wilson, both good preachers in their own right. Now it was my turn. Since I knew I was better than either of them, I was sure to get the call. Unlike the wise old hen, I was cackling before I laid the egg. I pictured in my mind the thrill of preaching to 700 people every Sunday. When they turned me down as well, you can imagine my shock when the call finally went to Jim Rendle, a man of inferior talent to mine (or so I thought). I was devastated. How could they have overlooked my superior preaching talents? If you think actors are proud and jealous, wait till you meet a few preachers like me. I felt like a failed politian who had just lost an election.

"What can you expect from the ordinary herd." said Alexander Hamilton to Benjamin Franklin, and then he added, "The people you so admire are a great beast."

On the occasion of my rejection by the Windsor church I so coveted, I concurred. The battle with ego had begun long before this episode and I was completely hookwinked. In other words, I preach on humility and 'how I attained it'. Now that I am retired, I always try to find ways to encourage my pastor and affirm his sermons, considering how criticized preachers are, I want to be an encourager. In my day I always appreciated people who did likewise. Here are some I remember,

"That was a good sermon." Now the test is to apply it to myself. I failed that test on too many occasions.

When I was pastor of the Ruth Morton Baptist Church, things finally caught up with me. Remember that I told you it was the flagship of the British Columbia Baptist Churches. It had fallen on hard times. No problem. I would build it up again, and its greater glory would also be mine. Things didn't go as planned. Our young couples were buying their starter homes in the suburbs. One by one, we would see them explain,

"The drive to downtown Vancouver is too far. We will be transferring our membership to a church closer to where we live."

I was pastoring a church in decline, and that surely reflected on my image. I was discontent and fearful for my reputation and not one bit ashamed of my pride.

Then, came a wonderful sweep of the Spirit that laid me low. I will not relate the details, except to say that like Isaiah of old, I got a glimpse of the holiness of God and the egotism of man. Mine! It was a liberating experience that left me with an afterglow that lasted for a week. I have a name for it. I call it the "baptism of the cross." That experience left me honest at last. It stripped me of the need to appear "successful" in the eyes of man. Of what consequence is that? Who cares? It's what God thinks that matters. In this revelation there is great contentment. It makes us into a person who is focused on others. It is the great leveler that makes us fit company for conversation. We become "child-like" in the best sense of the word. The wonderful thing about Jesus is that he was easy to be with. Imagine, the King of the Universe, yet his presence was non-threatening.

A true disciples should be the same. We are always in God's presence, in awe but also at ease with Jesus because he is at ease with us.

Chapter 40
What is a Charismatic Experience?

During the Sutera revival meetings in Vancouver that I have just alluded to, my wife and I would counsel Christians from many backgrounds who were longing for a fresh touch from the Holy Spirit. This often happened at the conclusion of a meeting when seekers were invited to come to the altar to pray. One such lady linked up with my wife, Joan. She prayed a moving prayer of devotion, inviting the Holy Spirit to search her heart. In the middle of her prayer to the surprise of my wife, this lovely Christian lady broke out into the prayer of tongues for about twenty seconds, and then reverted to English. After the "Amen," she turned to Joan and pologized. The revival meetings were not to be in any way linked to Pentecostalism. Ralph and Lou Sutera preached the baptism of the Holy Spirit without praying in tongues. That's why the lady in question apologized. Joan promptly excused her for her "slip of the tongue" but has thought about this incident many times since. When she told me the story later that evening, she said, "It sounded like the voice of an angel and very beautiful to hear."

I mused about this a great deal and decided that whatever praying in tongues might be, it ought not to be forbidden. However, the real question was, as a Baptist, should it be encouraged? Surely this was something to consider.

-oOo-

Enthusiasm takes many forms in the Church. It is amazing to me how over time, "Baptist Enthusiasm can become "Baptist Amnesia." Before the advent of radio, the only entertainment in town was the local church, especially the evening service. From the advent of gas lights, when the church could be illumined after dark, the evening service was the gathering market where townspeople could socialize once a week. "Why, they can make the church auditorium bright as day," was the amazing revelation of the nineteenth century. In every town and city, the Sunday evening attendance at church exceeded the morning worship by twenty percent. For entertainment there was nothing else. Congregations sought out the preacher-orators of the day. Every preacher alive sought to outdo his peers. It was a day of oratorial enterprise, and if preaching skills were lacking, there was always the perennial enthusiasm of the crowd. If Sunday services did not suffice, there were always the travelling speakers who made their livelihood by titillating their audience with the latest fad or humour. The best example of this is Mark Twain who was the standup comedian par excellence. He became wealthy by entertaining his audience who were used to the concept of sitting before a good speaker. Politicians also reaped a benefit. By virtue of church attendance, people were well trained to listen.

At Stanley Avenue Baptist Church, back in the nineteen twenties, there was a colourful preacher that everybody remembered. His name was C.J. Loney. No one ever called him by his name; he was C. J. Loney. A small man with a big voice, he knew how to preach the gospel with wit and wisdom. C.J. knew how to "pack them in," a phrase that meant, attract a crowd. His favourite way to celebrate was the "Victory March." In Billy Graham fashion, he would preach up a storm and then give the invitation. That is, he would ask the penitents to come forward to the "altar," which meant kneeling at the front of the church before the puklpit. This was called "harvest time." Whenever there was a good harvest, the members engaged in a "Victory March." To have a Victory March, you needed a church with a good broad aisle all around the perimeter of the pews. After an evangelistic service when several had come forward to be saved. C.J. would declare a Victory March. On queue, the congregation would head to the perimeter aisle, and the piano and organ would strike up the chord to "Onward Christian Soldiers." The march would begin with C.J. leading. The new converts would follow and all the congregation after that. Round and round they would march, singing hymn after hymn, until C.J. closed in prayer. These services could last up to three hours without a complaint. Baptist enthusiasm was contagious. Everybody went home rejoicing. Pentecostals did not have a corner on enthusiasm. They simply cast it in their own image.

" *A Good Minister of Jesus Christ.* "

   Then in 1927 came radio. Everybody bought one and with it reaped the comedians who dominated the Sunday evening routine, and what's more, their was no church collection. Church attendance declined. On a Sunday evening, the congregation shrank to two-thirds of the morning attendance. C.J. Loney would rail against the comedians of radio to no avail. There was a reprieve during the war years. From 1939 to 1945, the evening service ranks were swollen by the advent of wartime sacrifices. War concerns made people think about death. Evangelism thrived and C.J. Loney revived the Victory March. Alas, with the advent of peace, by 1946 the evening attendance at churches everywhere was once again starting to slip, although morning worship services were still well attended. The death knell of the evening service came with the advent of television. With it came the decline of Baptist enthusiasm. People forgot about the days of the Victory March. Church was where you came to worship in reverence.

Young people in the church grew older and imagined that services were always this way. I call this "Baptist Amnesia". So when the Charismatic movement (based on praying in tongues and singing in the Spirit and the raising of hands) came along – well, you can guess the rest for yourselves.

-oOo-

Two years after the Vancouver Sutera meetings, I was in my next church, Stanley Avenue Baptist, Hamilton. With the exception of the older members, most of my congregation was oblivious of the colourful C.J. Loney and his antics. I had been greatly impacted by the Vancouver awakening, and it showed in my preaching. That's when the old timers told me about C.J. Loney's revival meetings. I would often speak of the need to be filled with the Spirit. I personally had experienced a "renewal," and felt liberated from a stuffy fundamentalism that stressed legalistic rules for Christian living (mine) and not the kind of confidence that left the "shades of grey" to the Spirit of God. There are times when the rules simply don't apply. For example, if someone was divorced or smoked cigarettes, I would not consider them as fit for the deacon's office. As for women, they need not apply. All that changed with my own "spiritual awakening." Now, I looked more for devotion to Christ rather than a rigid standard of do's and don'ts.

This new emphasis did not sit well with some of my stalwart but rigid Baptist members. My church treasurer told me she had issues with me and wanted to speak her mind. Jesse Blair made no effort to be diplomatic. She flat out told me that my "Holy Spirit" preaching was stirring up trouble. By this she meant, too much enthusiasm. She informed me that she would resign from the office of church treasurer and leave the church for another Baptist church more to her liking. Then she pointed her finger at me and quoted a Scripture, "Where the Spirit of the Lord is, there is unity!"

While I was concerned with her accusation, I couldn't agree with her inflexible standards. All the way home, I wondered if somehow I had gone astray. When I arrived at home, I looked up that troubling verse (II Corinthians 3:17). I discovered she had misquoted it. The verse reads,

"Where the Spirit of the Lord is there is liberty (freedom)."

Relieved, I reflected on how rigid Christians imagine themselves so biblically versed that they often don't take the time to check their facts. Jesse's triumphant quotation was in error. If anything, her idea of what the Bible really says reads more like this: If the Bible agrees with my prejudice, than I'm for it. If not, I refuse to change. What Jesse Blair was really concerned about were the "errors" of Pentecostalism or anything that smacked of "emotionalism," as defined by her standards. So many traditional Baptists I have met would agree. However, by 1976, I had concluded that praying in tongues was biblical. Not a requirement for spiritual life, but nonetheless a legitimate expression of piety. The fallout then was for a true standard of leadership. An enthusiastic lover of God is what counts. My guidelines had changed. The best church leadership did not reside in a person who kept all the rules but in someone who was open to the prompting of the Spirit. In the eyes of some Baptists, I was on the slippery slope to error.

One day, I was reading Catherine Marshall's book on the Holy Spirit. I was struck by her testimony of how she entered into the experience of praying in tongues. She described it as something rather pragmatic as opposed to something overwhelming, like the experience of Pentecost, as described in Acts 2. She writes, "It was as though some Divine quartermaster was passing out equipment and said to me, Here, you'll need this.'"

I found my own experience of esctatic glossolalia much the same. I wish I could tell you it gave me extra power, like I had hoped. It didn't. I rejoice to pray this way before God. It gives me a new freedom of prayer expression (like the flurry of trumpets after a symphony). Baptists are limited to a "Hallelujah" or "Amen" (provided they are still enthusiastic about their faith). Pentecostals top their prayer with verbalized enthusiasm that frankly is edifying. On the other hand, I would never pray that way before someone who disapproved of praying in tongues. No charismatic I know would either. That distainful disapproval would quench the Spirit, within me and I couldn't do it anyway. (Baptists need not worry, God is not going to give you a gift you don't want, besides, that kind of enthusiasm doesn't fit their temperment). I love Romans 8:26 which calls this experience "sighs too deep for words." I could say a lot more but there are plenty of books on this subject by others more skilled than I.

For me, the "baptism of the Holy Spirit" really came to me when I was in the Vancouver revival. The "praying in the spirit," as Pentecostals like to call it, came later, rounding out my prayer life. In the final analysis, the proof of a Spirit-led people is that they practice love and tolerance. In that kind of church, there is room for everybody, and someone who enjoys a different experience of God is not "verbotten!"

Chapter 41
Chasing Retirement Blues

When I look at my wife, I smile. She's eighty now, but in my mind's eye, I roll the clock back sixty-eight years to see an energetic twelve-year-old cartwheeling all the way from her house to the corner. That amuses old man Martin who loved to watch the Amys. Who wouldn't, with all those children playing on the street? Is this the same girl? Perhaps, but things change with age. I guess I've changed a little myself.

In March 1997. my dreams for Hamilton Christian Fellowship were shattered. My Elders' board (unwisely I felt) suggested that since I was now sixty-five (1996) a role reversal, was in order. My associate pastor would become the senior pastor, and I would be the associate pastor. The church was now up to 170 in attendance and growing. Reluctantly I agreed.

Now a word about that wonderful organism called the Church. Note I did not call it an organization. An organism is a living thing; an organization is not. At times, it seems as though the organism is overshadowed by the organization, but that is beside the point. No Elders' board ever made a decision which they felt was against their church's best interest. Sometimes unwise decisions are made, but you have to look at intent. As a living organism which the Bible calls the body of Christ, the Church with all its faults is nonetheless the body of Christ. Christ loves the Church. From the beginning, He knew that it would be a blemished organism. How could it be otherwise? It is made up of sinners saved by grace, just like you and me. Just the same, it is supernatural. It is alive, and it will endure, because overall supervision is in the hands of God. Sometimes in the decision making, mistakes are made and people get hurt. I'm one of them. However, because Christ loves the Church, I love the Church; and I have confidence in that Church here in Canada and abroad. I had made this point sufficiently clear to allow my former congregation the liberty they needed to feel free under the new leadership. As a result, I was able to leave without any rancour. My relationship with my former friends at Hamilton Christian Fellowship is intact, and I am always welcomed when on rare occasions I return.

While all this was going on, Joan and I decided to take in a concert at Hamilton Place. The orchestra was playing a magnificent piece. It was something I have long forgotten because I was preoccupied with my circumstances. At my age, I would not be the pastor of another church. I would no longer be preparing sermons, eagerly looking forward to Sunday by Sunday to preach them to a waiting congregation. (That proved to be an assumption in error. I have preached many sermons every since in many churches). But for all practical purposes, my life as I had known it was over and my future uncertain. To add to my concerns, my security for retirement was in jeopardy. I had been persuaded to invest in a financial scheme for my retirement that looked good at the start, but in the end had cost me over $100,000. The investment that was too good to be true turned out to be a ponzi scheme. Why did I make such a foolish investment? My friend and church elder who was a finacial consultant recommended it. I learned too late in life, never make an investment in anything until you have consulted a third party.

It all caught up to me at the concert. When Joan looked over at me, she saw the tears trickling down my cheeks and asked what was wrong. When I failed to reply, she nailed it exactly. (I remembered C.J. Loney my predecessor at Stanley. When he retired, a few months later he lost his beloved wife. He would come to church sitting under Ernest Nullmeyer his successor and silently weep.) Now it was my turn but I still had a wife who understood me. After all, as my lifetime partner in the ministry, she knew me only too well. She had lived through all this with me and she had shared my lifetime with all its ups and downs. After the concert, we talked late into the night. Retirement! I just never ever considered that somehow the day would come when I had no responsibilities in a local church. After a lifetime of preparing and delivering sermons, things seemed to be coming to a conclusion. I didn't like it one bit. Then of course there were the finances.

While we weren't exactly destitute, I was not financially robust either. Due to my disastrous investment for retirement, I was out $100,000. What were we going to do? Financially, we couldn't keep up our house without a divine intervention. And that is exactly what happened. At that time, we were in trouble with no place to turn. Due to (yet again) bad financial advice, our RRSPs had shrunk from $60,000 to $20,000. I kept this latter information from Joan because I didn't want her to worry. Now I was beginning to worry. That's when God stepped in with two miracles. The first was my drama ministry which I have related in a previous chapter; the other was a new church. Between these two rewarding pursuits, our financial needs were fully met.

I have a wonderful band of Christian brothers who meet regularly on Saturday morning. I was at one of our Saturday meetings in May of the year 2000. There were ten of us that morning when Dave Arnold said to me,

"Bruce, do you ever think of starting up again and initiate a church from scratch? If you would, my wife Michelle and I would back you."

Art Sullivan, overhearing the conversation chimed in,

"And Betty and I would join you as well."

Grist for my faith. I had been considering that very idea but I just needed a little encouragement. The highly successful Hamilton Millennial Festival had concluded just a month before, and I was ready for a challenge. In September of that same year, we started a new church. I had visions of a repeat of the Hamilton Christian Fellowship when we grew from twenty-five to one hundred in five weeks. It didn't happen that way. We did struggle from twelve to forty over a period of six years and then joined the Congregational Church denomination.

At approximately in this period of my life I had a wonderful dream. I was in heaven. I cannot tell you a thing about what I saw. It is erased from my memory. What I can tell you is I experienced the overwhelming presence of God and it was wonderful. In all my days, I never felt so comforted and accepted. I remember thinking, "If death takes me into a world like this, the anticipation of heaven is truly glorious." I awoke and entered into the next day greatly comforted. The afterglow of that Divine encounter stayed with me for a while and then faded. Yet another reminder that I am a pilgrim between two worlds. Meanwhile our fledgling church had begun and grew to forty-five then waned until we were down to twenty. We had a wonderful time of spiritual growth and life and loved every minute of it. I especially enjoyed our monthly communion service. In many ways, with our prayers for healing, and the intimacies of a small group, God took us to a new level, we had never experienced before. By 2006, however, I was now seventy-five, and we all realized that we would be better off closing down, and joining a church, as we felt led. With no regrets, we disbanded and have found ourselves spread out and making our contribution elsewhere. Amazing! Our little group reorganized into a house church which meets to this very day. All of this released Joan and me. We are now at last fully retired.

One thing needs to be added. For the whole six years that we met as a formal church, our little congregation simply didn't have any musicians, but God wonderfully supplied a Roman Catholic couple who did music. Except for prayers, they always abstained whenever we had communion but participated in everything else we did. They would go to Mass on Saturday night and worship with us on Sunday morning. Victor and Mary Liskauskas are, in my books, the best worship leaders any church could ever hope to have. Their devotion to Christ and their willingness to serve blessed us beyond measure. If I were young again, I would invite them to team up with me, and we would start in afresh with the "mostest and bestest." I'll bet we could build one of the finest congregations in the city.

Real retirement has come upon me in a most remarkable way. Dear Christian friends right out of the blue gave us a check for $10,000. That gift provided for me enough financial support to write my first book, Between Two Women. It has not only been a writer's success, but also it has been a financial help. The Lord has provided for us in such wonderful ways that the house we thought we'd have to sell is still our home. From this house, I wrote my first book and now the sequel as well. At age seventy-seven and still going strong, I have had the adventure of a lifetime. It all began when two months before I was seventeen, penniless and without a roof over my head, I became a follower of Christ. He has never let me down, and I look forward to the day when I will see him face to face. Next on the list will be my Mother, to tell her what a wonderful heritage she gave me. After Mother, I will have a conversation with my grandmother and tell her much the same thing.

Chapter 42
Psychoanalyzing Mother

My mother died on a cold bleak day, January 31, 1975, one day short of her seventieth birthday. To borrow a book title, her death was a Complicated Kindness. For me, her passing was a time of sadness without tears. She attended our church for eighteen months (after her third husband died). Her marriage to Sid Jones was for companionship. It was the best of all possible worlds, and in many ways her best years, if indeed someone who continually suffered from depression can have best years. Unfortunately for Mother, her sad life degenerated into schizophrenia. Fortunately, for all of us, her illness was not as acute as some cases I have seen. Yet nonetheless, it deprived her of a genuinely happy life. She often wished for death. When death came, as Christians with a happier future world before us, we "sorrowed not as those who have no hope."

Mother at her 40th birthday

Mother suffered from paranoia and heard and spoke with different voices. Yet she was sufficiently a part of this world that, when we caught her talking with "the voice", she would return to reality. She lived on the brink, but somehow avoided the abyss of insanity. I now make my attempt to explain her mental illness, and what I might have counseled had I enjoyed the maturity of hindsight and experience. The question begins with the anomaly of how someone born beautiful, intelligent, and gifted could come to such an unhappy life. Detective-like, I will list the facts of her downfall, as I see them in retrospect, and let the reader decide if my observations are true.

Observations that beg for an explanation are as follows.

1) How did the death of Mother's best friend affect her? Alice Ballard was only fourteen and the loss left Mother broken-hearted. It set the stage for further losses to come.

2) The move from rural Camrose, Alberta, to industrial Stratford was an adjustment that she never quite successfully made.

3) At nineteen, my mother misunderstood the intentions of a boy who, after a dance at the Stratford Casino, took her for a walk down Lover's Lane. After they stopped for an occasional kiss, the late night walk turned into a date rape. That fate befalls one Canadian woman in every five. Small wonder psychiatric problems abound.

4) Bruce Senior came into my mother's life at a time when she was ripe for picking. Ethel fell for Bruce. With his worldly-wise ways, Ethel was no match for this Casanova. Next, came sex and Grandma knew it. The fear of pregnancy plagued Ethel, but the obvious solution eluded her, because her parents were opposed to their marriage.

5) When Mother fell in love with Bruce Woods, Senior, Grandma saw past his smooth talking ways, disliked my father from the start, and expressed her disapproval. Rather than face her parents' objections to a marriage, Mother simply sidestepped the impasse. Unable to cope with her impossible situation, she opted to run and hoped for the best.

6) At twenty-one, Mother eloped with my father. No church wedding. All the things a girl dreams of were forfeited by this impetuous but understandable decision.

7) Two weeks after the civil weddomg, my father took off for a six-week tour of the west, selling magazines for Macleans. Mother, left alone in St. Thomas, fell in love with Dad's brother Wray. It wasn't love; it was infatuation. They dated while my father was away and broke off the relationship when he returned. Talk about a conflicted beginning to a marriage. Who does Mother love: Bruce Senior or his younger brother, Wray?

266

8) Mother gradually figured out Bruce Senior's unfaithfulness, and that didn't help her sexual relationship that should be a part of a normal marriage. How do you cope with an unfaithful husband? She told me once, "I said to your father, I wish I could cut that part out of my body out and just give it to you."

9) My Aunt Anna told me, "Your mother was frigid in her relationship with your father. Obviously not all the time or you wouldn't be here. Nonetheless, in that vital area of married life, she just wasn't quite able to be comfortable with sex." My father's sales trips away from home didn't help. She knew too much. Bruce Senior had a way around women, and how could this not affect any wife's affection? At times, Mother was three months alone with no idea where her husband was. Bruce never wasted a postage stamp to keep Mother informed. Divorce was not an option in 1929; besides, even though my father didn't deserve it, she loved him.

10) The other woman. Phyllis Christian and my father had an affair. One of many, but this one proved permanent. His brother Jim was no different. They encouraged one another to marital unfaithfulness.

11) In order to save her sickly baby (me), Mother returned home. She never dreamed that her leaving my father would be permanent. She was devasted at the thought of divorce. Divorce in 1931was humiliating. It implied guilt and failure.

12) Mother never stopped loving my father. How much punishment can the human psyche stand? Knowing that she had been betrayed was a dreadful burden to bear. The "if onlys" of life. In contrast to Bruce, Wray was an honourable man. Her fling with Wray while Bruce Senior was away never crossed the line, something that Wray was careful to tell me later when we became friends and fellow Christians.

13) Wray never had children. I became his favourite nephew. Nonetheless, Mother in daydreams wished she had met Wray first. Later, when he married Irene Wright, for obvious reasons they kept their distance.

14) Trying to adjust to a single lifestyle was made easier by having a good friend. Yolanda Latter was that friend until tragically she died of cancer. (shades of her youth) Loneliness was my mother's constant tragedy; that loneliness led her back to church.

15) Mother became a born-again Christian at age thirty-six. Her Christianity, however, quickly became conflicted when she found herself in love with John McLeod, the minister of the Congregational Church. Her comment to me was, "When we shook hands, the sparks flew." This unfortunate experience shows how desperately Mother wanted to love and be loved. Alas, it was not to be.

16) Realizing she could no longer attend her beloved Congregational Church, Mother switched to Memorial Baptist. Less than two years later, John McLeod left his thriving church for a run-down Baptist mission in Montreal. Later, when John and I became friends, he said to me, "Worst decision I ever made." I have often wondered if John left his church for a bad reason. I guess I'll never know for sure.

17) Mother tried the Pentecostal church for a while but finally stopped going to church altogether. It was in 1942 at age thirty-seven that she finally imploded under her ongoing tragedy. Paranoia quickly followed. Next, it was schizophrenia. Next, it was living in two earthly worlds, sometimes real and sometimes divorced from reality.

18) I remember an ugly scene when I was twelve. Mother was weeping and railing at Grandma and blaming her for all her misfortunes. I couldn't process her statement at the time when she said, "I might as well walk down the street stark naked, because everybody looks at me 'that' way."

19) I have observed that in mental illness, a misguided view of sex plays havoc with the mind. So does moral betrayal.

20) Mother's best years (her last eleven) were salvaged by her marriage to a widower by the name of Sid Jones. She loved to go to the Pentecostal church, something at the time I couldn't understand. When I would ask her why that was so, her reply was, "Because they are so happy and they express it in their singing." Mother finally was able to overcome (in part) her life-long sadness. After Sid died, she attended my church in Hamilton (Stanley Avenue Baptist). The incredible paradox in all this is that through her unhappiness, she gave me my legacy. My happiness is surely from my God whom I serve. After that, I have to thank my mother for all the love she lavished on me.

21) The only other male that Mother trusted was Wray Woods. A

few times she even mustered the courage to correspond with him. Whenever I was with Wray, he always inquired about Mother. Romancing your brother's wife two weeks after their marriage is unusual to say the least. I will put that down to youthful folly and my father's irresponsible behaviour. I confess I did wonder about their six-week fling. I put the whole thing down to the worst of circumstances. The fact that mother trusted Wray speaks for itself. Given her tragic circumstances, small wonder she was afraid of men.

22) Wray always admired me as the son he wished he had. After Mother died, he set up his will with me as full beneficiary. However, his wife Irene outlived him. Since she did not share Wray's Christian faith compounded by a long memory, she had the will changed in favour of her nephew (her sister's son). He was not well off and had three children, maybe he needed the money more than me.

Given my mother's sensitive nature, she developed a mental illness. Life had overwhelmed her, and in her desperation she blamed Grandma for her mistakes: "You didn't warn me about men." How often have I heard her say that. The truth was, she did warn her about my father, but love is blind. If knowing what I now comprehend I could magically return to 1942 and counsel my mother, I would say,

"Mom, you fail to understand the depth of God's compassionate forgiving love. Not only does God forgive all our sins, he ALSO redeems our mistakes." It was this latter redemption that escaped her comprehension. She never ceased to lament her mistakes. Given the hypothetical opportunity I never had, I would reinforce this kindly counsel with a lesson on unnecessary shame. For the child of God there is no shame. Our reputation is of no consequence. Christ is our reputation, and we are a new creation – as the bible says in Jude 24, "faultless"; or in I Thessalonians 5:23, "May God himself, the God of peace sanctify you through and through. May your whole spirit, soul and body be kept 'blameless' – the one who calls you is faithful and also will do it."

I do not reveal these things to embarrass my mother. Where she is now, and with better understanding, she would approve, if it helped somebody else along the way. She was always so caring about others and especially me. I write these things to encourage some mixed-up pilgrim who shares a similar but unnecessary guilt. I regret that Mother never had the privilege of understanding the Spirit-filled life. It would have given her the power to overcome her past. Throughout history, the church discovers this truth, and loses it again. It is the stuff of great revivals. She was converted at a time when legalism was taught as a substitute for the Spirit filled life. It was the common error of the times and was called the separated life. Legalism and rigid rules for Christians always ends in failure, and guilt because it makes Pharisees of its devotees and offers impersonal rules to obey instead of the joyous Spirit-filled life that ought to be the norm for every child of God.

Conclusion

As long as I continue to live in Ancaster (now thirty-seven years), I still have the stray lamb that crosses my path from time to time. Some of them are healthy, others quite sick. One of these is Sandy who called the other day (not her real name). Sandy grew up under the arm of Children's Aid.

Her dysfunctional family of eleven (how different from another family of eleven so dear to me) were raised through a series of foster homes, and you can almost guess the rest. Sandy was a beautiful girl and won an Ontario-wide contest, as Miss Teen Ontario. Her inward scars not healed, she quickly descended into a series of relationships that further added wounds to the scars. Shades of another example fresh in our minds. Eventually, she ended up in the Galt Training School for girls where she and others were raped by the director. Later, he would go to jail. Sandy and the other girls received $26,000 in compensation money.

I first met Sandy when Diana, a friend, brought her to Stanley Avenue Baptist Church. Her friend also had a story (her husband did time at Kingston Penitentiary). They were both discipled by me. The wounded (Diana) seem to know the wounded (Sandy). Sandy was like the woman at the well that Jesus ministered to. She received Christ and I had the privilege of baptizing her. Her troubles were far from over. Her brother, who lived with her for a while, was like a stranger and yet her kin. He caused Sandy no end of trouble. Eventually, one day, when Sandy came home from work, she found him dangling from a rope. Suicide!

Sandy's two children (a girl and a boy) seem to have inherited all the troubles this fallen world can heap on two kids who have the capacity to make all the wrong choices. Trevor (not his real name) was the innocent victim of a drug-related shooting that took place in Hamilton's east end. The perpetrator of the crime mistook him for somebody else who owed drug money and will shortly stand trial. Trevor, now blind in one eye, suffers from epilepsy. His common-law wife couldn't face the problems. She took their child and left. To Trevor's credit, this little kid I remember from Sunday School, now

271

grown up and at age twenty-three is facing his twenty-fourth operation, is standing tall in his faith.

Thank God for downtown ministries. I am no longer his pastor; Al and Karen Craig are. Their ministry that issues out of Living Rock, a church located in downtown Hamilton, cares for Trevor's spiritual needs. Al and Karen have a thankless ministry that cares for hundreds of damaged youth, and their story would be a book all by itself. But who ministers to Sandy? She has long since stopped going to church. Overwhelmed by her troubles, apart from her daily prayers to God for help, she struggles on alone. Her damaged personality has made her hard to befriend. Poor Sandy.

As Sandy said on the phone the other day, "When will it ever end?"

All I can do for these wayward sheep is to hear them out and pray for them. I have a few more like that as well. From time to time, they contact me, and I do what I can, which really means I listen, trusting that a burden shared is half as heavy. For some inexplicable reason, it seems to help. I have learned one can retire from ministry, but ministry never retires from us. Do you know what? I like it that way. At age seventy-seven, every day is an adventure. It all began sixty years ago, when this wayward waif was rescued by Jesus Christ who picked me up in time to spare me from the troubles I counsel in others less fortunate than I.

Epilogue

From time to time, I pick up the apologists who reason from historical evidence that Jesus Christ is real and the resurrection beyond doubt. I appreciate their work. I wouldn't really need the evidence, although I enjoy reading it. The transformed life is, in the end, the best evidence of all. And I have a lifetime of examples. Research shows that people who attend church regularly, on average, live seven years longer than those who don't; If you love life that should say something. On the other hand, I am constantly running into people who denigrate religion in general and Christianity in particular. So what is the best proof of the worth of the gospel? My answer is always the same. It is the transformed life. There are many reasonable proofs for the existence of God and the truthfulness of the Bible. I no longer resort to these to convince the unbeliever. When you see a former Marxist, become a church historian or an ex-biker feeding the poor that's good reason for pause.

As for proofs of God, I have my own categories as to why I believe in God. The first is communication. Speech is the possession soley of human kind. The complexity of thought reduced to words that can be written for succeeding generations is my first category of proof for the existence of God. The next is music. Instruments of music are in themselves an infallible proof, especially when they come together in a symphonic masterpiece, such as Beethoven's Fifth. Add to this the possibilities of the human voice, and I am speechless before God, lost in wonder. Congregational singing makes us all into God's maestro (which we can take into our private devotions). It not only makes room for our own voice, but it places it in concert with others for a sound that is still the best of all musical worlds. The third is dance. I love to watch the ice dancing of the Olympics. It seems to add so much grace to skill that is improved by practice beyond my simple steps of dance. That God could and did design the human body for such beauty is for me simply amazing. These uncomplicated proofs of God are for me enriching and convincing.

Turning to the brevity of human life and the daily God ordained surprise that we all should enjoy, I have a healthy habit of doing twenty-two minutes on my treadmill, every day. True, it hardly counts for dancing; still, at age seventy-seven, I enjoy it. I can play my CD's and sing with the best of hymn writers. (Did you know that singing is therapy and can add years to your life?) I also put on my earphones and listen to the Bible (King James Version). I especially love the gospels. As I recount my life (from memory; I never kept a diary), I am amazed at my recall of events gone by. I also think about those authors, two thousand years ago, who gave us their accounts of the life of Christ. The idea of exaggerating the facts never occurred to me when I wrote my book. Why would it occur to them? Rarely do people say to me, "Are you sure all those things really happened?"

I suppose the obvious intent of what I write is so patently true that people trust that I have told them the facts without distortion. I found the first book easier than the sequel, even though the events I related in Between Two Women are more distant in time than what I relate in Between Two Worlds.

In the first book, I stated, tongue in cheek, that the events described were 97% true. I wanted to give leeway, in case my memory was faulty. However, as I now write in this book as I did in my former treatise, I can tell you that what you read squares with the facts. Now, let's consider the Bible accounts of Jesus. Can we trust that those ancient authors didn't exaggerate or in some way embellish the truth? Impossible; either Jesus Christ fed the 5000 with five loaves and two fish or he didn't. You can't have it any other way. The astonished disciples saw it with their own eyes. Furthermore, to suggest some kind of collective agreement to subvert a generation of readers at another place in another time with a story like this is nonsense. Sooner or later, the fabrication would break down. Someone would crack under the strain and admit the subterfuge.

Truth is truth. Either it happened or it didn't. Move past all the miracles that Jesus did and go to the resurrection. Fabricate this and convince a skeptical world? Impossible. I have given an autobiography of my life. Suppose my friends who knew me decided to do another version from an outsider's point of view. The essential story would remain unchanged. I know that I have told my readers the truth. I know that Matthew, Mark, Luke, and John also did the same when they, as eyewitnesses to the life of Jesus, wanted to tell the world about the greatest story ever told.

I had to write my book alone, although from time to time I consulted others whenever I was in doubt as to the facts. A few times, I was in error, but not often. As soon as those who corrected my memory shared the truth, the fog lifted, and I could piece the story correctly. Imagine now the biographers of Jesus. With the impeccable standard of truth that Jesus set for them, can you not see them doing much the same as I did? I can almost hear Luke saying to one of Jesus' disciples.

"Now, let's get this thing right" You can fill in the rest of the conversation. Still the skeptics will not listen to reason. For this cause, Peter was compelled to write,

"We did not follow cunningly invented stories when we told you about the power and coming of our Lord Jesus Christ, but were eyewitnesses of his majesty."

II Peter 1:16

It is amazing how memory and consultation with others can confirm the reasonable faith the disciples of Jesus left for us in their reports. How's this for an understatement. The Bible is certainly as reliable as my account – frankly, given the meticulous care the disciples would surely have supplied, better than anything I have told you, isn't that enough? As I listen to my talking Bible (walking on my treadmill), the gospel accounts, the stories have the ring of historical truth. I often think about those writers and compare my technique to theirs. It's the little innuendos that are so revealing, like the woman who washed Jesus' feet with her tears and "wiped them with her hair." An unusual statement to say the least, but written this way because that's exactly what happened. I have compared my story with the now 2000-year-old stories of the biographers of Jesus. I see the same patient attempt to tell what they saw as they saw it. I did that too. I smile at those who so easily believe the unbelieveable and then dismiss as facile the stories of Jesus. Eventually people wise up to the distortions they so easily mistook for truth. Oh, how I long that people would just read the Bible. I long for people who are curious enough to check out the Gospel records on the life of Christ. I know I told the truth with my story; I have no reason to doubt that the four historians of the life of Jesus did the same. Jesus has now gone to that other world, and at age seventy-seven, I am not too far away from that other world myself. For this reason, I have great hope that the future can only get better. To be between two worlds is not a prerogative of ministers. Every christian is a citizen of the world to come, and if you live in Canada, still be a responsible Canadian. I am proud to belong to both worlds.

The ministry has given me some wonderful opportunities to meet some very special Canadians. To name a few, there was Robert Thompson, leader of the Social Credit party. In 1963, he became the second most powerful politician in Ottawa because he held the balance of power in a minority government. Prime Minister Lester Pearson always had to check with Thompson before any legislation was proposed. Rex Heslop, who developed Toronto's Rexdale Plaza, was another of my friends. Oscar Bisnar, the ambassador to Canada representing the Phillipines, was another. I performed his daughter Olivia's wedding with distinguished guests from many countries in the audience. Mayor Bob Morrow, who held his office for eighteen years in the city of Hamilton, and who made it possible for me to meet Dr. Robert Schuller of the Crystal Cathedral, is another of my friends. Paul Henderson, who scored the most famous Canadian goal in hockey history, is another.

I, Bruce Alexander Woods, am a Canadian. Canada has shaped my life. I have experienced the Vancouver blahs when it rains and rains and rains and its exquisite beauty. I have marvelled at the Rocky Mountains and gazed at Lake Louise. I have seen the golden grain in Saskatchewan like a restless sea rolling in the wind. Winnipeg is the home of my oldest son (also a minister). Needless to say, my son made sure that I would see the landmarks that make that city so special.

Ontario born and bred, I have loved its towns and cities and especially Stratford where I grew up. I have made my pilgrimage to St. Joseph's Oratorio and tasted Montreal smoked meet before there were a hundred copy-cat brands showing up in supermarkets all across the continent. I have missed Fredricton, but knowing Dr. Molly Abraham as I do, I feel as though I could be a citizen of that city too. Molly was born in India, emigrated to Canada, and gave me a vision to reach international students. I have a son-in-law from Liverpool, Nova Scotia, who made sure that we visited that province in depth, as well as Prince Edward Island. I have been to Newfoundland. I have made the drive up Petit Nord Peninsula to see the L'Anse aux Meadows National Historic Site. I was in Bonavista when Queen Elizabeth addressed the crowd celebrating Newfoundland's 500th Anniversary. I am weak on my French attachment. But hear this, Fernand Petit-Clerc is my fellow Baptist pastor and French-speaking friend. Yes, I am a Canadian through and through. I love this country. With the exception of the far north, I've experienced Canadiana through and through.

Who would have thought that to do all this, I would have to become a Baptist Pastor. If I had not been a minister, I would have lived my whole life in one province and merely been a tourist in some of the others. However, who is a Canadian? I go back five Anglo-Saxon generations. Dr. Molly Abraham came from India; her daughter is a distinguished professor in English at the University of Toronto. Or how about the many wonderful Canadians I have met through my various churches. I select but one. Henry Sienko was born in Poland. He was a look-alike of Pope John Paul the II. Dress them the same and you couldn't tell the difference. He fought the Russians in 1920 who tried to conquer Poland and make it Communist. Under Marshall Jozef Pilsudski, Henry was a Cavalryman who helped turn the Communists back in the Battle of Warsaw. He emmigrated to Canada in 1925. Henry could speak six languages. After World War II, his shoe repair shop in Georgetown became the focal point for many eastern European immigrants making their transition to the Canadian way of life. When I met Henry, he was a deacon at the Maple Avenue Baptist Church that I pastored from 1960-66. All these and more are Canadians just like me. That said, I am a Canadian through and through and I have lived in Canada for these now seventy-seven years.

Courtesy of Vatican Library Archives People often remarked how much Henry Sienko resembled the Pope who also was from Poland
Henry Sienko repairing shoes in his Georgetown Ontario Shop. Henry fought in the Polish army against the Russian communists before he immigrated to Canada

Much as I love my country, I cannot have this priviledge forever. How wonderful to know that like the saints of old we seek another country. The Bible calls it a better country. We get a few glimpses of that second world in Scripture. Someday, I hope to write another book about the country that I have yet to see. In the meantime, I content myself to be a citizen of two worlds; one for now, the other still to come.

Appendex I:

For Baptists Only? Denominational Controversy

In 1983, I became the most talked-about pastor in our denomination. My notoriety or fame (depending on your point of view) came unexpectedly over the publication of an article I wrote, which is the classic example of how to make a mountain out of a molehill. You can say what you want to, but be careful what you write.

When I crossed over into Charismatic experience, the invisible walls came down between me and other denominations. I always thought of myself as a Baptist (still do); however, some others did not share my viewpoint. In experience, I was one with Pentecostals, therefore ipso facto, I am no longer a Baptist. Maybe in the end, I am just a Christian. With new eyes I looked at the older denominations that I had previously labeled as liberal and therefore hopeless. Perhaps God has good things in store for them as well. I found myself believing that anybody could experience the sweep of the Spirit. In other words, I had no denominational barriers. This included Roman Catholics. Father Bill Trusz I count as one of my dearest friends. I can't think of anyone I would sooner have pray for me than Bill. Of course, I knew that some of my exclusive Baptist brethren would disagree. (Woods has no convictions anymore). I had lost the us and them mentality. It's not that any of my doctrines had changed. It's just that I now had such a great optimism for the future of the Church that I even wrote a book – The Coming Great World-wide Revival. It was never published and is now collecting dust in a filing cabinet. On the other hand, I was afraid to tell anybody these things and so I remained a "closet Charismatic." After all, I valued my job. Years later when I established Hamilton Christian Fellowship and had the liberty to pursue my heart, Father Bill Trusz and I established a Roman Catholic/Protestant dialogue that reulted in a TV interview on Crossroads Television. I have personally met and prayed with Bishop Anthony Tonnos of Hamilton and Bishop Mathew Ustrzycki of Guelph.

I read voraciously every book I could on the "filling of the Spirit." I finally decided, after no less than forty books, that this is an open ended subject which although partly revealed also remains in the realm of mystery. Nonetheless, my first impulse was to reach out to any who

279

would talk to me. So why not start with those "other Baptists" at McMaster Theological Seminary. This included both Ivan Morgan and Melvin Hilmer, successive principals of the seminary. However, the real connection came with Dr. Clark Pinnock, professor of theology.

In my reading research, probing into the secrets of the ways of the Holy Spirit, the name Clark Pinnock kept popping up. I especially rejoiced to read his article on the gifts of the Spirit in Theological Renewal, a journal out of Britain. To my utter amazement, I was thrilled to discover that he would be coming to Hamilton in 1977 as Distinguished Professor of Theology at McMaster Divinity College. In my enthusiasm, I wrote a letter to Dr. Pinnock before he arrived requesting an opportunity to meet with him. That meeting indeed took place and I asked him to preach for us at Stanley Avenue Baptist. Later on, I wrote a letter to Dr. Hilmer offering to sponsor a faculty retreat at a place of their choosing to explore the workings of the Spirit. Stanley Avenue Baptist would pay for it. I secretly dreamed of a healing between the two Baptist denominations. I never considered a reunion of the two denominations. I was sure that was not likely to happen, but some kind of rapprochement, YES.

Dr. Hilmer graciously declined my offer for a faculty retreat, but Clark Pinnock proposed instead that I bring a paper on how cooperation between the two Baptist denominations might be possible. A planned symposium made for the opportunity. In October 1982, I found myself in McMaster Seminary, delivering my paper entitled "Theological Directions and Cooperation Amongst Baptists in Canada." This paper later found its way into print: first, in the Canadian Baptist 1983 July/August issue and in September, second, it was published in a book entitled, "Canadian Baptist History and Polity, the McMaster Conference" published by McMaster Theological Seminary and edited by Murray J.S. Ford. From my notes, I reconstruct the opening remarks. I began with a little joke as follows.

"I am pleasantly surprised and thrilled to be invited to this Baptist Symposium. Remembering that I represent the Fellowship Baptist denomination and that you are members of the Convention is in itself significant. The split amongst Baptists took place in 1926 in the church which I presently pastor. This fact alone adds significance to my address. If I may be a little lighthearted about all this, I say this; 'Many a child who watches TV for hours may go down in history.' I'm not sure if I'm a candidate for historical reference, but perhaps this is an event that may be the catalyst for better relations between our two denominations."

Little did I know what was waiting for me. My paper was included in a later publication of several lectures taking place in the symposium, but it was also reproduced in the Canadian Baptist, the official denominational magazine of the BCOQ (Baptist Convention of Ontario and Quebec). When a copy of the magazine landed on the desk of Roy Lawson (a former classmate), who was now executive secretary of our Baptist denomination (FEBC in Canada), a firestorm of protest irrupted.

To the casual reader unacquainted with our Baptist ways, a word of explanation is needed. I have previously alluded to the issues that divided Baptists beginning in the very church I pastored. Approximately thirty pastors representing as many churches met to form a protest Baptist denomination over the liberalism of McMaster Theological Seminary. I had heard those stories over and over again from the very warriors who were in the thick of the "McMaster Controversy," and reveled in those stories. As a young pastor, I was glad to follow in their train and preached against those wayward Baptists who succumbed to the wiles of liberalism. What I didn't know in those early days was that quietly, and without fanfare, the B.C.O.Q. had cleaned house and frankly stood for the same things as we "independent" Baptists believed. An excerpt from a letter written by W.H. Jones, editor of the Canadian Baptist, to Clark Pinnock is revealing.

"Woods uses the term 'liberalism' fairly freely when referring to BCOQ. I doubt if there are very many staunch liberals among us - anywhere. I can think of about a dozen at the most. Frankly, they have so little influence, that the use by Woods of this term is a caricature. It will, in fact, be a barrier to reconciliation which he correctly urges. I would suggest tempering that word 'liberal' or 'liberalism' as much as possible. There is much 'inertness' in our midst, but little 'liberalism'."

Enter Roy Lawson, our general secretary and titular head of the denomination of which I am a part. I first met Roy Lawson when he and I were fellow classmates at London Bible Institute. We had this in common – we were both Fuller Brush salesmen, working our way through Bible school by selling brushes door to door. Everybody liked Roy Lawson; he was our class comedian. I was sure he'd never amount to much. How wrong I was. Behind that Churchillian face was a first-rate preacher who not only knew how to preach but also entertained his audience while he was at it. Needless to say, I was not a little jealous when he became pastor of Central Baptist Church, London a place I was sure God had reserved for me. Roy and I were and remain friends. It was always a pleasure to chat with Roy at our various Baptist events. For us to become protagonists in a controversy of "epic" proportions (I use the word "epic" with tongue in cheek) was the last thing I could have imagined. So on with our little "tempest."

Revealing how easily we imagine ourselves pure and others as apostates, Roy Lawson took several letters and phone calls of protests from the "elder statesmen" of our denomination. My little submission on the reunifications of divided Baptists was the cause. Roy felt he had to do something drastic to put me in my place. He drafted a letter of protest and sent it out to every pastor in our denomination from to coast to coast. It reads as follows.

September 19, 1983

To All Fellowship Pastors

Dear Pastor:

A number of you have written and phoned to share your concern regarding the series of two articles by Rev. Bruce Woods of Stanley Avenue Baptist Church in Hamilton, Ontario, that appeared recently in *The Canadian Baptist*.

At the Executive Council meeting September 14, 1983 the following action was taken:

1) That a committee of three meet with Pastor Woods to express our concerns and regrets regarding the writing of such articles.

2) That the General Secretary write the editor of the Canadian Baptist regarding our disappointment in publishing these articles, and that a copy of the letter be circulated to our pastors.

3) That the General Secretary seek an opportunity to meet with the board of Stanley Avenue Baptist in Hamilton to voice the concern and disappointment of the Executive Council in this matter.

I trust you will keep this matter upon your heart rather than upon your lips in these days so that Satan may not gain ground in hurting the testimony and unity of the Fellowship of Evangelical Baptist Churches in Canada.

Your servant for Christ,

R. W. Lawson
General Secretary

Quite a letter! Naturally, I received a copy just like all the other Canadian pastors. My reaction to the reading of that letter was, "Wow, Roy, you have to be the best promotion manager the author of an obscure article published in a relatively unknown magazine could possibly have." The response was obvious. Since very few of our pastors subscribed to The Canadian Baptist (those other Baptists), with curiosity peaked they immediately went out of their way to find the article which otherwise they probably would have ignored. I was "infamous" overnight! (The law of unintended consequences: since the only people who had the sought-for-magazine were BCOQ pastors, men who might never have met were now talking to one another). On another level, in no time the younger pastors were phoning me or writing to me their approval of what I had written. Not exactly the kind of reaction the Executive Council in mind.

Talk about "does God have a sense of humour?" Roy Lawson was to be our anniversary speaker scheduled to speak in our church in just ten days' time on September 25. We had responded to an earlier appeal for funds on behalf of a deficit at head office by voting to give Roy a check for $1000.00 for the general account when he was scheduled to preach. In regard to "speaking" to our church board, I quickly freed him from that (I suspect Roy was relieved). Ours was a healthy, happy Baptist church that was completely in the dark about this self-made tempest-in-a-tea-pot affair. Lawson concurred. September 25 came and went. Roy preached at our church, and not a word was said about this issue. I duly presented Roy a check for the thousand dollars which he graciously accepted on behalf of the Executive Council. I sometimes wonder if Roy was really acting on his own initiative, or if he was pressured by the "old guard" and felt obligated. I guess we'll never know the answer to that one.

This Baptist in-house rhubarb had one more episode with two parts. The pastor's letter with the signature of Roy Lawson on behalf of the Executive Council had mentioned that a committee would be set up to speak to "Woods" for the purpose of addressing the "concerns and regrets" that the Executive Council had over the issues I had raised. The committee was made up of two elder pastor statesmen and a younger man: Robert Brackstone of Chatham and Donald Loveday of Brantford (later president of Central Baptist Seminary) plus Doug Blair of Bluewater Baptist, Sarnia, composed the committee. We had an amiable chat in which they agreed with my article in spirit, but not in letter whatever that means. I think in the end they were embarrassed at the difficulty of their position and were releaved to have it over with. All this happened one month later at our denominational annual meeting which was held in Niagara Falls.

In the days leading up to our annual convention, a mixture of hardliners young and old wanted to frame a resolution to put "Woods" in his place and make a strong statement about our Baptist distinctives which they erroneously imagined were not held by the BCOQ. It failed because of procedural difficulties. Resolutions of any kind have to be submitted in writing to the executive council thirty days before the annual meeting. There was nothing left for the hardliners to do but filibuster and reaffirm an old resolution about the reasons why our Baptist denomination was different (better?). Everybody knew that I was the intended target, and now the old guard had their say. The reaffirmation passed easily. Then at last with everyone having said their piece, I stood up and requested permission to speak briefly. This required permission from the parliamentarian, John Armstrong, and always my friend. Permission granted, I spoke briefly, avoiding the issue completely, and said,

"Our fellowship of Baptist churches means a great deal to me. I was converted and baptized in Wortley Road Baptist Church, in London, Ontario. I have now served in our denomination for twenty-six years as a pastor and have enjoyed every minute. I love our churches and am grateful for the enrichment you have been to me and my family. Our fellowship of churches is a wonderful place to serve, and I personally believe we have a great future to look forward to."

What a moment! As I was sitting down, the place errupted into a standing ovation for my remarks and congratulations all around. The old guard was taken completely by surprise, and I never heard another word from any of them after that. I still wonder if that published article really was the issue. It had been standard rumour for some time that "Woods is a closet Charismatic and must be watched." A whiff of Pentecostalism in Baptist circles was heresy. During my ministry, I always had enquiries from churches that were looking to fill a vacancy. From that time forward, the silence told the story. Either I stay at Stanley Avenue Baptist Church or step out and start an independent church. Backed into a corner, I chose the latter. In 1989, I started Hamilton Christian Fellowship which grew into an active church of 170 members.

The ultimate irony is that for the last nineteen years, I have been absent from the very Baptist people I wished to encourage for interchurch fellowship. The issue is now put to rest. Everybody knows that liberalism is dead and buried. Occasional pastoral exchanges between the two Baptist denominations reveal the evidence. We are basically no different from one another. The only thing left would be for both groups to realize there are no outstanding issues between us. We ought to merge our forces and get on with it.

The article I wrote was widely read, and I have received many letters of appreciation. Here is one of many from my author friend, Hugh Steven of Wycliffe Bible Translators:
"Actually, what I wanted to comment on was your very fine article. Norma and I read it together and I just couldn't help but be amazed at

how well-thought-out and insightful your articles were. It's my opinion that this article should be spread abroad widely to all of your Baptist brethern. It's probably one of the most beautiful documents, free of cynicism and party politics that I have ever seen. It is certainly one of the most Christian documents that I have ever read."

After the whole matter was laid to rest, I had a friendly coffee with Roy Lawson at Muskoka Baptist Conference two years later. We chatted as we would have in days of old and swapped preacher stories. In general, we had a grand time of it.

The strong crosscurrents of the Holy Spirit are always at work and are missed by many of us who are busy in our own place of ministry. There are two first-rate Baptist seminaries twenty-five miles apart in Ontario. Heritage Baptist, which is the Fellowship Baptist stronghold in the east is located in Cambridge. The McMaster Divinity College continues as it always has on Hamilton's McMaster University campus, representing the BCOQ (The Baptist Convention of Ontario and Quebec). In 2006, the office of Registrar fell vacant. McMaster Divinity College approached Stan Fowler, who holds the senior position of Distinguished Professor of Theology at Heritage Baptist. Talk about the fat in the fire. Maintaining a first-line theological seminary is an expensive business. It complicates things when two Baptist seminaries with identical theological perspectives are only twenty-five miles apart. In these days of financial meltdown, the logic of amalgamation is hard to resist. What can be far behind? Why should Mount Forest have two viable Baptist churches serving a community of 3000? It is time to lay down the outdated issues of a bygone era. They were relevant in their day. In our generation, the prayers of Jesus for church unity are hard to resist.

The invitation given to Stan Fowler to assume the position of Registrar at McMaster Divinity College would have vitiated Heritage College of a Canada-wide recognized theologian. It put Stan Fowler in an interesting position, to say the least. It touched off some informal discussions which raised the issues we have put forward. In the end, Stan was not ready to be the tinder for the conflagration such a move would have set in motion. The time is ripening fast, and I for one personally look forward to see the ultimate reunification of the BCOQ and the FEBC within Canada.

About the Author

Bruce Woods is a retired minister who spent 37 years in the Baptist Church. He spent the first sixteen years of his life in Stratford before he moved to London, Ontario. He received his B.A. from Western University and his M. Th. from Dallas Theological Seminary. He is married to Joan Amy of Waterloo with four children and ten grandchildren. At his wife's prompting (she also suggested the title) he has written his memoirs of his early years growing up in Stratford. Rev. Woods has been a contributer of many articles to his denominational magazine 'The Evangelical Baptist'. He was in Vancouver from 1966-1972 where he participated in the 1971 Centennial producing the reenactment of the coming of John Morton, Vancouver's first settler for CBC Television. He is also the playwright of two 'one man' dramas 'David and Bathsheba' and 'James a Skeptic Believes', which he regularly performs in both Canada and the United States. He has lived in Hamilton, Ontario for the last 35 years where he has pastored three different churches. He was the founder of Hamilton Baptist Non-Profit homes for low-income families. Active in local ministerial affairs, he was a co-founder of the Hamilton Theological Society, teacher of the downtown Business Luncheon for Men and Women and co-chaired with Mayor Bob Morrow the Millennial Christian Festival. From time to time, he has been interviewed by Crossroads TV. for 'One Hundred Huntley Street', The Hamilton Magazine as well as The Hamilton Spectator. He presently holds his credentials with the Congregational Christian Churches of Canada.

If you would like to communicate with Bruce A. Woods you may contact him at

167 Fallingbrook Dr.
Ancaster, Ontario L9G 1E7
E-Mail brjwoods @ sympatico.ca
Phone 905-648-1589
Web Page: www.betweentwowomen.net

Between Two Worlds
by Bruce Woods

What People are Saying about this Book

In this his sequel to his best selling book 'Between Two Women', author Bruce Woods has given the reader a folksy, uninhibited winsome story that is written in a warm conversational style that engages the reader to turn the pages to see what happens next.

Hugh Steven, Author at Large Wcliffe Bible Translators, (retired) Santa Anna, California

Heartwarming! Wood's book is a wonderful account of how a young adult, against all odds, became a Christian minister growing up in the post-war period. With a warm and engaging knack for story-telling, Bruce (now in his seventies) takes a retrospective look at half a century. Bruce began life with very few natural advantages: he was an only child, growing up in a broken family and raised for the most part by his mother, who was psychologically unstable. With no self-pity at all, but with complete honesty, Rev. Woods recounts his exodus from darkness into a full and fulfilled life as a preacher of the gospel. Along the way are many interesting and amusing companions. We meet girlfriends, a future wife, and alienated youth who become productive citizens. For my part, being a Catholic priest and pastor and, therefore, very much of an outsider, I found in Bruce's story a fascinating look into the inner life of the Baptist church. What emerges is a portrait of a very close-knit church family, and not always a happy family, but a real, live, down-to-earth family nonetheless. If you wish to read an uplifting account of how 'all things work to the good for one who loves God', then this is the book for you."

Father Bill Trusz, resident priest and pastor, St. Margaret Mary Roman Catholic Church, Hamilton, Ontario

I applaud you for your diligent work. Your story is a testimony to God working faithfully in your life. The writing is clear, the material very absorbing and the spiritual applications strong. I like your title. There is a lot of good stuff in it that people will profit from reading. You do write of winners and losers but often come across as saluting successfulness. Consider Henri Nouwen's "Here and Now" which Clark (Pinnock) and I use occasionally. The sentiments expressed here came to my mind as I read the "human achievement material" in your manuscript as the definition of who people are. I like Nouwen's antidote to that.

Dorothy Pinnock for Clark Pinnock, Hamilton, Ontario

Rev Bruce Woods has written an interesting account of his unconventional adult journey through the evangelical church world in south western Ontario. His sincerity and deep faith are never in doubt, but his energy and open heartedness sometimes lead him to butt heads with the conventional thinking of the different factions. It will be of interest to open minded evangelicals, and anyone curious, about that corner of the Christian community.

George Breckenridge, Political Science Professor, McMaster University, [retired]

In his first book, Between Two Women, Bruce Woods proves that he is a man with a story to tell. We are not disappointed in the much awaited sequel: Between Two Worlds. In his latest book, the reader is allowed to continue the journey with Woods, as he embarks on the difficult path towards adulthood. To begin, the setting is post WW2 London, Ontario,and we re-join the youth who struggles to work his way through a high school education. Woods knows what it means to be an outsider looking in, whether he is comparing himself to his carefree peers, while hoping against hope for funds to supply books for his schooling, or literally gazing into homes from the winter street, glimpsing the warm bustle of family life, so alien to his own experience. The onfolding of his story reveals the bittersweet combination of longings both fulfilled and thwarted. The reader will travel this dogged, unwieldy journey along with Woods to western Canada and back again to Ontario, never being sure what lies around the next bend. With him, we will experience surprise, love and hope. We will be entertained by the people he encounters and the details of a Canada that exists today only in the stories of those who give us the gift of their telling.

Between Two Worlds is a gift of memory, and the analysis that can only come from a mature perspective. Bruce Woods' understanding of his 'mentally ill' mother is generous and compelling. With him, we mourn her sorrow, 'her demons', and celebrate the love and spunk that she was nevertheless able to impart on her son. Woods is able to deal generously with so many situations that would have made others bitter, and the reading of these is inspiring. Many times I had a smile on my face as this ever-optimist worked his way through yet another tight spot. Woods' humour is contagious, and he is willing even to laugh at times at his own folly – this is indeed a mature perspective. It is a privilege to share in the details of this remarkable life, and to discover with the author what it means to live within the tension of two worlds on so many levels.

Nancy Spring, London Ontario, High School Teacher